Trevor Rogers

If we Lived

in the

Highlands

A life style adventure

First published 2008

by

Alsia Wells Publishing

ISBN 978-0-9556918-0-5

Front cover design from original painting
by Ann Atkinson

For Irene

Contents

CHAPTER ONE

The Start of a Dream

It was a moment of supreme satisfaction as we sat in the warm spring sunshine, our backs resting against the house which during the past year we had built with our own hands. From the makeshift bench we gazed out onto one of the loveliest views in the Western Highlands: a mirror-calm sea-loch shimmering in the early morning sun, the air so clear that one might see the very crystals of snow-capped mountains outlined against the distant blue sky. Was it a dream – could this beautiful shoreline really be ours? Clearings and woodlands lapped by the sea and gardened by nature: oak, elm, alder, and birch; thickets of sally willow hung with silver catkins, and blackthorn smothered by snow-white blossom; everywhere wild flowers – primroses, celandine, violets and more, and honeysuckle where small birds busied themselves at their nests. The sea, no more than a stone's throw away: the rocky headland green with new-grown heather and, along the margins of the shingle cove, a profusion of golden broom. Yes, it was easy to believe it was a dream.

Spring comes late to the Highlands. Such is the weather that often greets the month of May, one might be forgiven for thinking that summer had begun without waiting for spring. From where we sat sipping coffee and toasting the culmination of our labours, we could see clear across the harbour to the village, and signs that the fine weather was stirring other activity. Newly painted herring drifters with tanned mizzens were active around the pier, readying themselves for the summer fishing. Along Shore Street we could just make out the villagers, leisurely strolling at the head of the pier where a cluster of stores made up the centre of the village, and rows of white cottages looked like toy-town models. The church was just visible, and beyond it the Royal Hotel, centre of social activity, stood prominent.

In such a state of pensive contentment it was pleasant to look back and remember the past, those holidays when living here was indeed a dream and might so easily have remained one. After all, we had had a business and other commitments to consider, family, friends and social ties. To uproot ourselves from one location to another was nigh unthinkable. In those days, if the idea had ever been there, then it had remained in our subconscious, appearing from time to time only as a fantasy.

Many phases of my life have had no definite beginnings. They have just evolved from circumstances, often occasioned by other people. The course of my education, the beginning of a career, and more – none had any overriding plan other than that my life should be one of fulfilment. A passing interest in one subject has often led to a passion for something else, the origins of which have become obscure over time. So many twists and turns. Going to live in the Highlands was neither deliberately promoted nor the result of a prolonged consideration. In the same way as so much else in my life, it just happened, in one defined and memorable moment of time.

Every year since Irene and I had first met we had holidayed in the Highlands, walking, camping, fishing and taking part in many of the other outdoor activities induced by the splendours of this wonderful wilderness region. Now we lived here, and as we remained seated in the sun my mind lazily slipped from one thought to another, finally returning to that point, a year and a half before, which defined our decision to come north. It was the end of the holiday season, our twelfth at Loch Broom, and we were returning to our home in Shropshire, some five hundred miles south. I had sensed that although we had enjoyed our break, Irene was getting restless for change. She had not said as much, but had talked of friends who had enthused about the Italian lakes, and others who had walked in the Chamonix region. I'm sorry to say that at the time I did not recognise it as a gentle hint, but even if I had, we still might not have been sitting here eighteen months later enjoying this wonderful moment. As we had climbed the steep narrow road from the lochside at the start of the drive home, we had turned momentarily, as we had done so many times before, for one last glimpse of the village. The white cottages around the harbour, and beyond, far out to sea, the dark silhouettes of the Summer Isles always evoked so many happy memories.

As usual, neither of us spoke for some time after that last backward glance. Then to my sheer astonishment and quite out of the blue, Irene suddenly broke the silence: "If we lived in the Highlands, we could go somewhere different for holidays."

When friends asked me, "How did you come to decide to live in Scotland?", I would relate Irene's astonishing statement. If Irene were there, she would immediately counter with her story of what followed, adding that hers had been no more than a casual remark. Apparently my first reaction was to accelerate the Landrover which, despite my having once been a competitive driver, I generally drove at a very leisurely pace. I admit to having been completely taken aback by this sudden revelation. I had had no idea that Irene had ever considered the notion of uprooting ourselves from our home in Shropshire. It is obvious now that although I had never dared contemplate the possibility, my subconscious readily took advantage of this unexpected opportunity and immediately began turning over the practicalities. Irene would say that, without my having said a word in reply to her proposition, I had made my mind up and was already speeding south, and that the very next day I had put our property on the market. This was a slight over-dramatisation of what really happened, but it is not too far from the truth. We did actually arrive back in record time, having talked excitedly non-stop of putting our home up for sale, how to deal with our business and the dozens of other practicalities we would have to tackle.

Going south one arrived first at Inverness, capital of the Highlands, which today is a thriving Mecca for holidaymakers from around the world. In those far-off days, when motorways and by-passes were no more than a Transport Minister's pipe-dream, one drove through every town and village journeying north or south. Despite its situation straddling the beautiful River Ness, Inverness was then dreary with dour shops and a gloomy seriousness. It would be many years before tourism would awaken the good people of the town to what could be theirs with a little imagination and investment. However, although there were many topics we could have discussed in the course of our first sixty miles south, the regeneration of Inverness did not feature amongst them. We were talking about moving to the Highlands, and so far everything had revolved around dealing with the Shropshire aspect of the equation. As yet we had given no thought to where we might live if we really did come north.

Ever practical, Irene had spotted a newsagent's and suddenly shouted out: "Stop! I'll get a newspaper. There might be House for Sale ads."

I stopped in a rather awkward spot and Irene ran back to the shop; in a moment she was back.

"Got a *Ross-shire Journal*", she gasped as she flung the paper behind the seat.

I moved off quickly, for the driver of a large van which could easily have got past us was stubbornly refusing to do so. In the distance, a red-faced policeman with the familiar Scottish chequer-banded cap was hurrying to the scene; he watched menacingly as I made off. It was an uncomfortable few minutes, so in no time we had forgotten the purpose of the stop. Indeed, incredible as it now seems, we were back in Shropshire before Irene or I remembered the *Ross-shire Journal.*

Our forgetfulness wasn't really that surprising, as our plans of implementation had been changing faster than the varied scenery through which we travelled. On and on we sped, through the little village of Aviemore, one day to become an international skiing centre, on through Pitlochry, Dunkeld, Perth and Stirling, eventually joining the old A74 and the slow procession of lorries trundling north and south between the great industrial areas and docks of the Forth/Clyde valley and the northern industrial centres of England. It was a slow and tiresome journey, but one in which we had had plenty of time to make our plans. And what plans we made! If I had been at the drawing-board the floor would have been knee-deep in discarded sketches and details. Each time we had an idea in focus another one began to materialise in its place. We were in one of those rare situations, suddenly set free to speculate, where every option within one's means and capabilities becomes a possibility.

I recall that as we were negotiating the pass of Killiecrankie, we agreed the benefits of buying a piece of land in order to build our own cottage. It was all so obvious. Both Irene and I had been allied to building since our student days. With literally hundreds of square miles of virgin land in the Highlands, it would surely be easy to obtain a small plot. Down at the water's edge would be ideal… perhaps an acre… maybe several acres… and so it had gone on.

Weaving our way through Perth we came upon an over laden lorry carrying a wooden shed-like building. With no chance of passing we had to follow for some miles even after we had cleared the city. Finally the lorry peeled off and let us by. As we passed, the wooden building revealed itself as having the appearance of a tiny cottage. It even had a stable-type door.

"That's it, that's it!" Irene had shouted out. "We can build a sectional wooden cottage. We could do that back home, then just transport it north. We would have somewhere to live almost immediately, just a small place perhaps no bigger than a caravan to start with. Later, when we're settled, we could extend it at our leisure."

And so we fantasised mile after mile. By the time we were running south on the A74 and negotiating Beattock Summit, the light was fading. In those long-ago days, the five hundred and twenty-five mile journey was a tortuous one, demanding at least one overnight stop. With the pass behind us we chose to spend the night at Beattock village, which is no more than an hour's run north of Carlisle. We had done well, for not only had we accomplished more than half the journey by taking turn and turn about to drive, we had decided to try to buy a plot of land on which we would initially erect a sectional timber building. In the distance of a little over one hundred miles this structure had evolved from a tiny caravan-sized hut to a small wooden bungalow. We had gone from galley to kitchenette, to kitchen and finally to kitchen-dining area. The shower-space had become a shower-room before becoming a full-sized bathroom.

"Well why not have a full sized bathroom?" Irene had said. "It's only a few extra square feet."

"True," I had replied, lest the dream should suddenly fade.

And so it had gone on, one bedroom, two bedrooms, felt roof, tiled roof. It was only as we pulled alongside the hotel that the creative process temporarily halted, though only for a while. We soon returned to the subject over dinner.

We had always fancied stopping overnight at Beattock when we returned from the Highlands, but we had never managed to get this far south. That we had come so far on this occasion was a measure of our keenness to get home and bring our plans to life. We were both in high spirits and, if we hadn't been so tired after our early start and an arduous day's drive, we would undoubtedly have continued discussing the project throughout the night.

Whether all this excitement would have precluded sleep I do not know, but the nearby main railway line settled the issue. The night was fine and unusually still, and I don't believe there was a moment when we could not hear the sound of an engine, nearby or in the distance. Beattock sits at the southern foot of one of the country's highest mainline railway summits with long severe inclines. So long and so severe are the climbs that additional engines are required to assist the train over the tops. Throughout the night the express trains came through, and with the help of the banking engine the fight was on to get the train over the top. No doubt it was all in a day's or night's work for the engine men. There are of course times of the year when nature is not so kind: the winter winds blow and snowfall turns to blizzard, and it would be then that every ascent and descent required the years of skill these drivers and firemen possessed. Long into the night we listened to the fast staccato exhaust of steam as express trains struggled to maintain their timetables. Engines in unison gave their all, and heavily laden goods trains emitted powerful deep-throated exhalations fit to burst the tops of the boilers. Occasionally a single engine would return, running lightly down the gradient like a ghostly apparition, set on taking the village by surprise. Until what hour we listened I do not know, for eventually we succumbed to the tiredness of what had been an exceptional day.

The euphoria of the previous day had to some extent evaporated by the time we came down to breakfast. We were drained by the undoubted effort of the previous day's romancing plus the exertion of the drive, to say nothing of a restless night – now all compounded by an early call that I dearly wished I could have cancelled, and would have, had it not been that at this late time of the season we were the only guests and the staff had turned out early just for us. Breakfast over, our host bade us good-bye, hoping we would take the opportunity of staying whenever we passed that way again. I said how much we had appreciated our brief stay, but made no promises.

The fine still night had turned to drizzle and it was now a great deal colder. At breakfast I had casually said to the waitress: "Looks like it's rain."

"Ay, it's raining right enough. Be snow on the tops before the week's out."

Her voice had a rather accusatory manner; maybe she was feeling as we were, that we had risen unnecessarily early. The coolness of the morning soon began to revive us as chill draughts seeped through innumerable joints, around the doors and the canvas top of the Landrover. Although the vehicle was still almost new and everything fitted and worked as well as it was ever likely to, it was even by the car-standards of the time rather primitive motoring. Nevertheless, thanks to the skill of the Rover engineers, the works were superb. A couple of hours and we were across the border.

The rain had stopped and the air had become very clear, so clear we could see the top of Helvellyn at the northern extreme of the Lake District. To our amazement, the top was powdered with snow. I don't know why, but the first sight of the coming winter snow, especially lying on high hills, never fails to bring on a feeling of invigoration. There is a freshness that urges me to be creative, to start new ventures. It just seems so miraculous that in so short a space of time a barren mountain-top can be transformed into a thing of such pristine white beauty. Irene was equally excited at the first sight of the snow, although the coming of winter was not a prospect she greatly enjoyed. However the exhilaration of seeing the snow set us going again with yet more plans. Now it had come to the point of debating the merits and the practicalities: but as far as the merits (de-merits) were concerned it was as if we both wished to avoid the subject lest some unforeseen obstacle might suddenly appear and scupper the whole concept. I raised a few minor points, not particularly because I thought them important, but because I felt that I should perhaps be taking the matter more seriously. After all what was being contemplated was a whole new pattern of living at a place almost as far away as one could get within the British Isles. Irene was behaving in much the same manner. In no time we agreed that we must already have made our minds up, and indeed I think we had.

As we approached the notorious climb over Shap in Cumberland the traffic consisted mainly of heavily laden lorries beginning to bunch. We knew that the steep ascent would inevitably reduce everything to a crawl as lorry after lorry fought to maintain its forward momentum without closing too tightly on whatever it might be following. With such a diversity of loads and vehicles the ideal was rarely possible despite the skill of the drivers and, inescapably, one or other vehicle would be forced down into its lowest gear bringing the crawl to a snail's pace. There was little chance of passing on the steep narrow road, and one just had to be patient. The summit section always seemed to me to be claustrophobic despite its open aspect and I was glad when we reached the friendly all-weather face of the Leyland clock. We passed the St John Ambulance box with its ever-ready complement of first-aid supplies. Accidents along this stretch of road were all too tragically frequent. At last we were on the descent, still at a crawl as drivers applied themselves to the problem of overworked brakes emitting the sickly smell of burning Ferodo which permeated through every following vehicle. Finally, as the gradient eased and we gathered speed once more, we passed a roadside institution: the Jungle Café.

This landmark denoted, for those going southwards, that the struggle was over and, for those going northwards, that it was about to begin.

Down through Kendal, still on twisting and winding roads, we reached Lancaster, where the countryside gives way to interspersed centuries-old urban development and industry, a far cry from the sweet chilled air of the mountains and glens of the Highlands. On and on, Wigan, Warrington, down across the Cheshire plain. At last in the early evening dusk we passed through Whitchurch, and into Shropshire – nearly there. We had said little over the last hundred miles or so and despite taking it in turns to drive the journey had been tedious. Only now, buoyed up by the fact that within an hour we would be home, did we begin to revive. The evening air was mild and we entered the narrower roads amongst farms that straddled the road and where one almost brushed rickyards with their fresh stacks of sweet-smelling straw. There were cottages with their scent of fruit-wood fires, and there was the damp mustiness of fallen leaves. We descended into the Severn valley and patches of mist invaded the road. As we ran alongside the river there came that unmistakable scent, and Irene quoted Rupert Brooke:

'That unforgotten unforgettable river smell.'

We were home.

CHAPTER TWO

Tentative Steps

We had been so drained, mentally and physically, by the adventure of the last two days that we had just flopped out on our return, taking no more into the house than the hand luggage. Refreshed by a sound night's rest, I was up early the next day and off to my nearby office to deal with the mail. Usually it conspired to be heaviest whenever we were away, but this time the mail was light, and so I was able to go back to the house to see how Irene was feeling. She was making a cup of coffee and wondering where our luggage had disappeared to.

I suddenly remembered our haste the night before. I rushed back out, shouting: "Get me a coffee and I'll get the luggage. It's been to the office and back with me – I forgot it was still aboard!"

Irene called after me: " See if the *Ross-shire Journal* is still there!"

The newspaper was of course just where it had been thrown two days earlier. Neither of us had yet referred to the pending move. I was rather hoping that Irene would be the first to re-open the dialogue, whilst she seemed to have been waiting for me. She took the newspaper and began to read. I was just about to break the silence when suddenly a look of amazement came to her face.

"Sit down," she said with authority. "You're not going to believe this!"

I took my coffee and sat down beside her, as she began to read an item to me. I could see that the text which interested her was under the public notices section.

"For Sale," she read; "West Shore Street, Ullapool. A semi-derelict cottage with side entry to a small garden area at the rear. Offers in excess of £100 to be submitted by Friday 16th November to the County Clerk, Ross-shire County Council, Dingwall."

Irene dropped the paper on the table and before I could even speak she cried: 'When can we go and look? It sounds perfect!'

I'd had my answer. Irene was still as enthusiastic to go to the Highlands as she had been when she first broached the subject.

"A cottage," I spluttered, after gulping a mouthful of coffee. "But we've only just arrived back."

It was no good. Irene was suddenly in overdrive. "Could we make the journey in one day?"

"You know we couldn't," I said with dismay.

"Ah well," she said, "you know you said yesterday that if we went to live in the Highlands we should consider having the new series Landrover? You *said*' – this was one of Irene's favourite phrases, always used to good effect when pressing home an argument – "you *said* that the new Landrover was not only faster, but more comfortable, even more economic."

I admitted that yes, I had said that, but reminded her that she had not been very enthusiastic.

"I expect I was tired," she replied innocently, and then continued: "Don't go back to the office now. You look so tired. Have the day off, and I'll drive you up to Shrewsbury to see the Landrovers." And so she did.

Just one week later, on a rather crisp Monday afternoon with the sun low in the western sky, we found ourselves just south of Shrewsbury driving a new Landrover. I used to be incredulous when people said to me that they had "found" themselves doing this or that and suggested that they had had a loss of memory. How could anyone find themselves doing something they did not know they were doing? I confess that now having found myself in just such an irrational position I can sympathise. Only one hour earlier we had been driving north to Shrewsbury in a perfectly sound vehicle which we had now exchanged for a similar vehicle, with a considerable cash adjustment not in our favour. The exchange was simply so that we could drive to the Scottish Highlands in one day instead of two, in order that to see a cottage which because it was for sale by tender we might not get, and which in any case we had already decided was not our best accommodation option – assuming we decided that we would decamp to the northern regions. Furthermore, as the whole idea had only occurred to us a little over a week ago, it was still all very tenuous. I'm not a worrier by nature but, even as we motored gently along on this late autumn afternoon, I could not help but think that the new Landrover was not the highest priority in the run-up to a move that might be months away, perhaps a year – or, I mused to myself, even more than a year. Moving house at this time of the year was not exactly ideal timing. Spring or early summer would be much more suitable. After a few miles enjoying the novelty of our new possession I felt obliged to unburden my feelings to Irene, but as I glanced in her direction I caught a look which I knew from experience meant "Listen!"

"Look here," she began. "You *know* you've already made your mind up that you are going to live in the Highlands – and remember, I'm coming too! Look at it like this: consider the Landrover as our first practical step. So now let's get home and start on the others!"

There were times when Irene could be quite abrasive in her manner. I particularly remember occasions when people who claimed specialist knowledge would attempt to take advantage of Irene's often down-to-earth approach to a subject. Unable to shake Irene's opinion they would resort to intellectual parrying. "And what did you study, Irene?" they would ask. Back in a flash would come Irene's reply: "Common sense." "Oh," they would exclaim, "you mean logic!" "No, I mean common sense." The protagonist would look confused, and perhaps uncertainly mutter "Was it something I mistakenly said?", but by this time Irene would have wandered off to talk to someone more interesting.

I had written to the Ross-shire Council asking for more details of the cottage and received a reply by return. Unfortunately it did not add to what the notice had already described, except that I learned that the offer should be by the normal form of Scottish tender for which one was advised to consult a solicitor. So, armed with a copy of the advertisement and the Council's reply to my enquiry, I went into Wolverhampton to ask whether our solicitor, a Mr Becket who had already very satisfactorily conveyed two properties for us, might in due course deal with the latest. I was completely taken aback to find he could not. He explained that Scottish law and English law were quite different and that a solicitor qualified in English law could not deal with a Scottish conveyance and that therefore I would need a Scottish solicitor. I was interested to learn that Mr Becket knew Ullapool, having spent a holiday there in 1938.

"A delightful spot and a very pretty village, rather primitive I recall." A faint smile crept over his much-lined face as he related the detail of an evening in the Royal bar and his stay in the hotel. "You know I think I'm a little envious, but what will you *do* all the way up there?"

I went cold with apprehension. It was a very good question. We had no income other than what we earned, and our capital would consist of what we got from the sale of the business and the house. We would have to live on (as little as possible of) that while we built our dream-home, and as soon as possible we would have to build a new business. Irene and I had ventured tentative suggestions to each other, but at this stage all were without substance.

Luckily for my credibility, Mr Becket's was a rhetorical question, for without waiting for my reply he was now looking through a directory. Then, peering over the top of his spectacles, he said: "Would you like me to give you the name of a Scottish solicitor?" and again without waiting for a reply continued: "Here is one: Stewart Rule & Co, Church Street, Inverness. David Wilson's your man, all good Scottish names you know. I'll let you have a letter of introduction. It might help. Be in the post tonight. Good luck!"

As an afterthought when I got up to leave, he added: "I expect you will be putting your present property on the market. Anything I can do to help, don't hesitate to call on me."

I thanked him, and went out into the smoke-tinged air to join Irene. Often when I went into Wolverhampton she would come along and take the opportunity to indulge in a little window-shopping and afternoon tea in her favourite store. When the weather was fine we would often meet up at the terrace of St Peter's Church, and perhaps wander into the church to remember the day when the Reverend Eric Waterhouse had officiated at our wedding ceremony a few years earlier. And so I made my way towards the church, an imposing edifice of red sandstone with a tall square finialed tower which had dominated the town for more than seven hundred years. The atmosphere was so clear that as I gazed westward from my vantage-point in front of the old church, I could see out beyond the bounds of the town and the low-lying countryside, on into Shropshire. As the vista widened with distance, I could make out the isolated mound of the Wrekin rising a mere thousand feet above sea-level yet visible from every direction of the surrounding county. If one climbs to the top and takes in the view, it is a veritable watchtower. I cannot remember how often I have climbed to its summit. A little to its south lies Wenlock Edge, immortalised by that great Shropshire writer Mary Webb in her tragic story *Gone to Earth*. In the far greater distance lie the great outcrops of the Stiperstones and near their summit the tiny hamlet of Shelve where my direct ancestors are recorded back into the 1700s. With a telescope I might have been able to see the exact spot.

It was not long before Irene arrived, and I could see that she was bubbling over with some item of excitement.

"Well?" I said, to which Irene countered, as she invariably did: "Business first."

So I outlined the meeting with old Mr Becket and the fact that we were on our way to having a Scottish solicitor.

"Good," she said, "but why are you so intent on the view?"

"I was looking out into Shropshire. See how clear it is! You can see out to the Stiperstones and the old Rogers home. It seems hard to believe we will be leaving the area to go to the Highlands."

"Yes, I see," she said hurriedly and took my arm. "Come on, we must hurry! I'm taking you to tea. They have the most gorgeous blackcurrant tarts with great whips of fresh cream."

Who could refuse such an invitation? I guessed however from experience that there would be something more. We would surely not emerge empty-handed from Irene's favourite store. But I was wrong for, having partaken of tea and the delicious blackcurrant tarts, we left the store without a single purchase. I said nothing as we walked in the direction of our parked vehicle, then suddenly felt my arm being turned obliquely to the left.

"There is a little antique shop I would like you to come and have a look at," said Irene.

Indeed it was a small shop, right at the side of St Peter's, the very church where we had stood earlier. We entered, the assistant smiled and Irene walked up to a small spinning wheel.

"Please may I buy it?" she pleaded. "Wouldn't it be a lovely thing to take up to Scotland?"

This was playing directly into the shopkeeper's hands and any chance of bargaining seemed already to have been lost.

"Welsh?" I ventured.

The shop keeper smiled: "More likely just this side of the border – Long Mynd, or the Stiperstones area – one of the little villages, Ratlinghope, Bridges, maybe Shelve. Do you know the area?"

Had I been set up? I still don't know and I had no intention of enquiring, then or later.

"Will sir be paying? That's twelve pounds."

It was half what I had thought. Both Irene and I grinned like Cheshire cats as we carried our trophy away.

Two weeks had passed since the day of Irene's casual pronouncement – "If we lived in the Highlands, we could go somewhere different for holidays" – and although we had mentally committed ourselves to the project we had as yet made no formal plan of action. Indeed you could say that the prospect had gone to our heads and that we were behaving somewhat irresponsibly. I was of course pleased with the new Landrover, and the little spinning wheel was charming, but they hardly constituted material progress towards our goal. True, we nearly had a Scottish solicitor, but that is not quite the same as actually having a Scottish solicitor – not the same as actually instructing a Scottish solicitor to move your affairs along. As yet we had done no such thing.

Subconsciously it was our business interests that were the cause of this indecisive behaviour. We simply had not been able to formulate a plan which would satisfactorily solve this problem. It is all very well uprooting oneself from one locality to another when only a house is involved. People do this all the time. So why not with a business? When selling a house one goes to an estate agent, and when selling a business there are specialist agents too. I selected the most prominent and made an appointment to meet one of the principals. I have never been enamoured with agents of any description. Cloaked as they are by their apparent sophistication, one is easily entrapped into thinking that they are the answer to the prayers of a person with property to sell. Mr Bullier sat impassively as I related the details of my business. It was really all very simple. We were architectural metal workers. In plain terms, any item of metalwork that an architect might design as part of a building's construction was our business. I had three years of certified accounts and our buildings were freehold. When I finished my description, Mr Bullier looked somewhat nonplussed and sucked his teeth for what seemed an interminable time. He then, with a look of total disinterest, came out with:

"Difficult one this. I suppose we could try an ad, but I can't think where just at the moment. Leave it with me."

I did just that, never going back and never hearing from him again.

Selling a business requires a certain strategy. The longer you advertise the less likely you are to get a sale or to achieve your asking price. A business placed on market is likely to come under much closer scrutiny than a house, and if for whatever reason your proposition is known to have been rejected even once, it is surprising how often the news finds its way to others. It is therefore vital to get everything right before going to the market. On the other hand, you must behave as though it is business as usual. You cannot afford to relax for a moment. Orders have to remain promptly executed, standards have to be maintained, quotations given and a constant search maintained for new orders. There is of course much else to do, but in short you behave as though it's business as usual. The psychology means that until the property is sold, you cannot entertain for a moment the idea that you won't be there for ever. No definite plans can be made until the deal is made. Both Irene and I knew this and had been instinctively holding back. Our acquisitions of the last two weeks were really only sweeteners aimed at keeping alight the fire of our enthusiasm.

Meanwhile the tender date for the cottage, 16th November, was getting nearer, and Irene was getting anxious. We provisionally set aside a few days just before the sixteenth when we might rush up to the Highlands. If need be, it could all be done very quickly: look at the cottage in the morning, instruct the solicitor in the afternoon and tender by midday on the following morning.

I ventured: "Perhaps we should go up on the twelfth?"

The decision brought a smile to Irene's face and I was pleased that at last I had taken a decision, but this was only a passing thought and my mind soon returned to the business.

That day I remained on hand in the workshop while a big steel section was bent to a very exacting curve. A lot of heat and a lot of force was necessary and whilst the struggle went on my job was close monitoring of the shape and the dimensions. I had not been looking forward to this operation and in fact had some doubt as to whether we would manage the work. When I arrived Ron, the foreman, had the work already set up. In a few minutes the blowtorches were roaring and the hydraulic jacks were pumped ready to knead the as-yet unyielding metal. It all went so incredibly easily that I had difficulty in keeping up with my part of the job.

The foreman stood back saying, "Owz that then?"

"Splendid," I replied. "In fact, congratulations."

He beamed, shrugged his shoulders and slightly shook his head from side to side. "Nothing, just a matter of knowing what you're at."

I would have given him a raise if he had asked, but he did not; a bit of praise in front of the others was enough.

Ron looked past me and pointed his finger towards the big doors: "There's a chap waiting to see you."

I spun round, and approaching was one of the most dapper
men I had ever met, a short slightly built man, perhaps in his
mid sixties. He was wearing an immaculately cut suit, elegant
tie and shoes that shone to perfection. He clapped his hands
enthusiastically as he approached. My immediate impression
was of a man who had spent his life greeting people, putting
them at their ease and generally trying to make them feel good.

"Well done, well done." He had obviously been watching the
bending operation. He held out his hand: "Joe Corkindale.
You'll be the owner. I'm very pleased to meet you."

I immediately recognised a Midlands accent, or to be more
precise a strong suggestion of the Black Country. Who was
this man whose new and rather extravagant car stood in the
lane outside? It was certainly clear, as he talked excitedly on,
that for the moment I was not going to find out more than his
name and I wasn't going to get a word in.

"I often come down and have a look at the lads. 'Spect they
are used to me by now. Mind you, I don't talk to them,
wouldn't want to stop them. They are hard workers, and of
course I never entered the premises. Took a chance just now
– thought you must be the owner – otherwise I promise I
would not have come in like that. Got a minute?"

Strangely I seemed to have all the time in the world. I had
fully expected that we would still have been working on the
beam. Joe Corkindale caught my arm.

"Come and have a look at the new car."

We walked outside into what was a rather pleasant morning
considering the lateness of the year. The lane was really no
more than a rough track and, although it was public, it was a
rarity to see another vehicle unless they were coming to the
workshop. I made to where the new car was standing, and was

just about to say how much I admired it, when Joe amazed me by saying:

"Forget the car. It's just another vehicle. I only said to come and see it to get you outside. I wanted to ask you something and I thought better I did so in private. Is that all right?"

I just managed to say "Of course," when Joe's enthusiasm got the better of him again.

"I heard that you might be going to live in Scotland."

I confirmed the fact, adding that it was not general knowledge yet, but he did not volunteer his source. Instead he went on: "I hope you will not think me too impertinent if I ask what is it that is taking you to Scotland."

I was floored for a moment and could think of nothing better to say than Irene's comment that had brought about the whole business. I had noticed that Joe never stopped smiling, and now he laughed out loud.

"Well I'm blessed! I admire you for your consideration towards your wife!" Then he quickly added: "But of course there is more?"

I said the next thing that came into my head: "Yes – great opportunities."

"There! I knew it! May I wish you all the luck in the world!"

By now I was thinking that Joe was just an interested retired gentleman who had run his car down our lane to pass the time for an hour or so, but no: Joe had my arm again.

"Come on, let's lean against the car. We might as well be standing in the sun – it's nippy in the shade. I'd like to talk a little business with you if you have the time."

"Always have time to talk business," I replied.

"You know that you have a saleable business here."

"Yes," I said, fully expecting him to say he might know someone who might be interested but, to my utter astonishment he changed the subject.

"Guess what I did in life."

I said that I had been trying to but couldn't.

"A tailor would you believe?"

At that moment the penny dropped. Yes! – Corkindale's, the bespoke tailors in the high street of a nearby town.

"Yes," I replied. "Of course, I know the shop."

"Then you have not seen it this last ten years, not since I sold out to a multinational, but that's by the way. I'll come straight to the point. In the last ten years I've bought a one-hundred bedroom hotel, refurbished it, run it and sold it, and in addition I've built myself two houses in different parts of the country and sold both. I now live just down the river from here and I tell you, I'm bored. I never wanted to be a tailor. I wanted to be an engineer and I would like to buy your business. Yes, I could buy something bigger, grander maybe, but I don't want that. Now – come on – what do you want'?"

I already liked Joe, not only because he had just expressed an interest in my business, but because I took him to be an honest man. I did my best to express shock but, as I had already agreed an asking figure with my accountant (on the day I had met the uninterested agent), I had no hesitation in disclosing the sum. To my amazement Joe had said it sounded fair. Would I accept valuation for the stock? Yes of course.

Joe held his hand out, I took it, we shook, and the deal was done, the business sold.

"Is it really one o'clock? I must fly. Come to dinner this evening – bring your wife, and we'll have a party to celebrate the occasion."

CHAPTER THREE

Travelling North Again

I did not immediately tell Irene that I had sold the business. I told her the story, all the circumstances leading up to the sale, stringing it out for as long as I could, before I made the actual announcement. Irene had quietly worried over the possible difficulties we might encounter in selling the business, especially after the very negative meeting I had had with the agent. When finally I made my announcement Irene was quite overcome with emotion, prompted no doubt by relief. Her only words were:

"Oh dear! Has your lovely workshop really gone? You were so proud of what you had built up!"

I have to say I felt a little emotional myself at this point, and suddenly remembered someone saying at times like this to try to think of a simple joke. I did my best, and said: "Think of the money."

It brought a smile to Irene's face and the quick reaction: "Can we make plans now?"

Joe Corkindale was an absolute dynamo. Not only did he chivvy his own solicitor to get on with the business, but he chivvied my solicitor and accountant too. Joe had stipulated only two conditions – that he take over as soon as possible and that I put him through an intensive three-month apprenticeship. I agreed to both. His plan suited me perfectly and gave me continued use of the workshop, a facility I was to appreciate greatly over the coming months.

It seemed very likely that Joe would take over before we needed to go to the Highlands to make our offer for the cottage. With the business in the process of being taken over, the need to minimize our time away had receded. Therefore we went ahead with arrangements to stay on the first night at Crianlarich, just north of Loch Lomond. The plan was that we would travel up to Inverness the following morning, meet our new solicitor in the afternoon, and make the west coast by evening. We were both excited at the prospect of what had now become a late holiday.

In what must stand as a record act of conveyancing, just over a week later Joe officially became the new owner of my architectural metalwork business. This was on the morning before we left for the Highlands – although in actual fact I had been quite unable to keep him away during the preceding days. The men had really taken to Joe. He had a wonderful way of putting people at their ease and, in the case of workers, knowing how to encourage their best efforts. There was certainly no lack of encouragement on that first morning of his ownership, for even as we toasted the success of the new business the local garage was delivering a brand new pick-up bearing discreet inscriptions upon its doors: *Corkindale Engineering.*

"Hope you didn't mind me jumping the gun a bit," Joe said with an impish smile.

Who could mind anything that Joe did? He was like a schoolboy whose favourite aunt had left him a legacy with the explicit instruction that it had to be spent.

It was still dark as we climbed steadily out of the Severn valley under a wonderfully starlit sky. Its clarity had sent the overnight temperature plummeting and left a glistening pure white coating of frost over everything. It was as though we were driving in a wonderland. The new Landrover moved effortlessly. Gone were the draughts and rattles of its predecessor. No more cold hands and feet, for the heater was more than up to its task. Gone too were the emotional troughs and peaks of the last few weeks, where excitement had been followed by disbelief at our foolhardiness, which in turn often turned to anxiety. Now the first phase of our proposal was accomplished, and the adventure had begun.

The early morning roads were almost devoid of traffic, with hardly a sign of life save at the occasional roadside farm, where in the dimly lit stockyards the steaming breath of cattle presented ghostly images. It was breaking daylight as we reached the first of the industrial towns. The workers had mostly already reached their places of employment but, save for the occasional newsagent, shops were not yet ready to

open. Our timing, though not deliberate, was just right and
we were clear of the urban conurbations much more quickly
than we'd expected. Perhaps it had just been less of an effort
than it had been when only a few weeks earlier we had
travelled south in the gathering dusk, tired after so many hours
of driving. Lancaster and Kendal passed us by. Even the
notorious descent of Shap seemed less arduous. No doubt it
had a great deal to do with the novelty of the new vehicle and
our buoyant spirits, and in such a mood we even forgave
Beattock as we sped through it during the afternoon.

However it all ground to a slower pace as we reached the
southern fringes of Glasgow, where although the city centre
still lay many miles ahead, traffic seemed to materialise from
nowhere as if it had been waiting just to slow us down. In
these post-war years the road north through the outskirts of
the city was lined with grim-looking buildings, relieved at
frequent intervals by interesting rows of shops. Each one
carried so many advertisements and notices entreating the
patronage of their customers that it was difficult to see from a
moving vehicle what goods were being offered. To add to the
uninitiated driver's difficulties, there were the trams with their
tram-lines always ready to steer you off in a direction contrary
to your intention. There were also miles of cobbled surface.
Woe betide any driver who did not take note of this fact –
especially if the surface were wet! For me, the biggest
nightmare was overtaking a tram. One would be just alongside
and the tottering, swaying vehicle would veer to the right, with
no signal but just following the tram-lines. When driving in
Glasgow one had to have one eye on the road and the other
on the tram-lines. No doubt the resident drivers knew all the
tricks of the tram-cars. It certainly never ceased to amaze me
how the Glaswegians passed so easily on the nearside of a tram

just as it might be stopping. I would attempt to follow, only to find myself amidst a mêlée of angry passengers attempting to alight and a conductor swinging around the platform pole and shouting something which I could not quite understand but of whose meaning there was no doubt....

Eventually we were in Argyle Street, where trams, lorries and cars packed the road and pedestrians thronged the pavements as they hurried in all directions before the brightly lit windows of the big stores. Eventually the traffic funnelled under the railway bridges that spanned the main thoroughfare, and the city-centre was left behind. Now down the Dumbarton Road the traffic, although no less dense, seemed to move a little faster, or perhaps it was that having run the gauntlet of the city-centre one had suddenly taken on a new-found confidence. The road followed the north bank of the River Clyde and, from time to time through narrow streets of houses, one saw the enormous prows of ships under construction and heard the unmistakable cacophony of a multitude of riveters hammering glowing hot rivets. In a few more miles Dumbarton was easily negotiated and now, even more quickly than we had entered the southern fringe of the great industrial area, we left it behind. In no time at all we were motoring along the western shore of Loch Lomond.

Remarkably, it had suddenly become almost daylight again, when not half an hour earlier under the pall of smoke in the city-centre it had been almost dark. Now the sky was clear and although the sun had gone down there was a pleasant quality of light. The mountain-tops were clear, with Ben Lomond and a few other higher peaks dusted with snow. We pulled into one of the many vantage-points where countless travellers before us had stopped to marvel at the sudden transformation of the scene. The air was chill but invigorating, especially as one looked back in the direction we had travelled where the mantle of industrial smog which overhung the city was still visible along its western fringe. By the time we reached the hotel at Crianlarich, night had fallen. Just as our day had begun under a beautiful starlit sky so we stood once more under that very same sky. It was as if we had not travelled at all.

Crianlarich Hotel proved to be fairly typical of many Highland hotels where the owner welcomes you not as a guest but as a traveller, anxious for your well-being.

"Come away in and sit by the fire for a moment. It'll be a hard frost the night. Will you take a cup of tea?" they would say, and then add in rather whispered voice, "Or maybe a wee dram?"

We chose the tea and sat close up to the roaring log fire. This habit of welcoming travellers goes back a long way, to the times when visitors to these often isolated hotels were the only source of news outwith the area. There was thus a natural urge to hear the news as soon as possible even when, as in days gone by, a traveller arriving on horseback might be near frozen to death on arrival, and even passengers arriving by horse-drawn coach might not have fared much better. Our host reappeared and for a while sat beside us, but there was now no need for news of the outside world – the wireless had already seen to that -- but nevertheless there was still a keen interest in our long journey.

When the last of the tea had been drunk and we were thoroughly warmed through, our host got up and made Irene smile when he had said that he had put us over the Aga, adding: "You will be nice and warm there."

Irene's immediate reaction was to conjure up a picture of hammocks slung from a clothes-drier above the cooker, but in reality it was a bedroom over the kitchen.

We had been advised to start as soon as it was light as there was sure to be a lot of ice on the roads, and we would have to go very slowly and carefully. The idea that we might have made the journey in one day was now revealed as the height of folly. The journey so far had been arduous enough, for even the main roads north had offered rare opportunity for overtaking slower traffic. Each of the many often congested towns had added to the delays, not least the long sprawl of Glasgow and the central belt, but these were as nothing to the road that skirted Loch Lomond on our final leg the previous day. Here the narrow road never ceased to contort, left-right, right-left, in seemingly never-ending loops which skirted the bays fringing the shores of the Loch. Add to this mile after mile of menacing rock-faces which came right to the very edge of the road and where one false move on the part of a tired driver might tear out the side of the vehicle. No: maybe in summer weather we could have done the journey of over five hundred miles in one long drive, but not in the winter.

Crianlarich is set deep in the heart of the Highland glens, surrounded on all sides by high mountains.. We were soon to learn that it had a microclimate all its own. On such days as this it was indeed very very cold. A heavy coating of pure white frost clung to everything. It was difficult to keep one's footing, and I was glad that on the previous evening the hotel had insisted that I put the car in one of their garages.. Had I not done so I might now have been embarking on a very difficult job of removing ice. The early morning sky was still grey as our host waved us off with a last warning to watch out for the ice. Irene affirmed for the umpteenth time that we would, then shouted "Good-bye!", and we were off.

Although the main route north was very narrow, the road was single track with sparingly located passing-places. Irene had been unnerved by all the warnings of ice and was already seeking reassurance.

I murmured: "I don't think there is anything to worry about. This vehicle could go anywhere. We will just take it slowly until I get the feel of the road."

No sooner had I said the words than we were sideways on as we came to a slight bend. The reason was soon obvious — water had been flowing down the road from a blocked ditch or some such, and the Landrover was now standing on a sheet of ice inches thick. With the vehicle at right angles to our intended route Irene could see back in the direction whence we had come and was telling me that she could still see the hotel in the distance. The Landrover with its nearly new and heavily cleated tyres and in a low-ratio gear soon had us out of difficulty. We were off once more, but this time even more slowly. From now on things got worse. The frequent water-courses had streamed onto the road and frozen. It was like driving along the bed of an ice-solid river, as it twisted and turned for mile after mile. As we climbed further into the mountains we pierced a veil of freezing mist and, for the first time since we had set out that morning, we came upon another vehicle — a large Humber estate-car. We were squeezed close together as we manœuvred to pass. When we drew level the driver inched his window down, and called: "How far to the next petrol? I've been crawling so long I'm nearly out."

We had by chance just seen in the gloom a mile-marker.

"Six miles," I gasped as the cold air suddenly entered my lungs, and with that the Humber moved off before I could enquire as to what the conditions ahead. Perhaps it was obvious from the other driver's comment.

"Six miles," Irene repeated. "That means we have only covered eleven miles in almost an hour."

Things were looking a bit serious. We had arranged to be in Inverness at two thirty to meet our new solicitor. We began to consider telephoning ahead when, quite unexpectedly, the road widened into a carriageway where two cars might pass. In fact it was a stretch of road as good and straight as any we had traversed since leaving Shropshire. So, despite the fact that it was still very icy and the mist was as thick as ever, I felt justified in going just a little faster. For the moment I believed we would reach Inverness on time. Mile after mile the road went fairly level. Then there was a bridge followed by a series of sweeping bends, and we were climbing again. From the map we guessed that we were crossing Rannoch Moor, although we could see little of it other than boulder-strewn verges with the appearance of a moonscape.

Then, as abruptly as we had found ourselves on this excellent road, it came to an end. We were back on a narrow, bending and steeply descending gradient with deep rutted ice. Soon we were at a crawl again. Down and down the road plunged. It suddenly seemed lighter and in a flash the mist was gone. Miracle of miracles, the sun was shining and what a scene we beheld! Towering mountains on both sides cast giant shadows as they blocked the sunlight so cleanly; ahead we could see the light reflected on even more high mountains, clad down to their lower slopes in fresh snow.

We had reached the pass of Glencoe. There were still long streaks of frozen runnels at intervals along the road, but these were less frequent than they had been. We earnestly hoped that we would soon escape the icy nightmare. Still descending we came to a junction. Ahead of us was the sea. Loch Leven is a sea-loch which at this point stands in the way of any further direct progress north. We had two choices – either to take a long detour via the head of the loch and the village of the same name, or to cross by ferry at Ballachulish. We chose the latter, thinking it would save us something in excess of a dozen miles not to mention a hazardous drive.

We followed the signs and in a couple of miles found the loading jetty. The craft was lying at the far end, where we could see the ebb tide running out like a fast flowing river. It seemed such a small craft to take a vehicle over such a treacherous stretch of water. Near the water's edge all trace of frost and ice had vanished, but it remained bitterly cold.

As no one appeared at our arrival I decided to go and investigate. The boat's engine was running and I could see from the wash under the stern that a propeller was slowly turning in order to keep the craft alongside, but there was still no sign of a crew. We were wondering whether we might not have done better to drive round the long way, when two men came sauntering down towards the boat. They passed without comment, and then without even looking up one of them signalled to us to come forward onto the turntable deck. The skipper increased the engine revolutions to prevent the craft departing before we had moved from the jetty to the ramp. Safely aboard, gates across our front and rear penned us like so many sheep, the engine went full astern and we were carried out to sea. At a suitable distance from the shore we heard the engines go full ahead. Very slowly the boat began to stem the fierce tide out in mid stream, clawing its way up the centre of the sea-loch. We kept going until we reached the point at which years of experience had taught the skipper to pause. From here we would be swept back to the jetty on the opposite shore. When the moment for the turn came, such was the ferocity of the current that it was only moments before we were alongside our destination.

It had all taken a great deal longer than we had expected but it had been a wonderful experience. Before the crewman set us free he came to collect the fare, and still barely looked at us.

"Did'na think anybody would be over before midday seeing how much ice they say is over the top, and we was glad seeing how strong the spring low is running."

I handed over the fare and bade him keep the change, then felt embarrassed as he slowly touched his cap and waved us off.

We were now, incredibly, in sunshine. We had escaped the shadow of Glencoe's great mountain ranges, although we could still see the mist clinging to their flanks. Soon we were bowling along in fine style, unable quite to believe all that had happened. In only these few miles Loch Leven had joined the wide expanse of Loch Linnie. All was now mirror-calm as the last of the ebb slackened. A MacBrain steamer was making its way towards the town pier, and there was not a breath of wind as we ran up towards Fort William. But for the cold it might have been a summer's day. Fort William was quiet as we slipped down the main street. We had passed through the so-called Gateway to the Highlands, and as we entered the Great Glen we knew that we would just make Inverness in time for our meeting.

All the same, we had sixty-six miles to go and no time to lose. Nevertheless, a little beyond Spean Bridge we stopped to look back at the massif of Ben Nevis, white-capped in its mantle of early winter snow. This was a rare sight – we had been told that more often than not Ben Nevis is shrouded in mist. The road through the Great Glen was far easier than we had anticipated. Although it twists and turns and continually undulates we made Fort Augustus a little ahead of our scheduled time, but as we had nothing spare for emergencies we pressed on.

Alongside Loch Ness, home of the legendary monster, we cast the occasional glance out over the dark waters, but saw nothing. At one forty-five we reached our goal, and fifteen minutes later were sitting in an Inverness café with a traditional Scottish high-tea – haddock and chips, the obligatory bread and butter, a pot of tea and not forgetting the other high tea accompaniment, a three-tier cake-stand loaded with scones, pancakes and numerous other goodies.

Irene had always looked unfavourably upon the legal profession and I had been unsure whether she actually wanted to meet our new solicitor. It turned out she didn't and, without our having to discuss the matter, she decided that her time would be better employed in exploring the Inverness shops. Although Inverness was full sixty miles from Ullapool it was the nearest main shopping centre. Thus with five minutes to spare I set off alone for the chambers of Messrs Stuart Rule, leaving Irene to contemplate the contents of the three-tiered cake-stand.

I had already located the solicitor's office, across the road from where we had just eaten our excellent meal. I was shown in to Mr Wilson's office without a moment's wait, so it was as if I had just got up from one table and was immediately sitting down at another. It was a rather bleak room, sparsely furnished and aged from lack of recent decoration. Indeed it had a Dickensian feel, with its shelves of marbled ledgers, its rows of red-covered law-books, its piles of documents tied with pink string, and a number of redundant cast-iron paper-presses with their unused platens and screws gently rusting with age. Mr Wilson struck me at once as a shy man, for he hardly looked up as he shook my hand and bade me take a seat. He was of slight build and average height with the appearance of an academic schoolmaster rather than a solicitor.

This impression increased when he began by giving me an explanation of how English and Scottish law differed in the matter of buying and selling property. In Scotland, and particularly in the Highlands, property sales were almost universally handled by solicitors, unlike in England where the business was more often than not dealt with by an estate agent. Another distinctly different procedure was that of the asking price. The English system was to state the highest expectation and then negotiate downwards, whilst in Scotland one stated one's lowest acceptable figure and asked for offers above it. Furthermore, rather than leave the length of the selling period in the hands of the purchaser, the seller set a closing date by which offers should be made.

The sellers never in fact bound themselves to accept the highest or any offer but invariably did so. During the whole of the time Mr Wilson was delivering his discourse on property buying and selling he had hardly once looked at me, but sat with head bowed and with the fingers of his right hand continually twiddling the end of his nose as if constantly tuning in to one or other thought-wave. He paused a moment and resumed in the archetypal manner of an absent-minded professor, and I was now even more convinced of my impression that he was an academic and not a solicitor.

"Now where were we? Ah yes.... It's all here in your letter" which he began to read quietly to himself. As soon as the letter was read and he had taken time to consider its contents (something which I would have expected him to have done before I came, but if he had he had now forgotten it), he returned to the subject with a particularly determined twiddle of his nose and a long-drawn-out "W-e-l-l,... yes... perhaps this is a bit different from what I have been telling you. This is, shall we say, a derelict cottage for sale at Ullapool. Am I right in thinking that?"

I recall answering "Yes", but of course I had no more information to go on than what he had just read for himself. There was another long pause for thought, and then:

"You might have to disregard some of what I have told you. You see, the one hundred pounds asking price may bear no relationship to the expectation. It is a sprat to catch a mackerel, if you get my meaning. What you really need is the advice of a surveyor, but you do not have the time for that as the tender must be in by the date stated. I really can't advise you what to do, but I will be happy to undertake whatever instructions you may care to give me."

It was an ominous reply. It amounted to: 'You tell me what to do and I will carry out your instructions within the framework of the law. However I cannot be held responsible for your success or failure. I will only be carrying out your instructions.' That first meeting with a Scottish solicitor revealed to me what was to be my experience for many years to come.

We agreed that I would look at the building first thing on the following morning and telephone my instructions regarding my offer. I was assured that this would be delivered to the Council offices by the appointed time.

Irene was back in the tea-shop and tapped the window as I crossed the road.

"How did it go?" she enquired as soon as I had joined her table.   I related the meeting in a somewhat less than enthusiastic manner.

"I'm glad I didn't come along then. Mind you, the shops are not much better – except for the tea-shops.   They're wonderful! Try these scones!"

Dusk was not far away as we left Inverness behind.   There was little cloud in the western sky and although the sun had long since gone down there remained a very pleasant soft pink-orange afterglow in the sky which remained until we were descending into the glen.   The river Broom flows from here before discharging into the loch of the same name. Even as we reached the head of the loch it was still not really dark, and although the lights of the village twinkled in the distance there still remained a glimmer of light over the faraway Summer Isles. We had made our destination just as planned and we could smile at our adventures. As we drew up in Shore Street, the speedometer trip clicked over to five hundred and twenty-five miles.

CHAPTER FOUR

A False Start and a True One

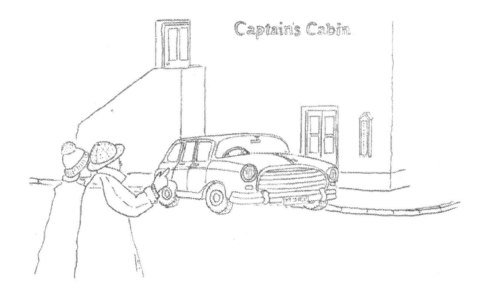

We had holidayed at Ullapool on more than a dozen occasions and during the years had made many friends. We'd never actually stayed in the village, preferring to take a delightfully situated lodge on the shores of the loch at Camas na Damph about a mile from the centre. We had had a special reason for wanting to be in this remote spot, particularly so when we took our holiday at the end of the season: we would pack up our company books and papers and, in the peace and solitude of the lodge, we would write up the whole of the year's accounts. Irene would then prepare the trial balance which, almost invariably, she would get right at the first attempt. It was a wonderful way to start our break. It was almost like re-reading one's diary – a review of a busy year successfully completed. Already the accounts were ready to go off to the accountant, everything neat and tidy. A very satisfying way to begin a well-earned break in this most beautiful part of the Highlands!

But this time in Ullapool was very different. For one thing, it was only a little over a month since our last visit, when we had as usual dealt with the accounts and followed that with a couple of weeks of walking, fishing, touring, visiting old friends and generally enjoying ourselves. But it was not only that now we had no company accounts to attend to, we had no company either. It was sold, and safely in the hands of Joe Corkindale. Further we had not journeyed five hundred miles for an early winter holiday, but for something much more serious. We had come to look at a cottage with a view to coming to live in the village. What better than to stay in the village on this special occasion?

We had thought carefully about this option before we set out from Shropshire, as it had certain difficulties. The principal problem was that Ullapool was very new to the tourist business, and many of our old friends were now putting out Bed & Breakfast signs. Whoever we chose to stay with we were likely to offend someone else. We could easily have avoided that situation by staying at the hotel, but that would defeat the whole object of being in the village – to get to know more about village life. At long last we chose to stay with a friend who lived on Shore Street. There were several advantages to our choice as we were no strangers and had many things in common. This would ensure one or two long evenings around the fire when we would be brought up to date with all that was going on, particularly the cottage which, very conveniently, was next door. We had plumped for the Shore Street lodgings just in time to write on ahead (I purposely did not reveal the object of our visit – that could wait). By return we had received an enthusiastic note inviting us to stay as long as we liked.

It is a strange feeling visiting a place outwith the seasons to which you have become accustomed. As we drove down the narrow street which separates the village from the shore, we could hardly distinguish the road-edge from the dark waters. An occasional light ashore was reflected on the top of the lazy swell as its momentum was lost in the pebbles of the foreshore. Lost in the darkness were the pretty gardens which line the seashore and which are so attractive in summer. There was little in the way of artificial lighting on the streets and, for the first time, we were seeing the village going about its business in the dark. True, we had seen the village in darkness many times during spring and autumn visits, when with only the sound of the lapping sea in our ears we had walked around a seemingly deserted community, but this activity in the darkness was intriguing. The first of the shops one passed was the chemist's at the corner of Mill Street. One would barely have known that the shop was open at all, the light glimmered so faintly from its tiny window. The same might easily have been said of the plumber's shop, which lately had expanded into electrical goods displayed in a window which never held more than an electric kettle, an iron and a one-bar fire. A low-wattage bulb glowed dimly in the interior and although the door was ajar there was probably no one there to serve a would-be customer. On the last occasion that I had called into the shop I had waited some minutes before a local seeing me waiting in anticipation called unconcernedly: "They're up at the water supply inlet. Blocked again. Dead sheep I shouldn't wonder."

As we progressed along Shore Street the first shop with any real illumination (and that only by comparison with that we had already seen) was Lipton's, the centre of supply for most staples and, not of least importance, a good selection of whiskies. There followed a general store, the Seaman's Mission and, next door, the Loch Broom Drapery. Then there was a green grocer's which, like most of the stores in the village, had been a simple cottage with consequently tiny windows whose dim glow was the only indication that they were open for business.

Finally, on the corner across from the pier, there was the village hardware store, the very centre of the commercial universe. Now if ever the Scottish Office had decreed that Ullapool should have diplomatic representation then Kenny would have been the obvious choice for the position of diplomat. The fact that Kenny's shop had no electricity but clung instead to the old-world charm of a very ornate oil lamp must not be taken as evidence that his stock similarly lacked imagination. This was by no means the case. You could not ask for the wrong thing: a bodger for making a peg rug, fish hooks of every size, paint for every type of surface, every kind of household cleaner, paraffin, turpentine, ammonia – whatever one might ask for he had or would get in a few days. Not only that, but several non-consumables could be had on approval. On one occasion I went in to buy a pair of wellingtons. I chose a suitable pair and, having enquired the price, I was admonished: "Just take them. How do you know they will fit until you have walked around in them for a bit?"

Kenny was always ready with advice, a weather forecast, the best place to fish or just a bit of local information, but like many people of such amiable disposition there was a sterner side. He was a staunch churchman, an elder and a man who practised what he preached. If something needed saying he could press home his point with authority. For example, one

Friday evening a year or two back I was down at the pier when a Buckie fishing boat had come in with storm-damage. I volunteered to help with the repair, and we toiled all though a long Saturday. In the late afternoon I saw Kenny shutting his shop, then watched as he walked purposefully down to where we were working. He had a grim look on his face and stood watching us for a while before turning to me. His demeanour made me feel that I was doing something wrong and his tone was one that I had not previously encountered.

"How is it going?" he had asked.

"There is a lot to do," I had replied.

"Then you had better get on, for you cannot be doing it on the Sabbath." He just turned and walked off.

Fortuitously, we did get finished just before closing time, and the subject was never mentioned again.

On this night, our first as prospective inhabitants, a few east-coast herring-drifters lay alongside the old wooden pier. In contrast to the village their decks were ablaze with light and fishermen busied themselves about the decks as they made ready to sail out into the Minch.

"The fishing must be good," I remarked to Irene. "They would be gone by now if the catches had been light."

Indeed had the catch been heavy it would have taken them until daybreak to haul their nets, and the rest of the day to get back to port and discharge the catch. Even then they might have to set to and repair nets. The only time for sleep might be a couple of hours whilst the vessel sailed out to the fishing grounds or whilst the boat lay to the nets, and even then someone would have to remain on watch. After that it was out onto heaving decks surrounded by the pitch dark of the open sea. Hours of non-stop back-breaking work; sometimes, when fish were scarce, all for nothing.

Leaving the glow of the pier behind, and as our eyes adjusted to a twilight that had not been obvious in the glow of the village, the object of our journey came unexpectedly into view. Along West Shore Street we could see the faint outline of cottages, one of which might easily soon be ours. The road was narrow and on its seaward side a wide grass verge was home to many small boats, now drawn up for the winter. Between the boats lay piles of lobster-pots and coils of rope, all awaiting a place in the various fishermen's stores, until the spring and the start of another season. As Ullapool Point opened up and we drew alongside the home of our hosts, the source of the twilight became apparent. Although the sun had long ago set there remained a thin golden line at the very edge of the sea and sky, the afterglow which was part of the evening magic of the north-western seaboard.

A quick greeting and we were installed without our having done a thing towards unloading our luggage or being able to get a word in, even to satisfactorily answer the non-stop questions. Had we really travelled five hundred miles? Did we come through Glasgow? They had heard there had been snow – was that right? What time did we start? And so it went on. They would be amazed by our tale, but it would have to wait. No sooner had we drawn breath than Morag, our hostess, was ordering Duncan to see to the fire (which was already going like a furnace), to bring the chairs in a bit, and "Will they want the table-light nearer?"

Irene intervened: "Everything is just perfect. It is so cosy, so comfortable that I don't think I will ever want to move."

"Supper will not be long if you would first like to see your room," Morag said, smiling perhaps with relief at Irene's enthusiastic approval of everything. There was some justification for Morag's seeming nervousness for she and

Duncan had only recently married, and they now shared the house where Duncan and his brother had lived as bachelors for many years. It was something of an achievement to have produced such a homely atmosphere into an establishment that had for so long been second to a fishing boat.

Although we knew Duncan and Morag well enough to have chosen to stay with them, we did not know them well enough to expect to stay without paying. We were simply bed-and-breakfast-with-evening-meal as the emerging Tourist Board was advising prospective participants in the new industry to advertise themselves. Morag busied herself in the kitchen whilst Duncan acted as waiter shuttling the dishes backwards and forwards as the meal progressed. Very little was said until Duncan came in to collect the coffee tray and Morag put her head momentarily around the door to enquire if we had enjoyed our meal and whether there was anything else we required. We had certainly enjoyed the meal and despite many snacks during the journey we had been ready for something more substantial.

Duncan hung about for a while as if he had something to say but could not think how to start. Suddenly and as if the question would not wait longer out it came: "And what has brought you back to the Highlands so soon after your holiday?"

Quite unthinking I answered truthfully, as indeed it was the only answer: "Oh, we've come to look at a cottage that the County Council are selling."

Duncan's face hardened and he turned so quickly to leave us that he nearly collided with the door to the kitchen which had slowly been closing of its own accord. We sat ourselves at either side of the glowing fire hoping that our hosts would join us, but they did not. All we heard were whispered conversations occasionally rising to agitated and almost audible discussion. It was as if an established friendship had just been terminated. Irene and I were genuinely too tired to care just then. It had been a very long day and we soon decided that it was time to retire. I called out "Good night!" The whispering stopped but there was no acknowledgement.

Breakfast was an equally frosty affair and we too took to whispering. Was it something we had done, or said? Irene thought that perhaps Duncan wanted to buy the cottage. I dismissed the idea, and added that it was more likely to be something to do with the placard we had seen outside a newsagent's shop that proclaimed: 'Outrage as outsiders buy up village homes.' Irene was clearly unnerved and suggested that perhaps we move elsewhere to pursue our quest from a neutral base. Since we had in fact only intimated a stay of two nights, we decided to tough it out and before leaving on the morrow, to solve the mystery of the frigid atmosphere that was in danger of engulfing our stay. The kitchen door was about half way through its self-closing act when I called out that we were off for the day and would be back in the late afternoon. At least Duncan acknowledged my announcement with a grunted "Aye."

The sky was a clear blue and the sun had just peaked over the snow-capped mountains in the east. The wind had dropped away completely and the loch was as smooth as a mirror. If last evening's afterglow had been magic then the morning was a miracle. Already one could feel a gentle warmth from the sun. It could easily have been the start of a summer's day. Our spirits lifted, and we jumped into the Land Rover and drove towards the pier. We'd already absorbed enough of the Highland approach to property dealing to be very circumspect about out interest in the cottage. We had decided not to look directly towards the cottage but instead to make a cursory inspection via the wing mirror, but it was hard to restrain ourselves.

"It's very tiny," Irene observed, and I agreed.

I don't know why we drove there, as we could easily have walked the few yards. Much to Irene's disgust I had stopped only a yard or two short of the ornamented cast-iron toilets overhanging the sea.

We were no sooner out of the vehicle than we were hailed by Willie Macrae. It had been Willie who on our very first visit to the village had persuaded us that no visit was complete without a boat trip to the Summer Isles. The Summer Isles were some twelve miles distant, out at the entrance to Loch Broom. This had been long before the days of organised boat trips, and there had been just the three of us in a rather small boat for the job, with a tiny Kelvin engine that ran as sweet as a sewing machine – not that it didn't stop occasionally. In fact it seemed to take frequent rests, something which Willie confessed was to do with the wrong clothes peg at the magneto. It is a day I recall frequently, the soft winter sunlight over a clear calm sea. We had landed on Tanera Mor, the main island of the Summer Isles group. Irene and I had walked over the island for a couple of hours whilst Willie remained at the boat smoking his pipe. From the highest point we had looked out over the smooth surface of the sea to the many other islands that make up the Summer Isles. No wonder they are called the Jewels of Wester-Ross! Looking across the sea to the north were the spectacular mountains of Sutherland, and to the south, beyond Gruinard Bay and more distant the high Torridonian mountains, we could see the Isle of Skye, whilst in the west, low on the horizon, were the Outer Hebrides. We had stood up there quite alone. We might easily have been the only ones in the world. I believe it was then that we had secretly decided that one day we would live in the Highlands.

Today Willie shook our hands until our arms were in danger of falling off. "Whatever brings you back so soon?"

Forgetting our vow of circumspection, I told him.

Willie stood dumfounded. I was uneasy and cursed myself for having been so unthinking. Irene was looking equally uneasy. Willie was obviously turning the situation over in his mind when suddenly he laughed out loud.

"What on earth interests you in that old place? It needs demolishing, and then what would you be left with? Nought but a pocket handkerchief of land! Don't you know Duncan keeps his fishing gear in there, and regards it as his?"

We were astounded, and the reason for Duncan and Morag's sudden offhandedness became clear. But before I could say anything he had his hand on my shoulder and was appealing to Irene in the way an expert salesman might make his pitch. Willie was an expert.

"Now look," he began. "You can do better than buying the old parish poorhouse! What you need is a fine stance down at the shore, a place where you could keep a small boat and build a fine cottage!"

We all smiled – who wouldn't at such a prospect? However there was only one thing wrong with the proposition: there was no such land in the village. I was about to say so, but Willie was unstoppable.

"What you need is to see the Major. Well, isn't that just the luck – here comes the very man."

We looked but saw no one. We were obviously were looking puzzled, so Willie enlightened us.

"The Humber estate car coming down Quay Street."

The car drew up on the corner below the captain's cabin. A dapper man of military bearing got out. He was dressed in a well-worn Harris-tweed jacket and matching breeches. Without another word, Willie marched over and accosted him.

"Good morning, Major!"

The Major straightened himself and seemed rather flustered. There was a lack of respect in Willie's approach and the Major's "Good morning, Willie" was rather abrupt. Willie was not the least put out.

"Major, I want you to meet two good friends of mine, Trevor and Irene Rogers."

We shook hands and I immediately liked the man. He smiled, and there was something friendly and welcoming about him. I could not say exactly just then. He introduced himself as Ian Scobie, but before any further word could be said Willie broke in.

"Now Major."

The Major's military moustache twitched and he frowned. Willie's approach was without question over-familiar, and the Major was clearly somewhat irked.

Willie continued unabashed: "My friends are looking for a building plot, near the shore if possible. I immediately thought of you, Major."

With that, Willie excused himself and hurried back to the pier-head and no doubt some other mission. The Major was the first to speak. He may have been bemused by Willie's informal style, or perhaps he did have land available – I could not of course say at that moment, but a twinkle in his eye suggested that he was by no means put out by the request.

"Land eh? What, what? Down by the sea, boat, eh what?"

"Yes, that's about it," I replied nervously. It seemed an age while the proposition was turned over in the Major's mind.

"Now then!" he at last said. "What d'you say to coming up to Rhidorroch Lodge, midday? We can have a dram and talk about it. I'm sure Patricia would like to meet you. Mid-day it is then!"

I thanked our new acquaintance and affirmed that, yes, we would be delighted to come along. Whatever the Major had come to the village for he had now clearly forgotten as he simply turned and drove back whence he had come.

To say that Irene and I were excited would have been a gross understatement. We were literally shaking with excitement, so much so that we just crossed the road and ensconced ourselves in the Tanera Café amongst half a dozen fish-buyers bemoaning the morning's poor landings. We sipped our coffee not daring to discuss the future. In little over an hour we would be up at the big house. Then all of a sudden Irene took fright.

"Suppose the Major thought that we had thousands and that we wanted to build a sporting lodge or something?"

"No," I tried to reassure her. "He wouldn't have thought that. Didn't Willie say that we only wanted to build a cottage?"

"No, he didn't. Remember – he just said we wanted a building plot."

I realized I could not remember what had been said, it had all been so sudden. Still the adrenaline was running, and time dragged as we waited. We had another coffee, and another buyer joined the circle with the news that the *Fragrant Rose* was in sight, an announcement that brought a murmur of encouragement and prompted a mass exodus down to the fish salesroom.

It was now eleven thirty and I judged that it was time to get started. Ten minutes later I knew I had misjudged the timing, for despite the roughness of the road up through the Rhidorroch Glen and our slow progress, we were already within sight of the lodge. We pulled in amongst the pines bordering Loch Achall. The only sound was the torrent of a nearby burn as it ran amongst the boulders. Rhidorroch Lodge is by Highland standards a substantial house; of typical early-Victorian design, it is situated amongst acres of Scots pine above the mile-long loch, with a magnificent view. The front door was open despite its being November and in a moment the Major appeared clutching a bottle of what I took to be sherry.

"For the ladies, what what. Come along in and meet Patricia." He shepherded us somewhere to the left. "Here in the with-drawing room, good fire, warmer, what what eh?"

Mrs Scobie could not have been more charming. " How brave you are tackling our road! Isn't it just frightful? I do hope it has not damaged your car."

I explained that it was a Land Rover. "Oh, how sensible!"

The warmth of the fire plus the Major's over-generous drinks soon had us chatting. I explained that my business was sold and, articulating thoughts that had barely entered my mind until that moment, said that having been visitors to Ullapool for a number of years that we had decided to come and live in the area and restart our business. The Major suddenly became a little more attentive and put his glass down.

"Does that mean that there are possibilities of local employment?" he asked.

My mind was racing ahead and I said "Yes, certainly."

I might have been mistaken, but I felt aware that Mrs Scobie was signalling her approval. The Major picked up his glass again, took a sip and announced that he thought they might have just the place for us, on the shore and a mile south of the village. Mrs Scobie rose. "You will stay and have a little lunch? Perhaps we could all go down and have a look afterwards. It would be such fun!"

Later, so as not to not to miss any of the fun, Mrs Scobie drove their Land Rover ahead of us as we bumped our way down the glen and on through the village. Eventually we stopped in a roadside lay-by alongside a spinney of oaks, birch, aspen and alder growing amongst the golden bracken which stretched down a steep slope to the shores of the sea-loch below. A dilapidated post-and-wire fence prevented access to the land, but even without it access would still have been difficult. The first few yards were in fact a steep embankment supporting the single track main road. I mentally noted this extreme drawback, and began calculating in my mind the expense and effort required to gain a vehicle entrance. As I might have expected even on our short acquaintance, the Major was already off scouting for an easier access, and it wasn't long before the command came for us to join him. He was standing at a point where the fence had disappeared and the embankment was less severe.

"Put your foot down hard, less likely to slip," he gently commanded Irene, who obeyed by stamping her way down through the bramble- and bracken-covered slope. At that particular point it was thankfully quite short. We were following her when suddenly the Major, bringing up the rear, missed his footing and sliding between us placed himself at the head of the party once more. It was surprisingly easy going now, the slope being quite gentle. Small patches had obviously been cultivated in the distant past, and marauding sheep had made something like a path for us as we threaded our way in and out of the profusion of small silver birch and bracken.

It was now becoming obvious that there was a great deal more land between the road and the shore than had been evident from the lay-by. At last we came out of the trees onto a headland where the Major delighted in telling us that the great smooth slabs of rock were the ancient bed of a prehistoric glacier. A short distance on, and we were at the point of the headland where the smooth slabs gave way to the more rugged coastline. Twenty feet below our feet, the land plunged into the deep water of the loch.

I caught Irene's hand as she leaned close to the edge. She gave my finger a long squeeze, and I knew that this place would one day be our home.

CHAPTER FIVE

A Highland Romance

We remained sitting on the rocks above the headland long after Major and Mrs Scobie had departed. It had not been more than an hour since we had first seen these seven acres, on one of the most beautiful shorelines in the Highlands: Creag nan Cudaigean. It was unbelievable that we were now its potential owners.

The light was beginning to fade in the east. Beyond the head of the glen, snow glistened brilliant white against the inky blue of the coming evening, whilst the west was still reflecting another spectacular display of golden light from the sun, long since set. The herring-drifters left the harbour, one by one, and became silhouettes receding into the distance. One by one, pinpoints of light from the village took on a fairy-tale image with a faint haze of blue peat-smoke rising above the rooftops.

Irene shivered. The temperature was dropping and it was time to leave our dream world. Away from the reflected light of the water the ground was barely visible as we stumbled back to the roadside. We sat for a while in the vehicle whilst the engine warmed the heater. I don't think either of us was thinking of anything in particular. Our minds and senses were drunk with all that had happened. It was Irene who broke the silence as the warmth began to seep into our numb bodies.

"Did the Major say where his solicitors were?"

I fished the card out of my pocket. He had written the solicitor's name on it, and which I could just read it in the dim light of the cab.

"Mr Wardle. Anderson, Shaw and Gilbert, Church Street, Inverness."

"That's the same street as Mr Wilson's office," Irene noted.

"Oh my goodness! Damn it! I forgot to ring Stuart Rule. I promised David Wilson that I would let him know not later than this afternoon what we wished him to do about the cottage." I was already shunting the Land Rover around in the narrow road. "I wonder if he will still be in his office. I must see if I can get him from the 'phone -box."

The unreliable village clock said ten minutes to five. Fortunately David Wilson's card was still in my top pocket and we always had change ready for emergencies. I dialled his number and almost immediately I recognised the voice of the lady I had spoken to on previous occasions. Incredibly, she recognised me.

"Ah, 'tis Mr Rogers. Mr Wilson was expecting your call. I'm putting you through."

I was relieved to hear the calm voice enquiring if it were now in order for him to proceed with the offer for the cottage. Then, in what I thought a light-hearted jibe, he admonished me for almost leaving it too late. I was breathing heavily from having hurried to the telephone – in fact I had a job to get my words out.

"We have decided not to proceed with the cottage," I managed to say.

"Not to proceed?" came the rather annoyed reply.

I imagined that he had before him the formal offer we had discussed and that it only awaited my instruction before receiving his signature. A moment passed. Mr Wilson had regained his dignity.

"Am I to take it that we are withdrawing from this negotiation?"

"Yes" I replied firmly, adding: "We have purchased a plot of land instead."

There was no reply so I began to fill in the details.

He interrupted: "Yes, yes, I know Anderson Shaw, and that Mr Wardle acts for Rhidorroch, but you might have discussed it with me beforehand. I'll telephone them in due course and see what's to be done."

I just had time to say goodnight and the coins were gone. The conversation with David Wilson had something of a sobering effect on me, but Irene was now warmed through and bubbling over with plans. So I just reported that everything was in order. We would not be offering for the cottage, but were buying Creag nan Cudaigean instead.

We drove down West Shore Street with a mixture of super-elation tempered with just a little trepidation – what would Duncan's mood be this evening? Morag greeted us at the door.

"Ah you're back," and added quickly: "There's plenty of hot water if you're wanting baths."

I thanked her and Irene whispered to me: "Round one."

Much refreshed by our baths and still in high spirits we decided not to mention the cottage or our adventures. No one had actually said at what time we might eat so we just appeared at about the same time as the previous evening. We might have been a bit late, as no sooner were we seated than Duncan appeared in his rôle as waiter, carrying two bowls of steaming hot scotch broth.

"Fine day" were his only words.

I replied: "Yes, just perfect," to which after a moment Irene whispered "Round two," as Duncan left the room.

Lamb casserôle followed, and then to finish the most superior apple dumplings I had ever tasted. When Duncan returned with the coffee, I said so. In fact I think I made a bit of a thing about it. This seemed to relieve Duncan of some of the obvious tension that had built up. He stepped across to the window and made to peer out, although little could be seen at this time of night.

He hovered for a moment and then quite abruptly came out with: "Well, did you buy it?"

"Buy what, Duncan?" I teased.

Now he was slightly put out. "The cottage, what else!"

I could not resist being jocular with my reply. "Oh no! We were never really serious about that. We've bought a plot of land instead – Creag nan Cudaigean headland."

"Well, well!" A smile of relief began to slowly spread across his weather-beaten face. He quickly stepped back to the window and pointed along the shore to the east. "That headland?"

I joined him, and in the clear starlight one could just make out the promontory.

"Yes, that's the one," I said with some pride.

"Well, well!" he said again. "You have bought for yourselves a near-forgotten piece of Highland history. Will you take a wee dram of whisky?"

Indeed I would.

"Morag! Come and join us! Trevor and Irene are to be the new owners of Creag nan Cudaigean!"

Morag was somewhat bemused. Being an incomer it's doubtful whether she had any idea where the object of our joy lay, nevertheless once general directions had been explained, she relaxed and joined in the excitement. Duncan's behaviour indicated a renewal of friendship, rekindled after the still inexplicable behaviour of the last twenty-four hours. Whilst Duncan searched out back for the whisky, Irene whispered "Round eight, a draw!." We both grinned.

With a dram poured and a toast proposed to all our futures, we settled around the blazing fire. The pile of twigs and dry peat was already giving off the aroma most evocative of the Highlands. Thus began one of those never-to-be-forgotten evenings where Highlanders pass down their stories in the grand tradition of story-telling that has gone on from generation to generation.

We sat in the glow of the firelight and a small table-lamp. Outside, the village lay silent in front of the black mirrored surface of the loch as it reflected the starlight. Indoors it was warm and comfortable, just sitting there in the soft light and thinking our thoughts. Had I been more enlightened in the art of the story, I would have know that as the visitor it was up to me to begin, by bringing my hosts up to date with my news. Even in my ignorance, I could sense them willing me to begin.

Highlanders are not generally shy of leading one on, and in due course drawing whatever they want to know from you. Someone had to begin.

I began. I related how we had started the day with thoughts of looking at the cottage and had returned the owners of seven acres of beautiful shoreline. Our hosts listened intently as I told how we had just happened to meet the Major. (I was very careful not to mention Willie as I knew well how these two fishermen had for years feuded over the supremacy of their profession.) I went on to say how we had had lunch at the Lodge, and how we had afterwards all visited the site at the shore, and how, finally, the Major and I had struck a bargain. This was the only point at which Duncan interrupted.

"A tidy sum I shouldn't wonder!"

I was not to be drawn. This particular piece of information could have been the crowning glory of the tale, but for me it was sufficient to say that it had been a very fair deal – as indeed it had been. Our story of the day was indeed news and, when I assured them that I had told no-one else and that I had wanted them to be the first to know, I could tell from their satisfied expressions that my initiation into the art of story-telling had gone well. Exclusive news is almost a currency in Highland communities. Although Duncan, unlike many Highlanders, was a very abstemious man and had only taken the merest sip from his drink, I noticed he still did not neglect to top up my glass. My meagre input had been approved but, obviously, there was more to come. We waited expectantly whilst Morag made some tea for Irene and herself, and then we settled down once more for a story. Part of the art is in building up tension. Everyone knows that a story is going to be told, but not exactly when. It's all pure theatre. The moment came when the tea-drinking was done and I had put my glass down.

Duncan began.

"Now about the Creag nan Cudaigean story and its brief but now near forgotten part in Scottish history. This came about as a result of the 1745 uprising. You will perhaps remember that on the 25th July of that year Prince Charles Edward Stuart landed on the shores of Loch Moidart. It was from here that the Prince and his ardent supporters intended that he should make good his claim to the throne. With his brave Highlanders he set out for the south, and there was little resistance as he advanced as far south as Derby, only a hundred and twenty miles from London. This advance towards the very capital itself had been a bold enterprise, particularly as the Prince's army was by no means large.

"The march south had been swift and orderly, enjoying an element of surprise to the English. Their parliament was indeed staggered by the news of a Scottish invasion. By the time the invaders had reached Derby, however, the English army had begun to muster. News reached the Prince that an army of twice the Highlanders' strength was now marching towards them with all haste. Considering the Prince's comparatively small army and the fact that it had already marched nearly five hundred miles, and come so near to its objective – London – one cannot but admire their daring and bravery.

"At this point the Prince had to make a decision. He took the only possible course a commander could take. He gave the command for an orderly retreat, knowing that the element of surprise had fallen just short of its objective and that, without the support of the promised French regiments, his army was too small to face the English now advancing towards him.

"The return to the borders was orderly and, although the English army caught up with the retreating Highlanders and rearguard actions took place, the Scots always successfully deterred their aggressors. This was no doubt due to their hardy nature. A measure of this was their steadfastness in crossing the Usk at Longtown near the border. It was well into a wintry December. The river was flooded and there were powerful currents but, undeterred, the men waded waist-deep through the freezing cold water, whilst the Prince and his officers crossed on horseback. The Prince now determined that his army should march as far as Stirling where they would take the castle and await the arrival of those long-promised French regiments, which were supposed to be crossing the North Sea with reinforcements and supplies. Stirling Castle could not be taken easily, it being one of the finest fortresses in the country, and so it was resolved to lay siege to it. Meanwhile the English army had re-formed at Edinburgh and set out once more to engage the Highlanders. The two armies met at Falkirk, in mid-January. The winter had now set in with a vengeance.

"The weather conditions were ferocious. Rain and sleet were driven by gale-force winds, and the visibility was so poor that the armies barely knew what was happening. Indeed it is said that at one stage the armies were unknowingly retreating from each other. Thus the English limped back to Edinburgh and the Highlanders returned to the siege of Stirling Castle, which had so far resisted all attacks. But disturbing news now reached the Prince: the French had withdrawn their offer of assistance.

"The Clan Chiefs and the gentlemen-supporters of the cause now urgently advised the Prince to return north to await the spring, when a renewed recruitment-drive would bring his army up to full strength. The siege of Stirling Castle was abandoned, and the Highlanders returned towards Inverness. There was no further talk of going south. Circumstances had so changed that their strategies were now all predicated on a firm stand in the Highland capital and rearguard actions from there. No-one dared say so, but no-one believed that success would be guaranteed even in a battle this far north.

"Indeed the odds against the Highlanders were considerable. A ship that had been bringing much-needed supplies had been intercepted by English warships and driven ashore further north. The Highland army had been fragmented by a combination of the winter weather, the lack of food and the urge of clansmen to visit their homes. It was almost impossible to keep it under close command.

"Meantime the English forces, all professional soldiers, were building up their numbers and their ships brought in regular supplies of everything the army needed."

The story-teller paused as hindsight recalled those desperate circumstances and the terrible aftermath of the battle of Culloden. "I expect you are wondering about Loch Broom and the story I promised you about Creag nan Cudaigean."

Although both Irene and I knew the essence of the story of the Culloden massacre, neither of us guessed what was to follow and we were on the proverbial edge of our seats waiting to find out. Another handful of sticks was thrown on the fire, and a shower of sparks was sent up the chimney. This was quickly brought under control with a shovel of peat, and Duncan resumed the story.

"The fateful battle should have initiated a great period in Scottish history, but once again in the last days before the fight circumstances altered the course of events. I mentioned earlier that there had been unvoiced concern about the outcome of such a battle – if the unthinkable should happen, then what of the Prince and the cause? If the Prince were lost then the cause would be lost, but as long as the Prince was safe there was always the possibility of reviving the campaign. At least one man was thinking of a contingency plan.

"If the Prince were defeated, then it would be necessary for him to return to France and renegotiate French support. The Prince's return to France would be fraught with difficulty, not least because the English would do all in their power to prevent it, but there was thus surely all the more reason to plan for it and not leave it to the luck of the moment. Obviously, any attempt to take the Prince out by the route by which he had arrived would invite trouble, as the area would be quickly overrun with English soldiers and escape rendered impossible.

"There was an alternative route, via Loch Broom in the north-west. This route had many advantages, not least that neither the English army or navy would be so far north. Furthermore the French were familiar with Loch Broom. A plan was formulated in great detail and the story has been passed down to us, one generation to another. Physical evidence of the plan remains to be seen to this day, but for how much longer, who can say?"

There was a lull in the tale. I wondered whether Duncan was marshalling his thoughts, or perhaps just working out where to begin the final episode of the saga, but it became clear that he was reflecting on those who might still have the details to mind. It saddened him to think that there were only two others.

"What a pity that no-one, as far as I know, has ever committed these details to print. Perhaps I should have done it myself but the written word is not my strong point."

The story now began again.

"Of all those who held the Prince and the cause in high regard and were aware of the dangers, the Earl of Cromarty was perhaps most conscious of what might lie ahead. The Earl's efforts to raise men to the cause had been untiring. His recruitment-drive had ranged near and far throughout the north, but alas it had only been moderately successful. It seems to have been at the Earl's instigation that the contingency plan to escape via the north-west and Loch Broom came into being. In 1746 there was no road to Loch Broom, just a bridle path over the mountains that separated east from west. It is important to know that Ullapool did not exist in those days. Also, in fact, it would be more than twenty years before there would be even a village at the lochside. What community there was was scattered or congregated at the head of the loch some seven miles away. There stood the small parish church of Loch Broom, and the Rev. James Robertson looked after one of the largest parishes in the Highlands. At the place that would one day become the village of Ullapool there was but a farm and a few huts that served the needs of a very infant and spasmodic fishing industry.

"To the north of this farm's land lay another small farm, Glastullich, occupied by Donald Mackenzie, and to the south-east and again bordering Ullapool Farm lay Corry Farm, occupied by Lieutenant Alexander Mackenzie. Corry Farm lay above a wooded glen within sight of the sea, where a small river gouged deep in the rocky escarpment gave hidden access to the shore of the Loch. It was to Lieutenant Mackenzie that the task of arranging the elaborate escape plan fell, should circumstances require it. He was to make his house available to the Prince and his immediate companions. As a contingency the farmhouse at Glastullich was also to be put at the disposal of the Prince. If Corry Farm was threatened he could be spirited away over the hills to the north and down to the house at Glastullich on the shores of Loch Achall, a mere three miles over the ridge which divided the two properties. In those days the area was thickly wooded and evading detection would not have been difficult. No one knew how long the Prince would have had to wait for a ship from France, but the whole of Loch Broom could be observed from Corry and a constant watch kept. Although there were no established charts of Loch Broom, a French ship would know how to find the loch. It was becoming well known to continentals who were now frequently fishing for herring in the local waters. To make sure that no time was lost the Prince would be brought to the shore as soon as a ship was sighted as it would be necessary for a rescue ship to run in and out as swiftly as possible.

"This was of course easier said than done, as the vessel would be at the mercy of the wind, but the same conditions would also apply to any pursuing ship. And remember, out-sailing an aggressor was an essential skill of the period."

The story teller had stopped from time to time to replenish everyone's drinks and to feed peat and sticks to the fire, which by now was throwing out the perfect glow for an evening of stories.

"Still wondering about Creag nan Cudaigean? We are coming to it now!" Duncan said as he gave the fire one last prod, sending another shower of sparks up the chimney. We really had no need of reassurance as to where the story was leading. We trusted Duncan and he had said that the headland had a history. We never doubted that he was going to tell it to us, and we were eager to know.

"Well, as you may have guessed by now, it was the Creag nan Cudaigean headland that Lieutenant Mackenzie chose as the best spot to embark the Prince, not because it was a headland, but because he knew that at Creag nan Cudaigean there was a cave, virtually undetectable. Should anything go wrong with the plan, the Prince could be hidden in a moment whilst the Lieutenant drew suspicion away from the spot.

"There was another complication. A small boat was essential. If speed were of the essence in embarking the Prince, then it would be easier for a small boat to put out from the shore than for a ship to lower its long boat to make its way to an unknown beach. Close by, to the east of Creag nan Cudaigean headland, there was a tiny cove where a small boat could be kept in waiting, but there was a big risk in leaving a boat far from habitation – it would surely arouse suspicion if the English came searching.

"The enterprising Lieutenant overcame this problem by having a port dug into the embankment just above the shore line. Helpers carried the excavated materials down to the sea where the tide washed away the evidence of the work. When the boat was drawn into the port it was covered in dead bracken which within a day or two had blended with the winter's decaying vegetation. The place later acquired the name of Port Aluinn, which means beautiful port, and so it is.

"One final thing remained. It was never intended that the cave would be used other than in an emergency, so some shoreline hide-out near the cave was also necessary. So, on a ledge under the low cliff of the headland, a rough stone wall was built across a recess in the rock face, creating a place where if one crouched close one could not be seen from above or indeed from the sea.

"Well now! That is the story of the Prince's cave, but not quite the end of the tale. As we all know, the Prince did not come to the north west and the reason is very plain. The minister at Loch Broom had preached against 'the rebels', imploring the men of the parish to stay on their land, and they had indeed had little enthusiasm for joining the Highland army. Although being tenants of the Earl they naturally felt under an obligation to him, they obeyed the minister, and did nothing until shortly before the fateful battle.

"Matters were forced to a head by the Earl's son, Lord Macleod (who had taken his name from his mother). He came riding over to Loch Broom and used brute force to round up as many men as could be found. He marched them east to meet the Earl of Cromarty's other contingent, where on the following day they were expected to march south to join the main army in readiness for the impending battle. Unfortunately they were surprised by Sutherland men and after a short skirmish were all taken prisoner – amongst them the Earl of Cromarty, his son Lord Macleod, and Lieutenant Alexander Mackenzie, with other gentlemen supporters and officers. They along with the others were all eventually shipped to London to stand trial for treason. The minister of Loch Broom, a great man, pleaded the case of his parishioners both at Inverness and later at the trials in London, but he was successful in obtaining pardons for only a handful. The rest, numbering about a hundred and fifty, were transported to the colonies. Lieutenant Mackenzie was never to see his native Loch Broom again."

The saga seemed complete and we began to applaud the story teller. But he raised his hands.

"No! There is still a little more to tell. Those who had played their part in the Loch Broom escape plan never had the chance to see their efforts recognized and its merits considered. History records that Prince Charles made his escape along a route that despite today's romantic connotations was one of great hardship, danger and deprivation. It all might have been less arduous if the north-west route had been used.

"There is another Mackenzie I have not yet mentioned, and that was the laird of Langwell, with lands to the north bordering Glastullich where Donald Mackenzie farmed, whom I mentioned earlier. All these Mackenzies appeared to be related including the Lieutenant, and in turn the laird was related to the Earl of Cromarty through his wife's kin. Now, following the battle of Culloden and the Prince's escape from the field, rumours became rife as to the Prince's whereabouts and it seemed no coincidence that an English sloop was dispatched to Loch Broom to search the area.

"It was perhaps no further coincidence that the ship, the *Furnace*, under the command of Captain Ferguson, went straight to Loch Kaniard. There the ship anchored, putting ashore a contingent of soldiers who, drums beating, marched up the glen to Langwell. The laird was not at home and the fact that the house at the time was plagued with smallpox possibly saved the life of the laird's wife and children. Nevertheless the soldiers ransacked the house and drove off the laird's livestock. The ship remained in the area for a week during which the soldiers terrorized the local community. Rumours persisted for some time that the Prince was in the area, until it was known that he had escaped to France."

Four decades on from the telling of this story and over two hundred and fifty years since the events it describes, the lookout which the Lieutenant built above the Creag nan Cudaigean headland remains untouched, and the site of Port Aluinn is still just discernible. Corry farmhouse is still occupied and Glastullich is a holiday home.

CHAPTER SIX

An Ideal Home

It would have been easy to stay on and have another day in which to explore our new acquisition and its historic associations, but after the story-telling Duncan did what he and countless other fishermen have done for generations. He went and stood outside "to get," as he said, "a feel for the morrow's weather." He returned with a noticeable shiver and pronounced: "A bit wind coming out of the south east. Likely back afore morning, and bring a bit of snow to the tops I shouldn't wonder."

Next morning his forecast proved right. The blue skies had given way to grey, and far away the east was almost black, smoked with the odd delicate white veil. The snow was coming, and we left ahead of it.

In Shropshire the skies were equally grey with the advancing winter. Trees and hedgerows lay bare, and the damp had begun to cling to everything. Even the river, now running dark and deep, had lost the unforgettable smell of warm autumn days. That fragrance was now smothered by the cold which was creeping inexorably over the countryside.

Joe Corkindale was pleased to see us back. I had promised not to be away any longer than need be, as I had undertaken as part of our deal to remain as a consultant. I wasn't surprised to see that Joe hadn't been slow in making the services of the business known. He had had cards printed and had been handing them out everywhere, and he couldn't wait to tell me the latest development.

A large national company had recently taken over one of the country's best-known manufacturers of wrought-iron gates and railings and, in a rationalisation programme, had closed its famous gate-shop division. That closure although regrettable had perhaps been inevitable, as the number of purchasers for Buckingham-Palace-style gates had been steadily dwindling for years. But Joe had seen his opportunity. These great gates last for centuries, but it doesn't prevent them getting accidentally damaged, usually by wayward lorries.

"Each gate weighs over a ton!" Joe babbled on, forgetting the gentlemanly demeanour of his tailoring days and lapsing into his native Black Country dialect. I recognized the enthusiasm peculiar to men who know that they have cornered a market in a rare skill. "Should see em! Twisted up like propellers! Defied every effort so far to get em straight!"

"Steady on, Joe!" I interrupted. He seemed to have skipped an essential bit of the story.

He backtracked and explained. Apparently the gates in question had been at the entrance to a park in Birmingham, and a very large lorry, having lost its way in the early hours of one morning, had attempted to turn in the park entrance. It had misjudged the space available with dire consequences, although it could have been worse: the lorry had been loaded with long steel joists, one of which had been forced through the cab by the collision with the gates, only just missing the driver.

When the park-attendants arrived in the morning they found the gates bent and the lorry immobilised. A crane soon arrived to reset the load, but it was soon discovered that the joist which had pierced the cab had simply jammed the gear-lever into a ratio too high for the engine to cope with. In due course the lorry was able to get clear and then the full extent of the damage to the gates became obvious. After much debate and scratching of heads the driver came up with a solution.

"Stands to sense," the driver had said. "If the lorry had the power to push um in, then it could just as easy pull um out. I'll get a chain."

The small crowd had gathered at the scene, and egged him on as he first attached the chain to the top of one of the gates and then to the back of his vehicle, and then, having ensured that the great centre bolt of the gate was fastened to keep the gate from swinging, he jumped in the cab and started the engine.

"Everybody stand back!" he called out. The crowd heard the click of the gear as it was engaged, and then, as the revolutions of the engine increased and tension grew in the hearts of the onlookers, the lorry took the strain. The chain was soon bartight, and the driver kept glancing anxiously in the mirror, but the buckled gate did not give an inch. Someone shouted "Give her a bit more, Jack!"

Once more the engine revolutions rose, and bystanders moved even further back, nervous of what might happen next. They had not long to wait. There was a great crash, and the enormous stone pillar on which the gate was hung came crashing down in a cloud of dust.

"It was all a bit of luck!" Joe beamed with an air of excited innocence. "Only called at the city office the day before, and there I was the very next morning, meeting the very same chap that I had seen at the office! Quite worried he was, but I soon assured him that the job would be well within the field of our considerable experience."

I was astounded. "Joe! Have you any idea of what you have taken on? A twenty-ton hammer powered by a one-hundred horse-power engine bent those gates. How on earth do you think you are going to straighten them? And what about the stone pillar? Are you going to rebuild that as well?"

Joe only laughed. "No, of course not! I told the chap we didn't do stonework, and he said not to worry. A firm of stonemasons down the Coventry Road would deal with that aspect of the work, but we would have to co-operate with them over the hangings. Not quite sure what he meant. Wragg I think the stonemasons are called. I thought you could perhaps speak to them in due course."

I was getting agitated, but tried not to show my feelings. Only two days earlier Irene and I had been sitting in the early winter sunshine gazing out across the sea, lost in a dream of escape that seemingly was not yet quite complete. And so, for a while, I found myself back in control of the business. You might suppose that mending gates like this is a matter of bashing them back into shape, but it is far more complex than that. The huge gates lay in what had been my workshop, and day after day we fought with the massive and intricate wrought-iron work to separate each and every one of its parts from the whole. No component in this type of structure was ever welded, and in any case these gates predated modern welding techniques. They had been built more as a cabinet-maker might work, with round or rectangular mortise-and-tenon joints, each tenon riveted over as it emerged from the mortise. It was these riveted ends that had to be laboriously heated and painstakingly dressed back to allow the tenons to be withdrawn from the mortises. Each component was then heated in the forge, returned to its original shape and alignment, and punched with a number to correspond with a drawing we had made of each gate. The only way to realign a gate of this kind is to relieve the stress on every member, and the only way to do that is to do what we did.

Irene had been busy preparing our house for sale even though Creag nan Cudaigean was not yet legally ours. We knew that to hasten our purchase might easily lead to disappointment, but a few items of correspondence had passed between David Wilson at the Inverness solicitors and ourselves, and all seemed to be progressing without a hitch. In fact we had been promised that we would be the new owners of the headland before the year was out. For me at least, having been so engrossed with the repair of the gates, time had passed more quickly than it might have done. With or without the gates to occupy me, one might have thought that we would have been full of Scottish plans, but we were not. The truth was that it all seemed a dream from which we would soon awaken. As each day drifted by the dream faded slightly more, and we slipped into limbo. Slowly, in our minds, we were saying goodbye to Bridgnorth and the years of happiness at our home by the river. We began to feel that we didn't live anywhere, and so at the last minute we decided to spend Christmas in a rented cottage deep in the heart of Wales, a sort of neutral oasis. We left our departure until the early-morning post arrived on Christmas Eve in the hope that the all-important confirmation of our purchase would arrive, but it didn't.

I hardly remember our drive into Wales or much of the holiday. We returned on the New Year's Eve, to a cold house and a mountain of post. Late Christmas cards, a New Year card from the Highlands, bills and trade circulars. Irene saw it first.

"Look, look, an Inverness postmark!"

"Open it," I said cautiously.

"No, you open it. I'm so nervous!"

Irene handed the envelope to me and slowly I slit it open with my thumb. It was a short handwritten note, not to easy b read but obviously from Stewart Rule and with David Wilson's signature. It was dated 25th December. I struggled a bit with the text before I finally got the hang of what had probably been written in haste. It read:

Dear Mr & Mrs Rogers

I came into the office this morning just for a few hours and suddenly saw in my diary that I was to let you know the outcome of Creag nan Cudaigean before the year was out. Well, I'm pleased to inform you that the title is now registered in your names. May I take this opportunity of wishing you every success and best wishes for the New Year.

Yours faithfully
David Wilson.

Irene gave a great whoop of joy whilst I made straight for the whisky and poured two large drams. We drank a toast, "To the Highlands!"

The new year began with a severe frost, and the countryside fell silent under the spell of the tinsel white coating. At the onset it was delicately picturesque, but as the days passed the unrelenting frost tightened its icy grip. Our workshop premises had for two centuries felt only the very localised heat of the blacksmith's hearth, and that only when it was called for. Joe was unaccustomed to being in such a freezing building, and had rushed out on the first day back to work after the holiday to buy the hardware merchant's last paraffin heater. Sad to say, it made little impression on the old ice box, and it was little consolation to remember how pleasantly cool it could be on a hot summer's day. Each day the river fell a little lower as its life-blood ceased to flow from its tributaries large and small, as in turn their supply congealed. Each morning Irene and I would go down to the water's edge and observe the latest ice-shelf. The intensity of the overnight frost would have solidified the slow-running water as it lingered along the fringes, and already the continued lowering of the starved river would be leaving yet another thin shelf of ice, giving the embankments a frilly lace ruff. No one, however old, could recall having seen such a sight before. The smooth iron handrails of the Severn bridge where countless passings had burnished the metal was now a trap to freeze the very skin from the hands of anyone unsuspectingly touching the crystalline metal surface. The joints in the ironwork, tightly fitting and smooth to the touch in normal times, were now gaping wide enough to accept the edge of one's hand. Within the week the piped water to riverside properties ceased to flow in the town mains. They had frozen solid as the ice penetrated even deeper into the ground.

The valley had entered a mini ice age. Emergency services were pressed into action and each day limited supplies of fresh water were delivered in tankers from an army base twenty miles distant. Winter held us besieged.

These conditions ran on for weeks, and had a profound effect on our plans – or, to be more precise, made us incapable of making plans. Finding a buyer for our home should have been a priority, but it seemed inconceivable that one could offer a property for sale where there was no water other than that frozen in the pipes, ready to flood the house when, or if, the thaw came. A trip to an estate-agent only added to our gloom.

The agent sat before a large coal fire. He informed us with a despondent air that the whole housing market seemed to have dried up. "Or perhaps 'frozen up' might be more appropriate", he added with a forced half-smile. He invited us to join him at the fire. We did not need asking twice, and were glad to soak in a little warmth.

The agent continued, with a look of unashamed melancholia: "This is all bound to have a short-term effect on the market, but what is more worrying are the signs of a slowdown in economy. You hear it every day – over-manning, de-stocking, time and motion – it's as if some alien culture is trying to take us over with all these new phrases. Where is it leading us, I want to know? My advice is let's get all the details down on paper, and then sit on it until, say, Easter."

I thanked him for his advice, but declined his offer to sit on the sale until such time as he might venture away from the fire. The sad thing for us about the agent's lack of enthusiasm was that we knew he was right. We went into a pleasantly inviting teashop and ordered a pile of hot buttered tea-cakes and a pot of tea. In these cosy circumstances, we came to the satisfying conclusion that there was no need to rush into anything. We had bought a piece of Highland land that had not been on the market for centuries, and the fact that we were not able to be there immediately made not the slightest difference. We resolved there and then we would not be rushed. We would take our time and prepare a well thought out plan.

Irene was thinking. "I was trying to recall what Duncan said about the Highlands... Yes, I've got it: 'When God made time he made plenty of it'."

To add to our feeling of well-being, the thaw began the very next day, almost imperceptibly at first. The ground remained rock hard, water remained locked in pipes and the level of the river was still falling. The ice-shelf frills stepping delicately down the embankment were such an amazing sight that they were attracting visitors. The phenomenon might not occur again in a hundred years – or so one newspaper said. But all the same, day by day the temperature began slowly to rise. Water Board men fought to induce the mains to resume the public supply, as consumers who while the frost had lasted had been resigned to its consequences became impatient to see the water flowing from their taps again. Someone somewhere brought enterprise to the situation by recalling that the temperature of water can be raised by passing a low voltage through it. The question was, would it work with ice? We never found out whether it did or not, as Providence intervened and it began to rain just in time to save half the local population from being electrocuted.

Next morning, as if by magic, water was trickling from one of our taps and a few hours later normal service resumed throughout our plumbing system. By some miracle not a single pipe burst, something to do with the very slow way in which the cold had initially descended upon us. The weather remained the dominant topic for everyone for some time until, one day in February, the sun shone as if to announce the early arrival of spring. With the sun, all thoughts of what had passed was consigned to the history books and we felt that the new year had at last begun.

The power of rational thought returned to our winter-weary minds, and we started to make plans. The estate-agent could have added yet another phrase to the alien words that troubled him: 'critical path analysis,' the straight line of objectives that lead logically from start to finish of a given project. We had originally, and perhaps mistakenly, believed that our first task would be to sell our house in Bridgnorth. That would certainly have been the case had we proceeded with the cottage, which would have provided at least a roof over our heads, but what we had actually bought was a piece of land, which offered only the shelter of the trees. That would clearly not do. Our first priority now was therefore to find somewhere to stay in Ullapool, and the obvious thing to do was to write to seek the Major's advice. Perhaps one of his estate houses, usually let for the summer, would still be free.

With his usual forthright efficiency, the Major replied by return. He was delighted that we had concluded our deal and he would be equally delighted to let us have the cottage at Corry Point any time after the end of September. He added that he had taken the liberty of pencilling in the booking in anticipation. I read the letter to Irene, who said: "When God made time he made plenty of it" and then realized the implications of the Major's offer. "End of September! Oh well, I suppose it *could* take that long."

A few weeks passed and spring had really arrived. We decided to go down to London for a short break. Irene wanted to visit the Ideal Homes exhibition at Olympia. I laughingly teased that I did not expect to find anything there relevant to the Highlands, and she agreed, but was still keen to go. The visit was mainly to give us a chance to catch up on the latest West End shows – perhaps, in view of the six hundred miles between Ullapool and the capital, this might be our last opportunity for such a jaunt. We drove down in the late morning, treating ourselves to a splendid lunch near Worcester. With every day bringing a little more daylight, we arrived safely at Richmond in the still of a warm spring evening. The hotel gave us a view over the river where mist was settling over the water. We were on top of the world.

On the following morning we went to the exhibition and stood in a short queue for tickets. Everywhere was bedecked with garlands of artificial spring blossoms set against scenic backdrops of the English countryside. Powerful spotlights not only brought synthetic sunlight, but their profusion provided a warmth that by contrast with the tingle in the outside air declared that at least here in the great hall of Olympia it was unashamedly spring. We had no hesitation in handing over our outdoor coats to the cheery cloakroom lady. Before we could even approach the main hall innumerable girls in pretty summer dresses surrounded us. Their patter was designed to lure us to this or that stand, where they each promised that their companies' products were the talk of the show and not be missed. If one looked doubtful they would add that whatever it was they were promoting had been reviewed in top magazines, and if that was not enough, there were the inevitable leaflets which one glanced at out of courtesy before struggling on. I supposed it was all calculated to build up the attraction of such exhibitions, and it was succeeding. Irene's excitement bubbled over as we entered this artificial world of sunlight and warmth. We stood for a moment on the soft green carpet of the huge main exhibition hall. Even above our heads the enormously high ceilings were hung in pale blue and white drapes simulating a sky, and soft back ground music only added to the theatre of it all. Recorded bird-song completed the fantasy of the Ideal Home. One could not help but marvel at the artistic forethought that had gone into the conception of this vast exhibition.

Irene's eagerness to start looking at exhibits was for the moment brought to a standstill as we pondered the necessary question of where to start. On the one hand, we were spoilt for choice, but on the other, there was nothing that I particularly wanted to see. In fact up until that moment I would probably have said that there was nothing there to interest me. Irene however while she too had no particular objective was in fact ready to look at everything on show if only time would allow. We havered until Irene suddenly spotted the row of about half a dozen show-houses as neatly built and gardened as if in a select suburb of the home counties.

"Look! There are only tiny queues. Later they will be half way round the hall."

Off she went with me following as close as I could. I need not have hurried for soon she stopped short.

"Decisions, decisions," she was saying to herself. "Which one shall we go in first?"

Each one of the houses was a masterpiece. One can only marvel at the energy, practical thought and organisation with which a builder erects an ostensibly perfect exhibition-house in the very short space of time available, only then with even greater speed to have to dismantle their painstaking efforts. The building operation is of course not as extensive as for a real house that has to rise from the virgin earth of an unbroken site. The exhibition-house is constructed in a weatherless environment, and has no foundations to impede the rapid rise of its brickwork from the concrete floor of the hall; there are no drains, and water need not flow from the glittering taps in the tiled bathrooms and immaculately fitted kitchens. But even allowing for all this, their internal and external finish is very impressive.

We joined the queue of about a dozen expectant viewers, waiting until the small party within had enjoyed its allotted five minutes of exclusive viewing. It was while we were standing there that I espied something that would soon occupy my every thought for more than a year and underlie the critical path to our new home in the Highlands. A less obvious house, partly screened by large tubs of leylandii, was standing just a little apart from what appeared to be its rather up-market neighbours. They had walls of neatly pointed handmade bricks and pantiled roofs. This house was different. Irene saw what I saw and grabbed my hand.

"Oh! Isn't beautiful!" she cried.

We stood spellbound in front of a small Norwegian log house, the first we had ever seen, and we were hooked before

we ever set foot inside. It was beautifully constructed with
fairytale imagination. We quickly swapped our allegiance from
suburbia to rural Scandinavia, captivated by the apparent
simplicity of the structure. Small, whole tree-trunks had been
cleverly machined into uniform sections, allowing each log to
sit neatly one upon another. At the corners the logs were
ingeniously notched together as one might place the fingers of
one hand through the fingers of the other.

Irene gripped my arm and whispered: "Isn't it exciting!"

"Yes, very!" I replied. My thoughts drifted to our site
immediately above the cove at Creag nan Cudaigean.

Now it was our turn to inspect the interior. The scent of the
fresh pine was heavenly, and pine was everywhere. Pine
floors, pine walls; the logs which we had seen on the outside
were the very same as those of the interior. The interior of the
roof was even more attractive with its exposed rafters and,
most imposing of all, a great round ridge-pole carved from one
mighty pine log. It was all so simple.

The more we looked the more we liked this dream of a home,
but there was scant literature available and a rather tentative
price-guidance slip. There was no doubt that the quoted prices
were high, but we knew the house was very special and the
enthusiastic representatives insisted that they were those ruling
at the moment. Our request for a quotation for building in the
Highlands brought forth sighs and ums and ahs. Yes, they
said, they were considering representation in all areas.

"How far away are these Highlands?" the saleslady enquired.

I replied "About six hundred miles."

Her face went blank. She confided that this was a new
venture, and that they had not yet had looked at the
possibilities beyond the south-east of England. She thought
that the best she could offer us was to say that we should stay

in touch and see how things developed, but her principal would be available in the afternoon some time after two o'clock and we could speak to him then if we liked. Extreme doubt set in as we left the stand, where an aesthetic boulder and some heather in coarse grass had suggested the landscape of our own site in the Highlands. Irene was very close to tears.

"Come on," I said. "Let's go and have a coffee and a think."

This was our well-tried solution in such cases. Something we really wanted was ostensibly available, but not to us. We found a coffee-bar on the upper floor overlooking the main arena. From where we sat we could see the Norwegian log house we had fallen in love with, and we began to consider our options. One idea was to wonder how the log-house people would have reacted if we had said that our site was in Shropshire rather than the Highlands.

The answer was obviously to go back in the early afternoon and try to have a more constructive discussion. It was still only mid-morning and we had several hours to kill. The main show seemed irrelevant to us now. We idly looked at a dozen or more stands exhibiting beautiful lounge furniture that assumed no lounge was less than twenty feet square. We gazed at kitchens with stainless-steel worktops for which the manufacturers produced a special polish. Irene decided against spending all her days just polishing her kitchen. No, none of this was for us. I had started to walk on when Irene's arm suddenly applied the brakes.

"Hang on! This is more in our line!"

We had drawn level with an area of the hall devoted to solid-fuel cookers. I hadn't yet considered what sort of cooker might be appropriate to our log house, but obviously Irene was ahead of me. The cooker is after all one of the most important items, if not the most important item, in a home.

As we made our way through the well-known and lesser makes I became caught up in Irene's enthusiasm. I needed no reminding of the virtues of a solid-fuel cooker slowly giving out its gentle heat in a living kitchen. I could recall the very smell of warmth when one comes inside on a cold day. It was as if we had held long discussions on the subject of cookers, for we both seemed instantly to know what was wanted. Our appliance would obviously have to cook food, but all these beautifully enamelled units had that as their prime object, and so we examined their varying claims for heating water, providing surplus heat for a towel rail and even central heating. It was not long before we had a young man in attendance whose enthusiasm for his company's product knew no bounds. Irene was soon locked in serious conversation with him while I was relegated to the status of a bystander. When she was about to pose a serious question Irene had a habit of looking her game in the eye and saying: 'Now listen!'

"Now listen!" she said to the young man, and he listened intently. Irene began: "Before you make any more fantastic claims there is something you must know."

I was as agog as the young man, with as little idea as he had of what was coming next.

"What you must understand is that possibly none of the fancy fuels you have been mentioning will be available in the Highlands. Did I tell you that we are about to settle in the remote north-west of Scotland?"

The young man shook his head.

Irene went on: "We may well have to burn what we can get— poor quality coal, wood perhaps, even peat. Not least, as there is no refuse collection, I will expect to burn certain rubbish."

It was the first time that Irene had taken the initiative in organising a phase of the critical path north, and it was by no means the last. I was seized with pride at Irene's capacity for such detail. It was at that moment that I knew for certain that any doubts that Irene may have had were gone. A mood of 'Let's get on with the job!' settled upon us.

CHAPTER SEVEN

We'll Build it Ourselves

We did go back to the Norwegian house and had a last look through it. The lady we had seen earlier introduced us to the company's managing director. He was perfectly frank in telling us that they had in fact completed only one house to date. He admitted that their participation in this exhibition had been really just a marketing exercise, and that he had been rather thrown by an enquiry from so far afield. Did I know if they might be able to ship directly into say Aberdeen from Norway?

Well, no, I didn't know, but I did know that Aberdeen was almost two hundred miles from where we intended to settle.

"Dear oh dear me," he replied. This was somewhat out of character with his general demeanour, but then as if a thunderbolt had jolted his mind he suddenly came out with: "I have just had a thought! I don't think our franchise extends so far north... Look, you're going to have to leave it to me. I promise we will stay in touch."

But he never did. Although I wrote to the company we never heard any more from them. Somehow even then, I had the feeling that that would be the case. Clearly, our enquiry had embarrassed the log-house people.

One way and another, we had had enough of London. We decided that it was all right for a few days, particularly if, as we did, one had some special object in being there; and it certainly added to the pleasure if one could occupy the evenings with a show or two to remind us the there were more things in life than gazing out at the countryside and watching the changing weather. But after only two nights in the capital the countryside had won.

The next morning we were heading west, away from the metropolis and glad to be on our way home to Shropshire. Today there was no need to watch the weather. The sun shone soft and warm, reminding us that spring was not far off. It was simply a gorgeous morning. As we passed through the suburban sprawl the countless houses that had looked drab in the late afternoon light on the day of our arrival now looked bright and cheerful, with splashes of forsythia around their doors. Clumps of snowdrops drifted in the rockeries beloved of the landscapers who design the upmarket houses fringing these roads which are neither town or country. Already the odd daffodil was adding further evidence that the season was on the turn.

It was quite usual that Irene and I would say very little during this part of the journey. The mid-morning traffic was still heavy and a failure of concentration might easily find me in the wrong lane and going in the wrong direction. It would not be the first time. Irene was aware of my tendency to put myself in the wrong position on the road. She reminded me that our turn north was not far away – and almost before her reminder was complete the road sign appeared. I read down the list of placenames, a quite unnecessary habit that to this day I don't seem to be able to break. It must be something to do with the romance of travel and the pleasure of anticipating the towns and villages that one has not yet reached.

"You've missed it!" Irene shouted.

"Yes, I know," I said in as calm a voice as I could muster, then quickly added: "We are going to Marlow. I fancy a walk by the river. Then I will take you for an early lunch."

Irene did not suffer fools lightly and I was expecting to hear more on the subject of lack of attention to the road, but the promise of lunch had done the trick. Irene's momentary flash of irritation subsided as quickly as it had arisen and the best reply she could manage was "Oh!"

Marlow was new to us. An attractive town set in a beautiful riverside location, it is a gem within the Thames valley. Exploring the town and the river banks on such a day could not help but soothe away the ordeal of even a short stay in a city so far removed from our normal surroundings. Refreshed by our brief sight-seeing foray, we sat in the window of a pleasant restaurant overlooking the river. A very attentive waiter advised us that we were just slightly early for lunch, but that if we would care for a pre-lunch drink he would be delighted to get what ever pleased us. In these relaxing surroundings, we settled down with a couple of gin and tonics. There could not have been a better moment in which to broach what was now on my mind.

We had spoken little of the Norwegian log house other than snippets along the lines of "Wouldn't something-or-other look good against the logs?" or "What about this or that colouring for the ceiling panels between the open rafters?." None of it very constructive. We had been unwilling to face the fact that the house had just been a show piece, a marketing exercise, one of those good ideas that might never make it. Was the company really going to get going, or was it only checking the possibilities? All we knew was that they had shown no eagerness for us to place an order. It was all very puzzling. Perhaps we should assume that the house was simply not available.

This unsatisfactory situation had forced me into considering the alternatives. I thought I knew the way forward but, although my confidence in the idea was growing, Irene might not be so easily convinced of its practicality. I was about to outline my ideas, but with the warm sun streaming through the window and the soporific effect of the gin and tonic, I was a bit slow off the mark. Irene got there first.

"I don't think we are going to get anywhere with that log-house firm. There was something – I just can't put my finger on it, but I bet we never hear from them again. So what can we do about it? I had set my heart on that little house! Well, perhaps not exactly that one, but one in that style. It was so beautiful, so cosy! It would have looked a picture built on Creag nan Cudaigean with the windows looking out to sea on days like this, and in the winter a big log fire. And, best of all, my solid-fuel cooker with a kettle constantly simmering away on the hob…"

I immediately regretted that I had not shared my thoughts with Irene earlier. I had come to the same conclusion about the company which had the house of our dreams. I doubted very much that we would ever hear from them again, and whilst what I had spent the last twenty-four hours turning over in my mind might not be practical, I was certain that I had the answer. I had gone through a myriad of thumbnail sketches and made hundreds of mental calculations.

"We will build our own log house. People have been building log houses for a thousand years, so why shouldn't we?" I said.

Irene's face glowed. "Could we?"

"Yes!" I said, with all the confidence in the world. I knew from Irene's look of intense pleasure that my very mention of taking on such a challenge had been enough to convince her. If I said we could build such a house, then we could.

We left Marlow more than satisfied by an excellent lunch, and with the bare bones of a plan to build the house of our dreams. We talked incessantly as we made our way north-west. The late afternoon sunshine was brilliant in a clear blue sky, which meant only one thing at that time of the year – frost. By the time we reached the Severn valley, wisps of mist added to the magic. The day was turning to night as we neared our home.

Back home again, Irene began to think about selling the house, which she had decided to do without an agent. My period of consultancy, helping Joe with what was now his engineering business, was at an end. I remained on hand, but things had settled down so well at Corkindale Engineering that I was now in effect free to pursue my own priorities.

The most important point to be settled before I could even begin to consider any other aspect of our proposed new home was: would I be able to find suitable timber? Canadian settlers in the wilderness might have built their cabins with whole tree-trunks, which was all very romantic but, it turned out, impracticable in the UK. The reason for this was not at first obvious to me, although I had spent some of my formative years studying timber and timber technology. Nevertheless I soon discovered that those old log-buildings of Canada, Scandinavia, and elsewhere had been built with logs cut from ancient virgin forests. There the trees grew close to each other and their need for light forced the canopy ever higher, producing long straight logs with virtually no tapering of the trunk and with virtually no side branches save those of the canopy itself. With an abundance of such timber the builders of days gone by could choose the straightest and most regular diameters. In the simplest structures logs were chopped to length and corners were pieced together by cutting interlocking notches with an axe. (Indeed an axe was probably the only tool used even in the most recent of the buildings.) In Norway buildings nearly one thousand years old remain in perfect condition to this day. Their walls were made draught-proof by caulking the joints with moss or a mixture of moss and clay. Roofing presented these early builders with no great difficulties: they spanned from gable to gable with one great round pole, from which they fixed rafters cut from smaller-diameter trees, all of which were notched into the main structure, again using only an axe. The roof was covered by laying even smaller timbers horizontally over the rafters, and then tying the structure together with creepers or peeled brambles in the absence of more sophisticated fixings such as wooden pegs. A much favoured primary roof-covering was turf, supported on slabs of birch-bark peeled directly from the trees. The joints in the turf were kept tight together and in no time at all the fibres of the still-growing roots knitted together to make an almost watertight covering. What damp might have percolated the turf in extreme conditions was prevented from penetrating further by the bark underlay. In turn the dampness of the turf ensured that the bark did not dry out and crack.

Of course knowing all this – eventually – only served to tell me that this type of structure is almost impossible to replicate in the UK. We have very little virgin pine forest. For a very long time almost all our sawmill timber has been from planted and sustainable forestry resources: it is a commercial crop and, like all such crops, the object is to grow as much as possible in the shortest time. Timber is indeed often talked of as if it were wheat or potatoes – but like them, it demands good husbandry. Trees are carefully raised from seed in forestry nurseries, selecting those that put on the most growth in the shortest time. After a few years, plantations are thinned and the small trees turned into fence posts. Sometimes further thinning takes place, leaving the best trees to grow on to become prime sawmill stock.

I was fortunate that the Dudmaston Estate, not five miles from Bridgnorth, was owned by Captain Wolryche-Whitmore, one of the most knowledgeable foresters in the country. At Dudmaston he had extensive plantations and a modern sawmill. If the Captain would spare me a little of his time, then he must be my first line of approach.

I lost no time in telephoning Dudmaston Hall. After a while a lady answered and I asked if I might speak to the Captain.

"He's away!" sang out the voice at the other end of the line; then: "Is it important?"

I explained that I wished to talk about timber.

"Ring the mill, not here."

The phone clicked but I held on for a few seconds, somewhat deflated. I had planned my conversation carefully, in case the Captain was taken by surprise by someone wanting to discuss log houses, but in the event I had been able to say nothing. I bumped the phone down in indignation. Whoever the woman was, she had at least pointed me in the direction of the mill.

This time I didn't telephone. I jumped into the Landrover and just went. Perhaps I should have done that in the first place. In ten minutes I was there. There is something evocative about the smell that permeates a country sawmill, conjuring up the past as portrayed in Hardy's *Woodlanders*. That delicate scent of pines, the pungent smell of fir-tree resins and that smell which only a country craftsman can appreciate, fresh-cut English oak. I had met Mr Elcock, the foreman, on a few previous occasions and he greeted me in his customary manner.

"Gud mornin sir! Haven't seen eh for a time."

Without another word he walked away from the mill. I followed knowing that to hold a conversation in a working sawmill is near impossible.

"Raw kind of mornin," he continued as the noise of the saws became less intrusive.

It was indeed cold and for the first time I noticed the rime of frost on the fields.

"Ave to watch the frost on my potatoes," Mr Elcock went on. "Put em sprouting in the shed at the weekend. Almost thought I shud have put en in the ground yesturday. Glad I didun!"

I explained what was on my mind and he looked at me in total disbelief.

"Can't be done! When was the last time you tried to handle a fresh-cut twenty-foot log?"

Before I had time to reply, a Landrover pulled into the yard.

"Here's the man you need to talk to!" Mr Elcock nodded towards the driver as he came towards us. "Mornin Sir! This is Mr Rogers from down the town. He wants to talk to someone about log houses." The foreman turned to go, adding to me: "I'll leave you to Colonel Haddock."

Colonel Haddock, I was to learn, was the estate manager. He looked me up and down, and then quite out of the blue asked if I played cricket.

Alas I did not, I replied.

"Pity. I'm looking for a bit of new blood, season soon be on us. Well, better get into the office, bit raw eh?"

The office was a timber building adjoining the mill. As we entered, a delicious smell of warmth greeted us. The pine lining-boards were darkened, and the ancient cast-iron stove gave the interior a timeless air. The building with its one old chair, tiny table with paperwork all neatly clipped or spiked, obviously doubled as the mill workers' refuge. One wall was lined with their coats above a low bench covered in sacking where no doubt they sat during breaks. The building was also the store: all manner of saw-milling equipment was ranged along the only remaining wall.

The Colonel closed the door and the noise of the mill subsided. The small room was a reminder of so many country businesses where a table, a chair and a few shelves served adequately as an office for generations. Their jumble of battered files and hundreds of orders and dispatch notes on spikes might have led anyone more familiar with a modern office to wonder how on earth they functioned. The answer is that they functioned very well. Their owners and users could recall past records faster than any dedicated system. However no one in these rural businesses expected to spend any longer in their so-called office than was absolutely necessary. They knew where the profit was made, such as it was: chiefly by manual labour, either in the workshop or out-doors. The office was there for scribbling a few notes, and providing a refuge for a well earned break away from the noise, the dust and, on a day like this, the cold. How cosy the small space was once the door had closed and the warmth of the log-burning stove began to penetrate cold faces and hands! What could be more soothing to the toiler than to sit clutching a mug of tea on a settle covered with a hessian sack!

The Colonel had made the tea almost as we had entered, the kettle having been merrily simmering away on the hot stove. No modern office was ever like this. The one small-paned window overlooked the farmlands of Severn Vale, where I could see the forestry plantations of the estate interspersed with stands of ancient hardwoods. I waited for Colonel Haddock to open the conversation. In due course he took a notebook and pencil from his pocket, and was obviously heading a page with my name.

"Better have your address and a phone number." He began in a relaxed manner, more reminiscent of one taking an order than dealing with an enquiry. "A log house you were saying? Well, I can't promise you that our timber will be very suitable. Grows with a lot of taper, you know!"

I saw his eyebrows raise at the thought that I might know such things, so I quickly confirmed that I was aware of this feature of plantation trees, and that I understood that it was not practical to use raw logs for my house. In the scheme I was considering, each log would be sawn to a predetermined size, and the two faces of the timber that would be visible on the inner and external face of the building would be profiled to simulate logs of regular proportions. The top and bottom surfaces of the section would have a double tongue-and-groove profile, enabling the logs to fit together with a wind- and water-tight joint. I interlocked the fingers of my hands to demonstrate how the corners and intersections were constructed.

The Colonel listened intently to my discourse, occasionally with a slight frown, and now with a hint of a smile. He sat thinking for what seemed an interminable time, then began slowly as if puzzling on some point.

"Um, I suppose you have special machinery for dealing with this process?"

I was shaken. This was the question I had not yet answered to my own satisfaction. I needed to remind myself quickly that I was only exploring an idea here, but I also wanted to tell the truth without admitting this major shortcoming. I simply answered that I had machinery that I would be adapting for the work.

The Colonel was obviously impressed, but hardly as impressed as I was with my sudden inspiration. Yes! – this was the way forward! My enquiry now became bolder: I explained that the wood I needed had to come from trees where the heart was as near the centre of the trunk as possible, so that shrinkage was more predictable.

"The size – seven inches by six inches – must be very accurately sawn," I went on. "I will need a few lengths of twenty feet and the remainder in various lengths, in all totalling approximately 1,080 feet." I felt a sudden flush of excitement as I quantified my requirements, and then just as quickly felt myself going cold as I envisaged the vast pile of material. I added with some haste: "Of course I would need to know the cost."

The Colonel looked mildly amazed as he dotted the last of the copious notes he had been taking. "That's a lot of timber, but let me say now, and say with complete confidence, that our timber is amongst the best obtainable, and that the price will not hurt you. Oh, and by the way, I think I will leave Captain Whitmore to advise you on species. I know you said pine, but we will see. The Captain is away for a few days, but as soon as he returns I will get him to telephone you."

As we left the cosy office, one by one the machines fell silent as the workers self-consciously took their places in the refuge we had just vacated. The Colonel caught the foreman's glance at the mill clock, and realized that it was past the normal break time. "Sorry, Mr Elcock! I got carried away with something you will find very interesting in due course."

"Not to worry, Sir. Hope it's a big order!"

We were all in good spirits at the moment of parting, but whether it was the cold or the realisation of what I was contemplating, I again felt a shiver run slowly down my spine. I thought once more of the mass of timber – at least two big lorry-loads. I thought of Mr Elcock and his "When did you last handle a fresh-cut log?", my answer to which if pressed would have been "Never." I thought of the machine I had so confidently said that I would convert, and of the corner-notching I had so simplified by interlocking my fingers.

Ten minutes later, I was back in our lane. Irene who had been to the town was just ahead of me, and we arrived at the house together. I hoped that I did not look quite as concerned as I was feeling. For all Irene's enthusiasm she was never reckless as I was. It would not do to let her think that I had the slightest doubts. I could see that Irene was 'not in the best of tune', as she would often say when displeased.

"Come on, let's get inside," she said. "It's freezing!"

"I've been up to Dudmaston to see about timber."

For some reason it seemed a bad moment. Irene shivered in front of the kitchen radiator, as I waited for some reaction and made a couple of mugs of coffee. Irene clutched hers trying to get a little extra warmth. After a few sips and when the agony of cold had receded, she seemed about to take an interest in my adventure.

"Oh." She shivered. "It's cold enough for snow." She went on somewhat dejectedly. "I think I have been wasting my time and money. I've advertised the house in two papers, three evenings in each."

She paused and I took up the conversation hoping to find the source of her dismay.

"Three evenings? I thought you were only advertising as a feeler to begin with."

"That was my intention." She was cross that I might be questioning her strategy. "The fellow at the office said that the property market is so poor at the moment that just one ad would be useless."

I tried to introduce a note of optimism. "It's probably not that bad. I expect the chap was just trying to get a bit more advertising business."

It was not the most tactful thing to have said. Clearly Irene thought my remark a criticism. She lost no time in cutting short anything else that I might have to say. "I hope you haven't ordered the logs! We need to know we can afford this venture before we commit ourselves further."

CHAPTER EIGHT

Timber!

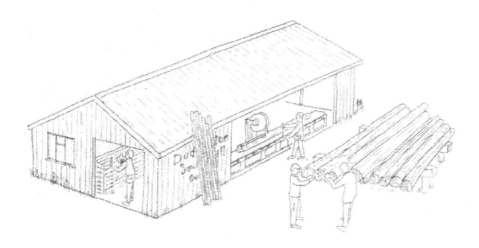

Irene's forecast of snow proved correct. The few days of spring-like weather had lulled us into a false sense of well-being. Winter and the cold had not gone. They had just been gathering their resources for yet another onslaught. A few inches of snow fell and then, as if to preserve it as long as possible against the awaiting spring, the frost returned with a vengeance. This brought more misery to the hill districts where the earth and frozen ponds still lay testimony to the Great Freeze. We only thought we had escaped.

Irene's advertisements duly appeared, without producing a single enquiry. The oppressive cold seemed to intensify people's uncertainty, and property was not selling. All this had the effect of pushing our venture to one side. Irene felt it more than I did. My mind was always so full of ideas that, racing ahead, I could easily put temporary setbacks to one side, but without Irene's enthusiasm my ideas seemed hollow.

More than a week passed and still there was no interest from the advertisements. We reminded ourselves that all the pointers had predicted that there would be no interest, and then we abandoned that consolation to blame ourselves for wasting money. It seemed irrational to want to find a buyer for our home – even if every thing ran to plan we would not be leaving Shropshire for at least six months. We felt rather foolish at having let our imaginations get the better of our judgement.

Nearly two weeks had passed since my visit to Dudmaston Sawmills and I had heard nothing. I was not really sure that I wanted to hear, but then everything suddenly changed. We were sitting over a rather leisurely breakfast listening to the weather report. The forecaster dwelt on Shropshire and the Welsh borders. He said that at last there were slight signs that the continuous frost of the last several days was coming to an end, although no significant improvement in this unprecedented weather could be expected for a few days. He went on: "All a very far cry from the west coast of Scotland, where they were having one of the mildest winters on record." He reported some unusual botanical phenomena from the subtropical gardens at Inverewe, which is near Ullapool.

Irene turned the radio off. "Oh, I wish we were there right now!" she cried. "And I wish your timber people would ring and that we could make a start at something!"

Within five minutes, the second of Irene's wishes was granted. The telephone rang and I answered. A man spoke.

"Wolryche-Whitmore at Dudmaston here. Am I speaking to Mr Rogers?" I assured him he was, and he continued. "My apologies for not coming back to you earlier. This weather totally disorganizes our style of saw-milling. However I have some encouraging news for you, I think. The chaps have started to take down a few trees, and I'd like you to come down to the Quatford plantation to see whether you approve. Could you be at the end of the lane by, say, ten thirty? We can then continue to the plantation in my vehicle. The going's a bit rough, you know."

My mind was racing. What did he mean, "taking a few trees down," "would I approve"? I was suddenly seized with the idea that Colonel Haddock might have misunderstood my enquiry and somehow taken it to be an order. The caller quickly brought me back to my senses.

"Sorry to have just sprung this on you. I could make it a bit later if it is inconvenient."

I answered quickly: "No, no. Ten thirty will be fine."

I had no difficulty recognizing Captain Wolryche-Whitmore at our meeting-place, as I had in fact met him before. At a much earlier time I had been one of a party of young people whom he had entertained with a tour of the plantation and mill on a quiet Saturday afternoon when the mill had been silent. Today the snow was hard packed in the lanes but, as the weatherman had said, there were slight signs of improvement. As if to prove his point, the sun had begun to shine over the forest canopy and cascades of powdery snow were beginning to fall from the topmost branches as they caught the rays of the gently warming sun. We chatted away as we made slow progress along the forestry tracks. The Captain said how pleased and encouraged he was at my enterprising interest in developing the use of home-grown timbers, and how my order had come at an opportune moment, and how he would personally see to my needs.

At that moment we entered a large clearing just in time to see an enormous tree come crashing to the ground. My heart shrank as I witnessed the scale of the operation. There were at least half a dozen men, a vehicle with a big winch, and a large timber wagon. It was difficult to imagine how the wagon had negotiated the narrow tracks. The Captain was enthusiastically pointing out how all the best and straightest trees were being left to mature to a time he did not expect to live to see, smiling as he made light of the life of a man compared to that of a tree. We examined the fallen giant and the Captain turned to speak to the man with the saw.

"About seventy, seventy feet would you say, John?"

"About that, sir. My father used to tell me these went in in the year I was born, 1927. Would that be right?"

"Indeed it would. How are they for ice?"

"Right through, sir. No chance of puttin um to the saw for a good few days. Saw ud be all over the place."

"Quite so," the Captain replied, as if that was just something to be expected. For myself I had never considered that a living tree could freeze through right to its heart. I was impressed with this and indeed with everything I had seen, and in no small way relieved that culling the trees to meet my order was all part of a greater plan. The trees that remained would become giants in their unrestricted domain.

The Captain talked to the men in turn and I took the opportunity to talk to John, who I had decided was the leader of the felling gang.

"Seems a pity to be felling such magnificent trees just to build a house," I said.

John looked puzzled at my sentiment. "Bless me! Why, they never bin used for anythin better than crates, posties and pallets afore! Why, the Captain's over the moon at your ideas!

He's a telling um all what you're agona do with it all! Guess we ul start acuttin in about a week's time if there is a thaw. I'll tell Mr Elcock to give you a call when we're ready, and you can come and see how we are on the sizing."

There was no longer any point in raising the question of cost, let alone of the order. Once I saw those great trees, and despite your mixed feelings about felling them, I was happy to accept the misunderstanding as a fait accompli. Every one seemed to have been swept along in the same wave of enthusiasm that had swept over Irene and myself when the idea of a log house had first struck us.

Irene was nervously excited as I related the morning's activity. "I still wish we knew what it is all going to cost!" She had a point.

"Whatever the timber may cost, just think of the savings with this type of construction. The foundations will be only half the requirements of a conventional house as there is only half the weight to support, what with no plaster or finishings either. It will be just like a giant Meccano set when it's made and, once we get the site ready, the house may not take much more than a week to erect."

Irene was smiling. "I was hoping you would have some news. Let's have a glass of sherry to celebrate the start of the log house."

"The log house!" we chorused.

Yes, we had really started.

A week went by. Each day the sun became a little stronger, and each day saw a little more snow turned to water. The frost had been holding back the river's water, its lifeblood, and the

111

river-level had therefore been steadily falling. However the thaw brought water aplenty, so that now the river was in spate, bank-high. The main roads were once more dry and clear, and snow remaining in the lanes was fast becoming slush. Grass was showing again in the margins of the meadows, and in the furrows of ploughed fields only white streaks remained to accentuate where the plough had passed. Winter had fought until the very last, but was finally defeated by the growing warmth of the spring sun. On the fourteenth of April we heard the first cuckoo, and a few days later a few timid swallows were perching gingerly on the telephone-wires. Each puff of the breeze seemed to threaten their grip; we feared that, weak after so long a journey, they might fall to earth. We also feared for their food, for this is a risky time for insect-eating birds. We could only hope that the warmish weather would continue and that a few insects would appear.

I took Irene to the mill on the day appointed to start the saw-milling. Cutting the logs had been delayed as it had taken longer than anyone could remember for the ice in the timber to melt. The Captain and Colonel Haddock were there, and the first log was set up on the bench. The sawyer pressed the start button on the carriage and the log moved forward. I saw the operator almost imperceptibly shake his head when the first slice of timber fell away and the log began its return. The two operators quickly reset the log, and away it went for the second cut. The sawyer still looked worried, and we watched as the process was repeated until the log of my specification was cut. The sawyer came over as the saw lost momentum and the mill fell silent. He shook his head in an unmistakable sign of despair.

"Wouldn't have believed it! Them still got ice in em! Not worth cuttin, blades all over the show."

I went over and attempted to turn the log just to see how straight the cut really was. Mr Elcock's words suddenly came back to me: "When did you last handle a fresh-cut log?" I could barely move the timber never mind lift it, and to cover my embarrassment I pretended just to feel the smoothness of the cut. Too late – nothing escaped the Captain. He came over.

"Don't worry too much about the weight," he said. "A great deal of the moisture-content quickly dissipates, although unfortunately what remains takes a great deal longer to go."

Irene whispered in alarm: "I don't like the colour one bit! It looks like cold pork, all pink – cold and dead."

Her description was very apt, and I too had my doubts. The Captain was standing close enough to have heard Irene's anxious misgivings, or perhaps he just guessed, but he looked around and caught Mr Elcock's eye.

"Can you find a piece of dry Douglas so that Mrs Rogers can see the true colour of the wood?"

Mr Elcock glanced around until his eye fell upon a planed plank. He brought it over and laid it on the saw-bench. We were amazed. Irene asked if he was sure it was the same wood.

"Ner been surer!" said Mr Elcock. "Only takes a day or two to lose the pinkiness, then it turns that lovely deep honey colour. Best of all the timbers – just look at that grain!"

Perhaps over the years the Captain's love of timber had transferred itself to everyone at the mill, perhaps that wasn't necessary, but I never saw men so proud of their product.

Probably our greatest problem was solved: we had secured the timber to build our new home. We had been very fortunate in having such material almost on our doorstep, and perhaps even luckier to have such expertise available. We had no technical decisions to make about the wood. But what had made it all so pleasurable was the sawmillers' enthusiasm. They genuinely wanted to see their labours translated into this revolutionary idea of building a solid-timber house. Of course the idea was not new. We had picked it up from Scandinavia, and they in turn may well have found their inspiration in the magnificent log-buildings of Switzerland, where the process of building from sawn logs goes back a long time. Indeed so fine and ornate are some of great Swiss chalets that they have become national monuments, part of the country's heritage.

Still, the timber was only the start of our project. Our dream was becoming a challenge – we seemed to have the knowledge to realize it, but not the practical experience. Apparently no one in the UK had the experience: we were to be the first to build a log house. We would not have to wait long for the first challenge to manifest itself.

The timber had now been felled and awaited my instructions. I went down to the mill to see whether the stack of saw material had shrunk. Under normal circumstances the timber would have been sawn as it arrived from the plantation but, as we had seen, the ice in the timber had prevented this, and so day by day the pile had grown to alarming proportions. The original stack of logs, lying where they had been dumped from the timber wagon, had seemed formidable. By the time of this visit, it had been neatly stacked, and I could tell from the way the stack stood that the wood had been well sawn. I judged there to be perhaps two very big lorry-loads, based not so much on the sheer volume as on the weight of the timber. I had not forgotten my nonchalant attempt to turn over that first log and how, in front of the assembly, my effort had embarrassingly ended in the pretence of admiring the work of the saw. Mr Elcock's friendly tease about handling fresh timber had begun to haunt me, and I had dreamed on more than on occasion that the timber was so heavy that I could get no further with the building.

The snow had now all disappeared, even from the high tops of the distant Clee Hills lying between the Severn valley and the Welsh border to the west. In the din of the mill I didn't hear Mr Elcock come up behind me, and when he spoke, I swear that a shudder ran down my spine despite the warmth of the sun:

"Come for your timber then?"

"Oh! you startled me."

He grinned. Still troubled by his taunt, I felt sure I knew what he was thinking, but it turned out to be something else.

"You can bring up your lorry any time you've a mind," was all he said.

A second shudder ran down my spine. "But I thought that you were to deliver," I muttered in mild protest.

"Lord no! We only got the old timber wagon and that's not rightly a road vehicle. If you're not fixed up, I tell you what, you just go and see that nice fellow at the bottom of the Stourbridge road. He'll fix you up, very obliging man. Bin up here a time or two, but for the lifer me I canna remember his name. You'll find him, though. Like as not you'll see the old lorry."

So here was my second challenge: would I be able to move my timber or not? I set off at the double to find the man and his lorry. If I could sort this out, I would have laid my ghost and return to nights of undisturbed slumber. I did not really expect to find either the man or his lorry. It being a working day, I thought he would probably be out transporting goods for someone else. I was therefore pleasantly surprised to find the lorry, and assumed that its owner would be nearby. My first impression was that the lorry had not been anywhere for some time. The spring weather was encouraging the growth of grass between the joints of the boarded platform, and for lack of polish the cab's paintwork had long since taken on a matt appearance. I wandered around looking for signs of life, but there were none. I had just begun to peer into the twilight of a building full of tyres, radiators, bits of engines and all manner of old vehicle parts, when there was a distinct cry of anguish from outside. I rushed out just in time to see a tousle-haired man rapidly extricating himself from the underside of the old lorry. He did not see me at first, as he danced uncontrollably clutching the thumb of his left hand whilst uttering not-so-ancient countryside curses. The utterances gradually subsided, and at last he saw me. To my surprise however he behaved as if I was usually standing there.

"Tham all right when they goes, these Commers, but tham beggars when they dosn't!"

"What's up?" I mildly enquired.

"Dunno. It's one of its dosn't days. So what can I do for you?" he said, finally acknowledging that I might be there for a purpose.

I explained and my possible haulier listened with great interest. The pain of the battered thumb had apparently subsided. He smiled.

"I be your man."

Then, patting the bonnet of the vehicle as one might pat a faithful horse, he began to extol the virtues of his means of livelihood.

"I be the man and this be the vehicle for your job. Couldn't have better. Had nine tons aboard once, but she's appier seven or eight. Always better to split a load if it looks too much. When's it to be then? Say ten in the morning?"

"Earlier if you wish," I volunteered, thinking he might just have said ten for my convenience.

"No, best make it ten. Give me time to get her started."

I might so easily have gone elsewhere with my transport enquiry, somewhere where my enquiry would have been dealt with in an efficient office and where in the yard outside there would have stood gleaming modern vehicles. In such a place, there would have been no hesitation about an eight o'clock starting-time. Each lorry would have started instantly, at the touch of a button. But no: I had engaged a man who needed time to get his vehicle started. What had he said? "When it goes it goes, and when it doesn't it's a beggar"—or words to that effect. I was unusually unconcerned, because my haulier had been recommended. That is the way of the country trader – no fancy advertisements promising the earth, no workmen who know their rights and no unsuspected additional costs that are always the customer's fault. No: country people generally live for their work. That is how it has always been and how it has remained – when there is a job to be done they just get on with it, the seasons often driving their effort. If there are obstacles they overcome them.

In spite of my unconcern, I can't pretend that I had a wholly restful night but now it was the following morning. If two hours were enough to get the old Commer started, then today I would handle my raw materials. I had known from the very first inkling of this enterprise that I would not be able to accomplish it alone. I not so naïve as not to know that long lengths of timber were heavy and that long lengths of wet timber were very heavy. I would need assistance. And so, now that I had reached the stage of a practical start, I had arranged with Joe Corkindale to have the assistance of Mick Rogers.

I could not have wished for a more able partner. In my workshop days Mick Rogers (no relation) had worked alongside me on whatever work we had undertaken. In all those years, I could not instance a single occasion on which he had been absent or even late. The workshop was getting along well now, and Joe had promised that I could have Mick for as long as it might take.

When I told Mick where we were off to that morning, I saw a flicker of mild amusement cross his face. I tried to make some comment about his mirth, but years of experience should have taught me that this was a useless pursuit. Mick never said anything adverse about anyone. And here we were at the Stourbridge Road site, and we couldn't see the lorry for smoke. I took the smoke as a good sign: the engine must be running. Sure enough, it was. The owner-driver, whose name I had learned was Harry, emerged from the fog and casually greeted me.

"See you brought along young Mick," he said.

Mick coughed and spluttered in mockery of the belching smoke.

"Just chargin the batteries a bit afore we go," said Harry. "Be all right when we are on the road."

I made for the Landrover, saying that we would go on ahead, but Harry would hear nothing of it.

"You're comin with me! You'll enjoy the experience."

Mick was beside himself with concealed mirth. We climbed aboard but not without difficulty. The whole floor on the passenger side was taken up with two spare batteries, a jack and its handle, and several coils of rope. There was only one seat, which Mick and I shared as best we could. We moved away with surprising ease.

We were on our way. At each gear-change, the engine seemed to die away, and then miraculously return to life.

"Six cylinder two stroke," Mick quipped – or was he being serious? "Steady up, Harry," he said. "Next left!"

"Good God, man! I know it's next left! I bin up here more times than you had hot dinners."

"Just saying like. I thought that you was concentrating so hard on your drivin that you might forget."

The banter might have continued except that we had arrived at the sawmill. As Harry had predicted, all signs of smoke from the exhaust had vanished. I tried to help with the loading, but it takes equal numbers to handle the lengths and I had to stand idly by. I became concerned at the way the vehicle was sagging over its axles. One of the mill-labourer shouted:

"Going to try to get half the stack on, or will that be more than the old heap can manage?"

Harry's face, already reddened from the exertion, turned a shade redder. "Could take the lot if I were a-minded!"

Everyone laughed, and at that moment there was a fearful crack from somewhere near the rear axle.

"There, Harry, the old girl's decided herself!" the labourer shouted excitedly.

"No er's not!" yelled Harry. "Er's just a-settlin, and any roads I'm the one that decides. Just to spite yer, I'll take no more. You all get back to cuttin up sticks and I'll be back when I'm good and ready."

I've never ceased to be amazed at the way a good lorry man can rope up a load, how in seconds, with a quick twist of the wrist, the doubling-up knot is formed and with another flick, the driver is pulling down on the load until the ropes form themselves into a veritable boa constrictor. Harry stood back and admired his handiwork.

This time there was no problem in restarting the engine. We waited a short while for the exhaust-smoke to settle from a belching plume to a gently smoking haze.

"See you in a while , Harry!" the labourer shouted as the heavily laden lorry moved off. "Got to give as good as you get, eh Mick?"

Mick nodded.

The exhaust left a faint trail as we headed out of the woodyard and into the narrow lane. Soon we were back on the main road and, although we were going at no more than twenty miles per hour, I was still surprised how effortlessly the vehicle was bowling along. I boked across at Harry sitting serenely behind the wheel with a quiet smile on his face. I remarked how well we were getting along.

"Ha! Her needs a bit of a load so that her knows her's wanted," he explained.

Maybe he was right, as we were already turning into our lane and minutes later we had come to a standstill in the yard of my house. Irene was there to greet us with a plate of ham sandwiches and mugs of tea. Just as we had been told, the colour of the wood was already beginning to take on the honey-brown hue of drying timber, illuminated now by the light and warmth of the mid-day spring sunshine.

Our first load of timber. We just sat around taking our well earned lunch-break. Perhaps we would still be sitting there dreaming of that not-too-distant future when the timber would become our home on the shore of a beautiful Highland sea-loch, had Harry not brought us back to reality.

"Come on then," he said. "We needs to get this lot off, although I don't thinks we'll get another load in today."

At last the time had come for me to slay my dragon. I had made ready an area for the timber several days before, where we could restack the piles and baulks, placing thin strips of wood between the layers to aid the drying, and with bearers in place to keep the wood clear of the ground. Soon I was going to know whether the nightmares were real – had I miscalculated my ability to handle such heavy material? and what would happen then? I had always managed to wake myself from the dream before the feared revelation was upon me...

Harry climbed up on top of the load. Mick and I waited whilst he struggled to slide the first length out over the rear of the pile. Out and out it came, until at last it reached the point of balance and slipped quickly downwards. Mick caught it just in time to prevent it clattering to the ground, and stood waiting for me to take the other end. That end was at an angle, still just caught on the edge of the loadway above my head, far too high for me to reach. There was only one thing I could do, and that was to get nearer the centre of the log where I *could* reach. I stood there and braced myself as Mick pulled the log free of the pile. With a sickening jolt the weight came on to my shoulder. My knees bent, and I know that I staggered. I quickly worked my way back to the end so as to halve the weight between the two of us. The saw-marks in the wood grazed my shoulder, and I was more than relieved when we had the first length safely placed. Mick was looking rather serious but Harry seemed to think it funny.

"Don't let it get you down!" Harry decided he liked his witticism, and just had to repeat it. "Don't let it get you down! Not many as long as that one. Must a bin two hundredweight or near. You need a shoulder pad, you do. There's one in the cab. Best get it on, or you'll have no shoulder come the end of the day!"

I put the shoulder pad on and the process began again. Maybe I was getting the hang of handling the load, or perhaps it was as Harry had said and there were not too many as long as that first length – whatever the reason, the pile on the lorry gradually got less and the pile on the ground grew. It was getting easier.

It actually took two more loads to get the remaining timber from the sawmill. As each length of timber left its place on the lorry to join the stockpile, my confidence grew. As our muscles met the challenge, I knew that what we had undertaken we would accomplish.

CHAPTER NINE

The Story of Altt-a-Choire

When the last of the timber had been added to the pile, I decided on the Captain's advice to leave it there for one month. This would help the timber lose its excess moisture more quickly, and, the Captain had promised me, timber with a drying surface was easier to handle. To assist the drying process the stockpile was on bearers that kept it clear of the ground; we had also been careful to leave small gaps between each piece, and at each layer we had inserted thin strips of dry wood, thus ensuring complete air-flow around every single piece of wood. The whole operation was going to plan. We were well satisfied with ourselves and our spirits rose accordingly.

It is certain that not a day passed without some thought of our newly acquired land in the Highlands and of our friends in the village. Amongst these friends was a couple who like ourselves had decided to move to the Highlands. Mac's ancestors had been Highlanders but had moved south to Liverpool many generations earlier. Mac, as every one called him, had spent his life at sea. He had been on convoy duty throughout the worst periods of the Second World War and was now a captain in the pilot service. He and his wife Jenny intended to retire to Ullapool.

Their plans were someway ahead of ours. When we first met in the village they had already secured a lochside site and engaged an architect. In the absence of a village builder, this architect had been trying with some difficulty to interest various tradesmen in combining their efforts in order to build the property. We had kept up a correspondence with them throughout the winter months, and we were delighted to read in a letter received on the same morning that our timber was safely stacked that Mac and Jenny had moved in. It had taken them nearly two years of visits, letter-writing and argument to get thus far. There were still many things to do, but they were in and clearly delighted. They ended their letter by asking whether we would like to go and stay with them for a few days – now, if we wished.

I wrote that very day congratulating them on their success. It had all been achieved by remote control, for they had not had any opportunity to visit whilst the house was raised from the bare ground to the finished roof. Since they as yet had no telephone, we calculated that if we suggested arriving on a date a week hence they would have time to put us off if it was inconvenient. Two days later Jenny rang us from a call box, and we went up the very next day.

Suddenly bringing forward our departure meant that we could not make our usual early start. However we were away in time to get up as far as Keswick, in the Lake District. We had never been particularly fond of the journey up the A6 over the high ground of Shap, and although there was no reason weatherwise to be put off at this time of year, the thought of all those crawling lorries negotiating the tortuously narrow roads made up our minds. We stayed at a house just south of the town, and learned that it had at one time been the home of the poet Shelley. I wished that we could have stayed longer, as the owner had many interesting stories to tell but, alas, we needed an early start. We still had three quarters of the journey to Loch Broom ahead of us.

With the pattern of our future now taking shape, the areas of uncertainty were slowly becoming tangible. We spent the whole journey making plans. Since that enlightening day at the Ideal Home Exhibition when we had seen the log house I had drawn up designs for several houses that would suit our needs and the site. We visualized a comfortable sitting room with a large window overlooking the sea, and – this was essential – an open fireplace where on a winter's night we could burn logs and driftwood. Irene's kitchen would of course have to house the solid-fuel cooker, already ordered. And there were to be two bedrooms and a bathroom.

After testing these requirements in a variety of arrangements I now had a planning proposal, but we had done nothing towards getting planning consent. This situation was horrifying our Shropshire building friends. I had in fact had no contact at all with the Ross-shire Council about Creag nan Cudaigean. This was not because I was being dilatory; it was that Irene and I could not agree on the best position for the house – not that we disagreed about it either. It was simply that with so many acres there were so many positions that might be suitable.

One of the prime objects of this visit was therefore to have Jenny and Mac along, in the hope that we would have the benefit of their advice. They had also had a number of options, but had finally chosen the one we had seen on their plan. Soon we would be looking out of their window. It would surely be late evening when we arrived, and we imagined seeing the lights of the village as one day we would see them across the harbour from Creag nan Cudaigean. We had no doubt that once on site we would soon come to a decision. Then I would be able to sketch in a site-location on the plan, and take the opportunity of meeting the planning officer during our stay. I was not in the least concerned that he might react adversely to our proposal, as I had been told that all reasonable development in the Highlands was being welcomed with open arms.

Even with the early start from the Lakes, four hundred miles is a long journey. By the time we were skirting the Beauly Firth, just north of Inverness, it would be fair to say we were tired. We might easily have called it a day except for the fact that the west coast was calling, and Jenny and Mac were waiting. Just over an hour later, and surprisingly still in daylight (for it was only the beginning of May), we rounded the last bend. There in front of us was Mac, his arms out, beckoning us into the new gateway. I was amazed – a proper gateway and fencing! The drive had even been tarmacked, and they had a new wooden garage. We came round the bend in the drive and faced the new house. It was hard to believe that it had only just been completed. It looked wonderful.

Mac was ambling down the road behind us and Jenny was at the door with a great big smile on her face. I just had time to say to Irene how impressed I was, what a magnificent job the architect and builder had done, and how all this talk of building problems in the Highlands must be a myth.

Irene sighed. "Oh, if only we could just do as they have done and have someone do all the work!"

"If only," I replied. "Of course, when you have the money you can do anything."

In the next moment I was shaking hands with Mac, and Jenny embraced Irene. As soon as I could extricate myself from Mac's crushing handshake I stood back and gazed at the house. I could still hardly believe that it had all gone so well. I could hardly find words to express my admiration.

"It's magnificent!" I spluttered. "I never expected to see you so well established. Gates, fences, a tarmacked drive – and just look at the house! It looks *perfect*!"

"Aye, not bad."

Mac had already returned to the mannerisms of his native Highlands. 'Not bad': he showed no sign of emotion as he uttered the words that constitute the highest accolade ever bestowed by a Highlander, however splendid the project being appraised. I have never been clear whether 'not bad' means that it's not bad but it's not good either, or whether it just expresses the natural reserve of the Highlander.

Whatever it meant, there was no more time to reflect on Mac's apparent lack of enthusiasm for his new home, for we were now being ushered through a glazed entrance porch full of wellies, walking sticks and waterproofs into a warm kitchen. The smell of a new building always overwhelms me with joy: the paint, the varnish, the wood, stone, plaster, a myriad of reminders of a building satisfactorily completed. It is to me as greasepaint is to the actor, new-mown hay and the harvest to the farmer, and the scent of flowers and blossoms to the gardener.

"What a triumph of your organizational ability!" I said, trying to convey at least something of what I felt.

"The porch was an afterthought" was all Mac said as we squeezed through with our luggage into the kitchen.

Jenny frowned as Mac made this revelation and for a moment I felt slightly uncomfortable. Perhaps we had after all descended upon them just a little too soon, perhaps we had been a little over-enthusiastic in taking up the invitation? No, I inwardly chided myself, it was they who had insisted that we come straight away.

In the next minute we were toasting Altt-a-Choire, as they had chosen to call the house. When we ran out of things to toast, Jenny served a magnificent dinner. Good humour had well and truly returned by the time I related the story of the timber now lying in our Bridgnorth garden, ready to be hauled north and turned into a log house. Both Mac and Jenny thought it highly amusing that I still did not know how much it was going to cost.

"That's the first thing I would have wanted to know!" persisted Mac. "You'll see, they'll wait until you've cut it up and then they'll drop the bombshell."

Mac seemed to delight in insisting on my ineptitude, but as we had all had a few gins and tonic and our share of an excellent wine, it merely seemed funny. Even Irene, who would normally have been unnerved by such a comment, just laughed.

It was dark now, and Mac stood up. We had dined in the kitchen and had as yet seen hardly anything of the rest of the house.

"I'll just go and see how the fire's getting on in the sitting room," said Mac.

Jenny added quickly: "And draw the curtains!"

"Oh, please don't!" Irene countered. "I have been so looking forward to seeing the village lights across the harbour!"

We went through to the sitting room, and Irene stood for a while staring out into the blackness. Mac was manœuvring the logs in the enormous stone fireplace that seemed to take up about a quarter of the room.

"I don't understand, Mac," Irene said at last. "I thought I would be looking out at the village, but I can't see it."

"You'll have to come and have a look through this little window at the side of the chimney-breast if you want a view of the harbour." Mac's voice betrayed his disappointment, and I began to realize with a sinking feeling something that had crossed my mind earlier. Whilst I hesitated, Jenny entered with the coffee.

"They faced the house the wrong way." A naturally handsome woman of fine bearing, Jenny's simple announcement magnificently conveyed that all Highland builders and architects were imbeciles. Up until this moment the conversation had mainly centred around our proposals and their progress. Now it was time to hear the story of Altt-a-Choire.

We already knew that it had been more than a year since they had accepted a tender for the building work. We also knew that when they had met the builder on site they had been so clear about the orientation of the property that they had had him hammer four substantial pegs into the ground there and then, so there could be no doubt as to where the house should stand. What could have gone wrong? Both Mac and Jenny were still seething as in turns they related the sorry tale of the woes that had beset their dream-home.

When Altt-a-Choire was being built there were no local builders. The contract had been placed with a joinery company some fifty miles away. This company had undertaken to deal with the woodwork element of the proposed house. Although they were referred to as 'the contractor,' in practice they had no responsibility for any of the 'subcontractors'. The other tradework was undertaken by men appointed by the man who had acted as architect. The first subcontractor on site had been the mason, whose job it was to lay the foundations and to complete the brick and stonework to roof level. The architect had arrived on site just in time to see the last of the marker pegs being hurled out into the loch and a very red-faced Willie the mason shouting to his little band of men:

"Come on, start here! It's a lot easier, less digging. What would they know about where to put a house? Lived all their life in the south!"

Now it is a fact that all Highland workmen are gentlemen. Whatever they are asked to do by their employer they do without question. These men only did what they had been told to do, and so the work progressed. A special feature of the house was to have been an external chimney breast with tiled shoulders that would look attractive as one approached the house.

"Nonsense!" Willie told the workers as they perused the drawings. "No need for such frills now. No one to see it now we've changed the position of the house, and anyway it will be easier if the chimney breast goes in the house."

Once again, the men did as they were bid. The weather had been exceptionally fine during the autumn and on into the early winter, and Willie the mason had kept his men hard at work. Soon it was time for the roof structure. It was fairly plain to the joinery foreman that the house was in the wrong place and facing the wrong direction, but he and his men had come fifty miles and his employer had been quite explicit with his instructions.

"Get that roof on as quick as you can. If you get a move on we will be in the dry before the weather breaks."

And, being loyal Highland workmen, they got on with the job and the roof was, as they say, soon on.

Mac got up from his chair and walked out, his face so drawn that I was concerned for him. As soon as he was through the door I asked Jenny if he was all right and noticed that she was also looking strained.

"He'll be fine." She paused then went on. "He's been waiting to tell you all about it. Do him good to get it off his chest. Can't very well discuss it with anyone in the village, and I know he would like to talk over some of the details with you. Perhaps tomorrow, if that's all right?"

"Yes, of course," I said without hesitating.

After a while Mac returned. I could see that his smile was rather forced but what he had in his hand was real enough: a bottle of brandy and four glasses.

"Thought we might need this. I knew we had it somewhere." He proceeded to pour four generous measures.

Jenny took up the story.

"At the beginning of December we received a glowing letter, about how well the work was proceeding, and how we were probably ahead of schedule, and how in consequence the architect was taking the liberty of enclosing statements in respect of the work to date: he had no hesitation in certifying the amounts as due for payment. As the sum amounted to at least half the contract amount Mac was just slightly suspicious. As you already know, and unlike you, he prefers to know what he is paying for."

We laughed easily. Jenny went on. "Mac decided that perhaps he should pay a flying visit."

Mac interrupted. "It's the closest I have ever been to a heart attack. I can't describe the agony I experienced that day. I saw instantly that the house was in the wrong position, but it was only later that I noticed the chimney breast and other things. I could have killed the architect, but it was useless even trying to remonstrate with him. It wasn't for want of trying, but he and Willie the mason and the joinery-contractor just closed ranks. It was clear that the architect could afford to fall out with me, but that it would not do for him to fall out with his contractors. He would need them long after my work was finished, whereas he could stay clear of me. People a mile away in the village must have heard me bellowing.

"What was most galling was that while I was saying for all to hear that they would have to knock it down and start again, a chap was setting the chimney-pot. I was obviously in a blind fury, for I never heard what one of the three must have said. The next instant everyone was packing up and in the space of five minutes I was alone. I can tell you that I never flinched through the worst the war could throw at the Merchant Navy, but just then I could have sat down and wept."

Out came the brandy and we fortified ourselves. Mac stirred the embers of the dying fire and whilst he did so I said: "If that was the state of play at the beginning of December, the restarted contract must have gone well."

Mac was clenching and unclenching his fists as he spoke. Whatever the memories, they were painful. Irene was weary, but there was no way of retiring yet.

"I'm sorry to inflict this on you, but Jenny will tell you that I've been bottling it up for weeks," said Mac. Jenny looked up and nodded.

"Well," he went on, "I sat there on a pile of concrete blocks until the cold struck through me. I jumped up knowing what I had to do. I'd sue them every one of them. It was still only early afternoon so I drove down to Dingwall where my newly acquired solicitor had his office. I was there in the hour, and by good fortune he was in and for the moment free. I told my story and waited whilst he thought up a strategy. But I was not prepared for his summing up.

" 'Well,' said my solicitor, 'I suppose this is a holiday home that you're building? So whether it is finished this year or next is of no real consequence, in which case we might consider a breach of contract if indeed that is what we could prove. I make no bones about it, there are difficulties. You say you definitely put pegs in so as to show the desired position of the house, but you would need independent witnesses to prove that and of course to prove that you had conveyed your instructions precisely. Now, as to timescale, I can easily foresee that a case of this nature could drag on, but then time is on our side as you have not paid other than a deposit sum. Of course they will counter-claim, and we will have to defend our position. Of course it goes without saying that in the meantime all works must remain at a standstill. We can try for damages in this respect, always assuming we can prove the rest of our case. Yes, it will all take time, however we can console ourselves with your Mr Johnson's words after visiting the Highlands – now, let me see, was it 1790? Yes, I think it was. Let me see if I have the right words: *"No man regards himself as a gentleman unless he is sporting with at least one action in the court of sessions in Edinburgh." ' "*

It was Jenny who put an end to the evening. "Come on, Mac. These people have driven four hundred miles today, and it's midnight."

"Yes, of course. I'm sorry for going on so, but I feel better for having talked about it. At least you know what I've been up against."

He put his arm around Irene's shoulder as Jenny led us to our bedroom and I heard him say: "Irene, you're lucky to be able to be here and organise your own building. You will know that it's all right and exactly where you want it on the site. Good night, sleep well."

The morning dawned with a clear blue sky, glorious sunshine and not a breath of wind. The loch was like a mirror, and one could sense the delicate smell of moss and peaty earth mixed with the ever-present tang of the sea. On mornings such as this that scent is incomparably delicious.

Jenny was in high spirits. "I think it's done Mac the world of good to talk about the house. It had completely dragged him down, all the worry and the felling that somehow there was just no way of getting what we wanted."

Mac was already pottering about in the garden, so Jenny rang the bell they had rigged up for announcing meal time.

"There's no point in my trying to shout," she explained. "I never know where he is, and he is beginning to go a little deaf."

The bell obviously served its purpose as we heard Mac in the porch. Jenny said. "Listen, he's humming to himself! I haven't heard that for a very long time. He's definitely feeling better."

There was no doubt that Mac looked infinitely better. The stress and pain so evident last night had all but gone as he joked about the porch. It was only half the size of the one they had ordered. He beamed from ear to ear as he related how he had taken the joinery contractor to task over the shortcomings of the structure, but his smile faded as he continued:

"Do you know what he said when I pointed out the deficiency? I used to think it plain cheek or indolence until I realized that it's just the make-up of the Highlander."

"Well? What did he say?" Irene asked, as Mac seemed to have forgotten to deliver his punch line.

"He said 'Ach, tis big enough.' "

We all laughed. Jenny and Mac promised us a grand tour as soon as breakfast was over.

We stood at the window where Irene had dreamt of seeing the lights of the village. It was now all too obvious that the house had been set looking out across the loch instead of across the harbour to the village. Irene was quick to point out that as the house stood it certainly got more sunlight, and then after a moment's further contemplation she all but exploded with:

"And just look at that view!"

Jenny was pleased with Irene's vindication of the position. Mac was not so easily persuaded.

"I wanted to be able to sit back in my armchair and watch the fishing boats come and go."

"But Mac, you wouldn't have been able to see the harbour over the window-cill!" Irene protested, but here she was on weaker ground.

"Quite right," said Mac. "That's something else that was supposed to have been done that wasn't. A french window giving us access to a terrace."

We looked blank as we waited for yet another saga.

"Simple," said Jenny as she took up the story. "They had made this window before they realized it should have been a french window and by then it was too late."

There was more. "In the bathroom serving the two bedrooms on the ground floor, the underfloor heating is under the bath instead of warming the area where you stand. But I don't know why I bother to mention such a minor deficiency. You must see the other bedrooms!"

We looked puzzled, as we had not seen a staircase. Jenny was beginning to see the shortcomings of their dream home as something of a joke. She laughed out loud: "The architect is known to be not very good with stairs. We'd been told that he tends either to forget that they were a necessary part of a two-storey dwelling, or more often he just finds that there's no room in the finished building for such luxuries. Of course it wasn't the job of the workmen to point out such limitations, and anyway a ladder had met their requirements up to the fateful moment when it was discovered that something was missing.

"The workmen had got used to the idea that the bathroom was the stairwell as this is where they had had their ladder fixed. Sadly when the plumber had installed the bath they could no longer get to the first floor and, sadder still, there was no room anywhere for a staircase or a ladder."

Mac produced a pole and was bringing down a foldaway loft-ladder. When it was safely secured we all trooped up to the loft bedrooms then trooped down again.

"What's the problem?" I enquired and then as if pierced by my own design pencil, I recited along with Jenny:

"If you are in the ground-floor bedroom and the ladder is down, you cannot get to the bathroom or indeed get out of your bedroom. Likewise if you are in a loft bedroom and the ladder is up…"

We did not get any further, we were laughing so much.

"Come on," Jenny said. "Let's go and have our coffee outside on the bench. It's far too nice to be inside on a day like this."

"Anyone think it strange if I have a brandy with my coffee?" Mac called out and I knew that while he laughed, his heart and mind remained in turmoil.

Altt-a-Choire is built in a clearing amidst a beautiful copse of silver birch that runs right down to the shore line. We sat in an area cleared specifically to provide a vantage point to gaze out at the whole panorama of sea and mountains. The loch shimmered in the morning sunlight and the sun warmed our faces as we sipped our coffee. Mac looked at ease, so I asked "How, with all the upset of last December, did it all suddenly come together?"

Mac was thinking long and hard. We began to prepare ourselves for another long session and were somewhat taken aback when he began:

"I came out of that solicitor's office and sat in the car for an age. At least the light was fading by the time I had made my mind up. The facts were simple. Here was a band of workmen building me a house, and no one could say that what they had done so far was not of the best possible materials and workmanship. They had placed the house where they thought it would best sit. They had disregarded my æsthetic chimney requirements in favour of a more practical build. What's more, they had really got on with the job."

I could see by Jenny's expression that she did not share this philosophical view, but Mac drained the brandy that he had brought down with tray of coffees and went on.

"Now, to my mind the solicitor was clearly either sympathetic to the builder or he relished the idea of a lengthy case. Whichever, he had given me no practical advice or comfort. Yet as far as I could see, no one so far had acted with malice. Being myself of Highland descent and with Highland blood in my veins, I should have recognised that they were only going about their business in a way that has served the Highlander well for generations.

"My only excuse for not seeing all this earlier was that living away so long I had lost half my Highland faculties. Whilst half my brain wavered about what to do, that which belonged to the Highlands had decided."

Jenny could stand it no longer and burst in on the conversation.

"And do you know what he did?"

We waited in anticipation. Mac looked at his boots, Jenny was quite agitated.

"He wrote the so-called architect a note saying how pleased he was with the progress and the workmanship. He said he knew he could rely on them to have the work complete by mid-April and, to cap it all, he enclosed the cheque as requested!"

Mac was playing the innocent child who has been scolded for something he had done but who still could not accept it was wrong. He looked up slowly and with a faint smile said:

"It got the house built though, and on time."

Jenny was going to have the last word. "Oh, that man! He simply can't imagine how I feel when I have to greet my guests in a wellie porch and escort them through the kitchen. It's not what I'm used to."

With that she rose quickly, grabbed the tray and stalked off up to the house. Mac too left us sitting there.

It was hard to take in the Altt-a-Choire story. There was no disputing that this was a dream location. The house would sort itself out one day. We just sat in the warm sunshine mesmerised by the grandeur of the scene and the knowledge that soon we would be sitting like this in front of our own dream house.

CHAPTER TEN

Planning Permission, Highland-Style

We had intended going along to Creag nan Cudaigean straight after breakfast, but had felt constrained by Mac and Jenny's totally unexpected saga. It had taken all the previous evening and most of the morning to tell. Jenny remained somewhat aloof over lunch and declined to come with us, and Mac decided to go out in the small boat he had just acquired, hopeful that one of his lobster pots would contain a lobster.

So it was the early afternoon before we arrived on what was now our very own land. Excitedly, Irene clutched my arm.

"I can hardly believe it is ours."

Neither could I, but there it was – a thousand feet of the most beautiful shore-line, made even more attractive by its edge of mature trees. Their lovely open growth gave evidence of more than half a dozen species. We followed our immediate inclination, which was simply to go and sit by the sea. We watched Mac's little boat in the distance. It headed out across the loch and into the narrows – the small strait before the loch opens up again into the vast stretch of the head waters. Soon the boat was out of sight.

It was less warm now than in the morning and anyway, it was really too thrilling to be sitting around. So we set off to solve our prime problem: where to site the house. We probably stood on at least six or eight spots, each of which offered some good reason or other for being The One but, after making reams of notes and analysing and re-analysing the Fors and Againsts, we finally came back to the site we had noted on our very first visit. It stood away from the shore, in an area of dry bracken and enclosed by trees and coppice on all sides except out over the loch. In the shelter of this site, it was suddenly warm again – so pleasant that we stayed there almost the whole afternoon, surrounded by primroses, tiny violets and celandine. Carpets of speedwell sprang from the few patches of well-cropped turf, the delicate blue of the tiny flowers sustained only by the glorious afternoon sunshine.

As we sat quietly thinking our own particular thoughts, I became aware that the trees and undergrowth were alive with small birds. It was a large family of long-tailed tits that first caught my attention, flitting and chattering amongst the profusion of silver birch. Typically, the longtails did not stay long. They always seem to think the next tree might be more interesting and then the next, until the distinctive chatter dies away. We spotted coal tits, blue tits and their larger cousins, the great tits, all intent on their own special territories. They were so tame that they came within feet of where we sat quietly observing. Perhaps they were just inquisitive as to who these strange invaders were. Although the land had once been occupied and worked, that had last been more than a hundred ycars ago. A little dunnock came, silently working its way through the moss and stone that formed most of the cover below the silver birch. The solitary little bird, normally so shy, moved like a little mouse, and seemed quite oblivious to our presence. Word was obviously going around that strange creatures were trying to establish nesting rights in territory that they had held unchallenged for decades. A chaffinch came and perched close, chirping out its questions as if in an interview. Within an hour most of the chaffinch's cousins had also come to have a look, although in pairs and from a more respectful distance this time: goldfinches, greenfinches and a rather aloof pair of bullfinches who only gave us a passing glance. It began to be amusing as one by one even more birds arrived. Just below where we sat motionless, a very tiny bird moved quickly amongst the twigs of the stunted sallow. The olive-green with a gold crest was unmistakable, the plumage that gives this smallest of the British birds its name: the goldcrest. It was by no means our last visitor. A wren and a robin joined the ranks, and then in a distant tree to our left a blackbird chattered. Further away a thrush had been busy the whole time we had been there, already settled into a feeding routine that would take him all the remaining hours of the day.

We must have been sitting in the middle of a prime nesting site. By this time, we felt ourselves to be intruders and so we left the feathered residents to what was rightfully theirs – for the time being! Now that we had been introduced, it was time to let them get on with the business of raising families. It would be the autumn before we returned and in the following winter we would do our best to become their friends.

Back at Altt-a Choire that evening, we learned that Mac had caught two lobsters. Both he and Jenny were certainly in better spirits as we related the story of the birds and, unlike our first evening, the second was relaxed. We sat around a roasting log fire, the fire being as yet the only source of heat. The electric underfloor installation was on hold pending the business of the bathroom (where, you will recall, the heating had been mislocated under the bath). In my opinion, the open fire was in any case preferable to underfloor warming. Such a system could take two days to heat the house and two days to cool if the weather turned warm again. Really, the only way the inside temperature can be controlled with such a system is by opening and closing the doors and windows, as you do with a greenhouse. However, in a region like this, of such changeable weather, it's impractical. Mac had calculated that the one or two years it would take him to get control of the trees around the house would provide them with a non-stop supply of firewood; but so voracious was the appetite of the dream fire that already he was finding the daily work of cutting wood a chore, and he was planning to replace the open fire with yet another electric appliance. It is truly a mistake to imagine the country way of life as no more than an extension of perhaps many years of very enjoyable holidays: so much of what seems a welcome break with city-life is soon revealed to have a very short-term novelty value. Although we had lived most of our lives familiar with the ways of the countryside, Mac and Jenny's experience made me wonder how Irene and I would fare when the time came for us to live here.

Later that night, I commandeered the dining table and got out my drawing of the log house. Previously, I had only 'eyed in' the contours at about five-foot intervals, but now, as I set about sketching in the details of our chosen location, I could see that it was going to be a major undertaking. For one thing, with no suitable machinery within a hundred miles or more, the job would have to be undertaken by hand. For another, the angle of the slope would at its worst point be almost one in five, creating problems for the entrance and driveway. And finally, even my rough draft of what would be needed to provide a level base for the house itself indicated that we would need to dig out over one hundred tons of soil. A good navvy in the heyday of canal building could dig twenty tons a day in easy-going loam, but here at Creag nan Cudaigean a trial-hole had shown that beneath six or so inches of top soil there was moraine clay and gravel so hard that you needed a sharp pickaxe to break it up before your shovel could lift it from the excavation. For some reason, I found the prospect of so much hand-labour not intimidating, but a challenge to be enjoyed rather than feared.

With the drawing finished, the next morning I telephoned the County Building Office, as it was then called, and made an appointment to meet the relevant officer. A very helpful lady asked when it would be most convenient for me to see Mr Stewart.

I half-protested: "When would it be convenient for Mr Stewart?"; but she would not hear of me giving consideration to him.

"No, no! You'll be coming a goodish distance and we must help you the best we can."

This attitude was quite different from that of any planning office I had previously dealt with. The norm is confrontation.

"Ten thirty," I said, and the helpful lady disconcertingly promised to do her best to have Mr Stewart there.

The time had come, all too quickly, to say our farewells to Mac and Jenny. I don't know whether we had been any real help to them, but we had been sympathetic listeners, and they were both in a more buoyant mood than when we had arrived. As for us, we had had the very considerable pleasure of

145

spending an unforgettable afternoon on our very own piece of the Highlands.

As we waved our last goodbyes and Altt-a Choire receded in my rear-view mirror, I was seized by an attack of doubt. Would our plans be acceptable at Dingwall? Hadn't all our professional friends cast doubts on my proceeding without first consulting the planners? As we drove, I looked at the local architecture. The journey to Dingwall from Ullapool is about forty-five miles, and although the countryside is sparsely populated, there were enough cottages built of stone to convince me that my log-built proposal would be an anathema to the average planning officer. The nearer we got to our destination the more uneasy I became. It took one and a half hours to travel the forty-five miles, which will give some idea of the state of the road: for the most part it was single track with passing places, and for long stretches there were just two strips of tarmac with grass growing between.

Irene suddenly broke my train of thought by declaring that if I did not want her at the Building Office, she would rather explore the small town. It would be our nearest source of many essential goods, although there would be many things for which we would have to go to Inverness, more than sixty miles away.

At last we arrived in Dingwall. I dropped Irene off in the main street and drove the short distance to the building I had supposed to be objective of my visit, only to find it was the County Court. With minutes to go and no one else nearby whom I might ask, it seemed sensible to go in and enquire. I went cautiously through the main door. From somewhere out of sight at the top of the staircase in front of me I heard whispering. In a moment I would be late for my appointment, so there was nothing for it but to go and find the source of the distant voices. I climbed the stairs.

Two young men sat on a bench discussing some topic in low voices and on seeing me made room for me to join them.

"What you up for?" the elder one enquired in a soft Highland lilt.

In a rather louder voice and with more than a hint of urgency, I asked if they knew where the Building Office was. They looked blank, but before either could reply, a door, obviously to the court room, opened. A tall thin-faced fellow stepped out with a finger to his lips, from which a low shushing sound issued. He saw me and advanced angrily. I feared he might grab me by the throat.

"You – Macdonald – you're late!"

I shook my head. "No, I'm just looking for the Buildings Office."

"Back down the stair, turn left, and through the door facing." And with that he swept back into the court. I went back down the stairs, turned left, and there was the door, with a brass plate indicating the destination of my quest: County Building Office.

I entered the foyer, tapped on a door marked 'Enquiries', and cautiously went in. I feared that it might be one of those general offices where half a dozen girls would pound away at typewriters and continue quite oblivious to your presence, each determined that she will not be the one to be disturbed by your intrusion. I need not have been concerned, for the only occupant was a lady of middle years who immediately jumped up and smiled such a welcome that I felt slightly embarrassed. I thought at first that she must have mistaken me for someone else, but my fears were soon allayed.

"Oh, you've arrived!" she said in a lovely west-coast accent. "Sit awhile and I'll make you a cup of tea. It is such a long way down from the west and the roads no better than they were."

West-coasters are very loyal people and it would have been treachery for her to have said that the roads in the care of her employers were bad, although they were. By suggesting that they were no better than they had been, she left it to me to decide just how good or bad they were.

The smiling lady reappeared with my cup and a couple of digestive biscuits. This was service indeed, and I said so as I thanked her.

"Ouished!" she murmured. "It's the least. Mr Stewart is not here but we can chat till he comes."

"How long will he be?" I asked.

"Oh, no longer than he need be, I shouldn't wonder."

I assumed that if he was going to be long she would have said, so I changed tack.

"Mr Stewart, I assume, is the planning officer?" I ventured. I sincerely hoped that he was, as this was the purpose of my visit.

"Oh no! Mr Stewart is the Master of Works," she said, with such reverence that I did not dare to say that I was not familiar with that title. There was no need to dissemble, however, as she had seen my blank expression.

"I see you have your plans. Well, Mr Stewart will look at them for planning. He will just need to see that you will not upset the neighbours, and maybe it will look right amongst the others."

"It's a long way from the nearest house," I said. I thought it worth mentioning.

"Well in that case your planning will be all right."

I was very confused. On what grounds was this very amiable lady suggesting that planning would 'be all right'? Did she mean that they would give consent just like that? I was sceptical as well as confused. It had been my experience over many years that the planning process was tortuous and antagonistic, not to say bureaucratic.

"But surely I need to know what the planning officer might have to say?" I said in disbelief.

"Mr Stewart is the Planning Officer," she calmly replied.

"But," I exclaimed in astonishment at this revelation, "Mr Stewart must be a very busy man!"

"Oh yes indeed! For he is also the Sanitary Inspector and the Petroleum Officer, as well as being the Burials Superintendent, and today he is the Meat Inspector too. Indeed the abattoir is where he is at this moment." She glanced up at the large wooden-cased clock. "Ten minutes to eleven. He will be leaving in a moment, and it's only minutes away." Having listed all Mr Stewart's official duties, she sat demurely, silently expressing her pride in working in this so-important office.

"It seems unbelievable! Mr Stewart must surely have assistants," I protested.

"Oh yes! He has Mr MacPhee out on the Islands. You see the travelling from here would just be too much."

Just at that moment the door opened and in walked a shortish man of light build. His bearing was such that he might well have been a military man, his tweed suit was immaculate and his brown brogues well polished. His hair was slightly greying and he had a small well-trimmed moustache. He walked straight up to me, held out his hand and smiled faintly as he introduced himself.

"Jack Stewart. It's Mr Rogers isn't it?" I only had time to nod in the affirmative. "Janet been looking after you I see! Can we have the same again, Janet. Any calls?"

"The messages are on your desk, Mr Stewart."

"Join me in my office," said Stewart, turning once more to me. "I know all about you. The Major's been petitioning on your behalf – told me all about this novel wooden house. It sounds interesting. Got the drawings?" I spread them on the desk. "Ah, just as I expected – it's between the road and the shore, so no problem there. Now let's look at the building. Ummm, five inches of solid timber – pity. You don't need a fire rating, so four inches would have sufficed. Just joking! How's it going to rate for insulation?"

"It has a better rating than an eleven-inch cavity wall," I assured him. This was my first opportunity of saying anything.

"Felt damp-proof course... Prefer three courses of slate myself, but it will do. Ah! oversite concrete – that's good – better than hot tar and sand. You've got roof tiles." I detected a note of disapproval. "Would you not consider Ballachulish slate?"

Before I could answer he observed that the pitch of the roof was insufficient for slate. At last I got a word in, explaining that it was important to have as much weight on the roof as possible. "This type of building requires logs to season in position, and it is essential that there is pressure from above to keep the logs pressed tightly together whilst the seasoning is going on."

"Ingenious," he said without looking up. His finger traced across my drawing as he quietly mentioned each significant feature as he came to it. "Septic tank well away from the water." He paused. "You know the well is not up to much. You might need to dig another – get some one local to come and have a look. Thcy can sometimes tell by the lie of the land where the water is. All you'll need to do is dig a bit of the bank away and see if the water begins to run."

He sat down heavily at his desk, no doubt already exhausted from having been at the abattoir since some early hour and then, without a break, going through all the details of my proposed house. I watched anxiously as he turned over in his mind the detail of my application. Of course, for all I knew, he was already dealing with something else. This man was a dynamo. At last he looked up with a kind of tired, far-away smile.

"I suppose you will want to start tomorrow, well that's all right, but don't get embarrassing me in front of my committees. No doubt the local councillor, Big Huw, will be looking over the fence on his way down to the next council meeting. Wait until you get the paperwork through before you get anywhere near the roof."

The telephone rang. He picked it up and said something. Holding the receiver and covering the mouthpiece at the same time, he held his hand out.

"Delighted to have met you. I'll try and call on you in due course if I get a chance. Leave the forms and your plans with Janet." He smiled. "And the council fee. Good luck!"

As I handed the forms and plans to Janet and wrote the modest cheque in respect of fees I glanced at the clock. It was eleven fifteen.

"Incredible! I think Mr Stewart has passed my plans."

"Yes, of course he has. I never doubted for a moment that he would not. Did he say you could start?"

"Yes!" I said, still in disbelief.

"Well, just go steady," she advised, and then glanced at the calendar hanging on the wall. Selected dates were ringed in green ink. "The building warrant and the planning consent will be with you in about five weeks. They have to await the committees, but it's only a formality."

I thanked her for her kindness. I collected my car from the County Court car park and drove slowly round the town looking for Irene whom I espied just as she came out of a haberdasher's shop. The town-hall clock was not yet at eleven thirty.

"We've got our planning consent," I told her. I felt breathless. "And a building warrant. That's an acceptance of the materials and the structure. We could start tomorrow if we were ready."

For the first time we travelled down to Bridgnorth in one run through the night. The early light of the spring dawn as we neared home was akin to waking from the dream of our future house by the sea. The weather had remained perfect over the whole period that we had been away. It had been warm and sunny with an occasional breeze, and the enormous pile of timber had begun to dry. There was a lovely scent in the air, the delicate and faintly perfumed resin peculiar to the Douglas fir, and the smell of the seashore which we had left less than twenty four hours earlier lingered with us. A fine layer of sawdust covered the yard: everything in it and everything around it was smothered. It was only the start of the fallout of sawdust and shavings – in the weeks ahead it would all but engulf us.

CHAPTER ELEVEN

How to Make Your Own Log House, Part One

The day arrived when Mick and I were to start the long process of machining the logs. We needed them in profiled sections with interlocking tongues and grooves on two adjacent edges, and regularised log-faces on the remaining sides. To achieve this I had built a machine which in some ways resembled a circular-saw bench, but which could also take substantial moulding-cutters. As I no longer had the use of a workshop, we set the machine up under an open-fronted outbuilding in the yard of our house.

The first job was to make provision for shrinkage. When a log dries out, the greatest shrinkage is in the outer layers and the least is around the heartwood. The consequence of this unequal drying-out is that thick timbers invariably crack, or 'shake' as it is called, down their entire length. Sometimes several splits will occur in one log. The object of our exercise was to provide a means of controlling the shrinkage and of obviating or at least minimising the cracking, especially on what would be the inner and outer faces of the finished log. To do this I proposed to make a saw-cut down the entire upper and lower faces of the timber, my theory being that these artificial splits would open and close to suit the relative moisture content of the inner and outer faces of the wood.

The time had come to put my theory to the test.

I set the saw to make a cut two inches deep, started the motor and selected the shortest length from the top of the pile. The surface of the wood may have become drier but the overall weight seemed as heavy as ever. Undaunted, we ran the log over the saw; and then, turning the wood over, we did the same along the other edge. I stopped the motor and we examined our first effort.

It was perfect. However, both Mick and I were sure that we had already injured our backs. It was not the weight of the wood that was creating the problem, although it was heavy enough; it was that, even with a relatively short length such as we had just cut, we had to keep the wood perfectly in position as it passed over the saw. It was no good – we could not manage the logs without more substantial guides and rollers to take the weight of the overhang at the start and finish of the cut. So we set about making them: two trestle rollers and improved saw-guides. But when the end of our first day came, all we really had to show for our effort was one short length of timber with a saw-cut on two faces. We reassured ourselves that our tool-making meant that tomorrow would be better.

The second day began with us in high spirits. Again we chose a short length, and again it went through like a dream. However, there were no more of the smaller logs accessible to us, and it was a struggle just the next length to get on the machine. We got halfway down the cut and the log jammed in the guide. I stopped the saw. Mick had the answer almost immediately: the log was thicker than either of the two we had already machined, by at least a quarter of an inch. In fact it was oversize by that amount, and we soon realized that varying thicknesses were a feature of the whole stack, the maximum variation being no more than that of the log that had stuck. I couldn't complain. A quarter of an inch was well within the tolerance allowable at the sawmill; it was just that in my enthusiasm I had not anticipated the problem.

Mick suddenly came up with the solution, something I was already turning over in my mind.

"We need sprung rollers," he said, "to take account of the variations and to provide the necessary pressure on the log."

"Yes I know," I said, "but we haven't got any."

"Joe'll let us in your old workshop and we can make a pair."

"Take more than a day, even if we can find something to make them from."

And so the second day passed, and a few hours into the night. When I finally got to bed, I could not sleep. It was thus an early start that I made on the third day. By the time Mick arrived, the rollers were fixed and we were ready to start once more. Picking over the shorter lengths we began to make real progress. It wasn't easy, but a stack of logs with saw-cuts was mounting up, and we felt we were getting somewhere.

Now we were into a layer of longer lengths, twelve and fourteen feet (although these were by no means the longest – a few were up to nineteen feet). Mick was having a problem with the trestle rollers: at almost every cut, at least half a dozen times already, when he had just lowered the roller, he would put his hand up for me to stop pushing the log. Now he was raising his hand again. I stopped the machine. We had finished only the tenth of well over a hundred lengths.

"What's the matter?" I shouted as the noise of the saw subsided.

"Dunno," said Mick. "One minute they won't go over the roller unless I lift un, then the next they're nowhere near the roller and I'm having to take the weight."

The problem was not difficult. Some of the lengths were slightly bent, making it like having to work with a banana. With the curve down the rollers too high and the curve up the rollers not high enough, there was nothing for it but to set the rollers low and take the full weight of each length. At least the roller was never more than an inch below where it should have been. And we soon learned to take a rest at strategic points along each length.

And so the first day of continuous work passed. By evening, we had worked through the whole stack. We were now ready for the second operation: the moulding. I knew that unfortunately we would never be able to do the work on this machine. It might be acceptable to have the saw-cuts at slightly different depths, but a moulding must be like the piped icing decorating a wedding cake: near perfect.

It is said that experience is an expensive school where only fools learn, and maybe I had been foolish. Hadn't Mr Elcock at the sawmill posed the question: "When did you last handle a fresh-sawn log?" I had simply not foreseen the problems of undertaking such a complex woodworking project with so few mechanical resources, and I had paid little regard to the weight of the material to be handled. It was probably foolish of me to think that with my primitive means I could emulate what the Scandinavian undertook with vast machining plants that had required equally vast investment. I had allowed myself to be swayed by the fact that I was only producing one house, while they aimed to manufacture hundreds. I should have accepted that the problems were the same: we were both working with very similar rough-sawn timber of very similar length and weight. I knew very well that if one wished to machine big timbers then one needed a big powerful machine. It wasn't that I had ignored that fact; I had been only too conscious of the ideal. But not only do such machines cost a fortune, they are big and weigh many tons, they take up a lot of space and they require substantial electricity supplies. And if this was not enough, their multitude of cutterheads will not operate without powerful extraction systems to vacuum up the colossal volume of waste produced. Yes, I had thought of all these things, and every single one was totally outwith my means.

The fact remained that although Mick and I had been working for three days, we had accomplished only one day's work and were now at a standstill. It was not as if we had all the time in the world. Irene's first foray into house-selling had met with a complete lack of success. Not a single prospective purchaser had shown any interest. However, Irene sensibly decided that this was because we were at the end of one of the worst winters on record. Now it would soon be glorious summer and, if the property-writers were to be believed, the house-market was on the move again. There was something else for us to bear in mind. Irene had confirmed to Major Scobie that we would take Corry Point bungalow from the first of October. This was only four months off, and was a very confining date. I knew that in practice only part of this time would be available for the work on the logs, which was now very much at a standstill.

So something had to be done, and quick. It was Mick who came up with an idea about which I was at first scathing. In self-defence he challenged me to think of something else, and I had to admit that I could not. His idea was to look around for a second-hand machine. My reply was that it was very unlikely that we'd find one, but that on reflection it was perhaps worth a try.

And so, armed with a couple of yellow-page directories, I began to search for second-hand woodworking-machinery dealers. Most that I spoke to didn't even know what I was talking about. Others only dealt in machines suitable for very small building or joinery businesses. After more than an hour of telephoning I suddenly found a man who not only knew what I wanted, but said he had just what I wanted.

"Admittedly," he said without concern, "it can't machine timbers of the size you want, but perhaps you could stretch it a bit, or use smaller timber. Come and see it," he coaxed.

Off we went. Mick was in high glee that his idea might bear fruit and I was in a state of disbelieving despair. Our destination was somewhere beyond Solihull, to the south of Birmingham. We had no proper address, for apparently the road had no name. It was unmade and "a bit rough," as Jack Smith, the owner of the business, had told me in his rather flat nasal voice.

"Yo cor miss it, old mate, right at the fruit-and-veg at the end of the High Street. A left in, and yom nearly there. Just ask anybody for Jack Smith an they'll tell yer."

What a contrast it was driving through the industrial Midlands compared to the narrow, partially surfaced roads of the Highlands! I wondered what Janet in her quiet little office in Dingwall would have made of these driving conditions. It was impossible to compare them to the roads of Ross & Cromarty, although I knew which I preferred. It took us nearly two hours to reach Solihull and another hour to locate Jack Smith,

Wood Machinery Dealers. I must have enquired of more than a dozen people about his whereabouts. Every enquiry met with a blank response and a slow shaking of the head, as one after another everyone said "Sorry." In desperation at about a mile from the fruit-and-veg I asked a rag-and-bone man.

He took his cap off, scratched his head and said: "Yo do mean Jack Smith the scrap mon, do yer, cos ifs yo do, he's down that rough road over yon. Watch the pot-holes – some's a foot deep."

We had arrived and there was Jack Smith. Sweat was pouring down his forehead as he excavated his way through a mountain of scrap of all descriptions. At that moment he was just beginning to uncover an ancient machine.

"Yer must be Mr Rogers. Yum just in time to help me off with the rest on this junk."

Unwillingly, we began to help, and in no time we were covered in rust and black grease, just like Jack. To give him his due, the machine *was* a moulder, a very old moulder. It had lain undisturbed in all weathers for at least twenty years. It was indescribably rusty and, even if it could have been resurrected, most of the parts were missing. Although it probably weighed five or six tons, no way would it have been big enough to deal with our requirements.

I tried to explain this to Mr Smith, but our parting was acrimonious.

"Yo promised to buy that machine!" he insisted. "Don't yo know I could have yo in court for breach of contract?"

I just drove away as quickly as decency allowed. I tried to thank him for all the trouble he had gone to, but that was only met with a shaking fist. I was relieved when we regained the main road and the fruit-and-veg. If there was a low point in the whole of our adventure this was it. Tired, hot, covered in bright orange rust with smudges of black grease and the prospect of Birmingham in the rush-hour: all with nothing to show for our efforts.

Days passed as we visited other merchants who promised that they would not waste my time and that they could practically guarantee that what they were offering would meet my requirements. One giant of a machine that the owner boasted weighed over nine tons and was a good eighteen feet long may well have done the job, but like most we saw it was devoid of many of its essential parts (including in this case the main gearbox). Even had this machine been usable, its sheer bulk and its nine motors (totalling over one hundred horse-power) finally convinced me that my original dismissal of Mick's bright idea had not been misguided.

Mick took it very hard when I finally said that it was a waste of time looking further. He had had no formal training in mechanical engineering but was very quick to grasp the workings and intricate nature of anything mechanical. He was thus bruised by the failure of our search, and his next inspiration came out rather cautiously, and not without some self-consciousness.

The ends of the lengths of timber looked like small rectangular dart boards. The annular rings indicating each year of growth were very pronounced, with a small spot, the heartwood, in the centre. A few of the longer lengths of timber projected at one end of the stack and made a perfect seat. What better place could one be when thinking about timber than to be seated in its midst. It was while thus seated in deep contemplation that Mick came up with his real brainwave.

"No more than a thought," he insisted. "But what about that old planing machine of yours?"

The planing machine had been lying in store alongside a small collection of antique woodworking machinery that I'd inherited. It had originally been installed in the estate workshop of a great country mansion where, before the days of electricity, it had been driven via line shafts and flat-belt pulleys powered by a waterwheel. My long-term plan had always been to set the machinery up as a sort of working museum. I had never developed any clear idea of how I would do this or even when, and this reminder of the existence of the collection only added one more problem to our migration north.

I quickly realized that Mick's idea had potential. The planing machine (or thicknesser as it is also called) was not a big machine. Constructed mainly of cast iron, it was six or seven feet long, about three feet wide and the same high; it probably weighed two tons. Mick looked anxiously in my direction whilst I toyed with the possibility. I was suddenly getting very excited. Even as I was saying that it was worth looking into my mind was racing ahead. These machines had become commonplace by the twenties and most builders would have had one in their workshops. They were intended to plane any item of woodwork that a building might require – components for doors, window frames, staircases and much more. On the one hand, rough material could be fed in one end to emerge at the other as a beautifully smoothed old-fashioned teak draining-board; on the other hand, they might be used to plane great gate-posts up to nine inches square.

It was still a bit of a shock to see 'Corkindale Engineering' over the door of my old workshop, but I was getting used to it. We went round there to borrow Joe's big trailer, for I had decided that we would bring the thicknesser back to my house if at all possible. Even if it could not deal with the tongues and grooves and mouldings, I knew it would it could solve the problem of the varying thickness and widths of the timber. Rendering it all to a standard size was well within its capability. We had no more than a few miles to cover before we reached the old barn-like store. I could hardly get the padlock off quickly enough.

I flung the doors open. The planer had been the last machine to go into the store, so it should be easy to get it out. In fact the block and tackle that had lifted it into its present position four years earlier still hung from one of the barn's great beams. Don't however imagine from my newfound enthusiasm that this machine was ready to use: it certainly was not. Not only was it extremely dirty from years of inactivity, every bright part was now rusty and, to add to its unserviceability, it was partially dismantled. As if all that were not bad enough, there was the drawback that this machine had no motive power of its own. It had been driven by a waterwheel and, needless to say, we did not have a waterwheel to hand. All these considerations might have had something to do with my failure to investigate the machine earlier. But now, after our repeated failure to find anything halfway suitable elsewhere, I was keen to use it. I began to look around for the dismantled parts; mercifully I found them all.

Mick organized the loading, which was a bit of a struggle. Either Joe had misled us over the carrying capacity of his new trailer, or I had under-estimated the weight of the machine. Whichever it was, the load nearly flattened the trailer. By now however, we were happy to ignore such problems, and made our way back to the house with the precious cargo.

The dirt and rust proved to be no more than superficial, and we soon cleaned it up. Brian, the local electrician, found us a second-hand electric motor and in less than three days we were all standing by while he tried the starter. Everything began slowly to revolve but, as it gathered speed, I noticed things were going backwards. I held my hand up and Brian hit the stop button.

"No problem," he assured us. "Phases wrong way round."

We watched as the cover came off the switch-box. In less time than it takes to tell, the cover was back, and off we went again. Now the machine was up to full speed.

"Come on!" Brian shouted, signalling at me to try a length of timber under the feed-rollers.

I set the thickness required and selected the shortest length of timber from the stack. If the machine had been new from the manufacturer, it could not have performed more perfectly or more easily. We were jubilant. We were off again.

There was a sort of compulsion to keep trying another length of timber and then another, as if none of us believed that this old machine could possibly have come back to life. All we were doing was loading the material onto the bed, holding on until the feed-rollers took charge and then watching as the wood slowly emerged reduced to the perfect thickness. It was hypnotic. The machine was in charge, and Mick and I became just labourers. One by one, the lengths were processed until the piles of shavings became a mountain. So began the bonfires that kept all the children of the surrounding area entertained night after night. They soon learned that we stopped in the late afternoon and would volunteer to barrow the day's waste to the open ground where it was burned. Despite the heavy labour of the day, every evening became play-time, and we loved every minute of it.

That task done, it was not difficult to adapt the machine to take the cutters that would form the tongues and grooves, and then finally to reshape the logs in the way which would be such a feature of the house, inside and out.

It was about this time that Irene had her first serious enquiry for the house. She came out into the yard to tell me that some people were coming down from Chester that afternoon. It was an exciting time. We were not to know that, even while Irene was excitedly telling us all she had learned about the prospective purchaser, a second lot of would-be purchasers who had travelled even further was at that moment viewing the property from a distance. They liked what they saw, and were ringing the bell just as Irene returned to the house. They only had time for a cursory tour but, even in that short moment, they made their minds up: they wanted the house. Irene did the only thing that was fairly open to her. She was perfectly honest with them, and told them that the people who would be arriving shortly were coming in the belief that they were the first serious enquirers. The couple were not put off, saying that if it was convenient they would come back that evening.

Irene was going to have a busy day knowing that we might have two parties fighting to be the new owners. Mr Powell and his wife arrived on the dot of two, just as they said they would. He was a man in his mid-sixties, wiry with hard features and a mop of naturally curling grey hair that seemed to grow upward from his scalp. His manner was abrupt. He wanted to know about us and, naturally, the house, but we found out little about the Powells other than they had just retired from a business. What business we never discovered. Mrs Powell smiled thinly from time to time, but never entered into conversation. It was a hard afternoon. There was absolutely no indication of interest from them, and as time ran on the one-sided conversation became wearing. I felt we were wasting our time, but then, quite out of the blue, Mr Powell turned to Irene and quite simply said: "We have decided to take it."

We were amazed. They had not even discussed it with each other, but there it was: they had decided. Irene had prepared a fairly comprehensive brochure on which she had included the name and address of our solicitor, and she handed Mr Powell a copy.

"What's this?" he said, rather rudely.

"Particulars," said Irene.

"Don't need them."

"Yes, you do. They have the name and address of our solicitors," countered Irene.

Mr Powell thumbed through, found the piece with the name, tore it out and handed back the brochure. He indicated that we would hear from his man in a day or two, and bid us good day.

We could only stare at each other as the car moved off. As one car receded into the distance, another one moved quietly to take the vacated space of the first.

"Oh goodness!" Irene gasped. "It's the people who were here this morning!"

They were quite the opposite personalities. With them, it had been Harold and Gwen from the word go. They were outgoing country people and didn't mince their words.

"Is the property still on the market? We thought the others would never go!"

It seemed to us that as they had seen the property first that they had some priority. Although they were forthright, one would not have called them pushy – 'jovial' might have been the word that best described them. It was no surprise to learn that they had a small farm south of the Lake District. Small farms were no longer viable so they were getting out. They expected to get a good figure for the property and had decided to have it auctioned.

"The neighbouring farms won't want to pay our price. Best to have a auctioneer clear the farm and end up with the house and the land as a desirable property." The way Harold put it, they were about to make their fortune.

"It seems a risky business," I said. "What if it's not sold and the highest bid is far short of expectations? Won't this set some precedent for the future?"

"Believe me, it will be sold," Harold said with conviction. "But you haven't answered my question – is the house still on the market?"

The truth was that he had not given me the opportunity to reply. Irene hated people who imposed themselves in this way, and I could see that she was already becoming irritable. Her monosyllabic answers betrayed her feelings.

It wasn't long before Harold began bargaining with the usual "How much will you take for a quick sale?"

That was enough. Irene looked Harold straight in the eye and very deliberately came out with: "Harold, are you really in a position to deal with a quick sale?"

Harold was stopped dead in his tracks and looked to Gwen for support. Gwen was as shrewd as Harold was brazen.

"Don't get ahead of yourself, Harold!" she said. "You're not selling sheep, you're trying to buy a house."

Harold looked hurt, and I guessed at that moment that it was probably Gwen, not Harold, who ran the farm. I felt more certain of that as she went on to say in a rather teasing voice that we still hadn't said whether the house was still for sale. Irene gave them the briefest details of the Powells' intentions, which were that we expected to hear from their solicitor within a day or two and that they had not questioned our asking price.

The steam had for the moment quite gone out of Harold, and it was Gwen who outlined their position.

"Our sale is in three weeks' time, and we are confident of doing well. Harold was rather putting his cart before his horse and, as you guessed, we can't possibly confirm any bid until after the sale. However it does look like your afternoon visitors must be serious – they stayed so long. So I'll come straight to the point, and make no bones that we love the town" – with its ancient half-timbered town hall set in the middle of the well preserved high street – "and we love the river and the countryside, and we've set our hearts on coming to live in Shropshire. We've thought it over and decided to offer you five hundred pounds over the asking price if you will agree to the sale now. Of course you'll have to wait until the day of our sale for the contract to be signed. I do understand how you must feel about having to wait three weeks for confirmation, but under no circumstances would I wish to mislead you into thinking that we could make the purchase out of our current resources."

Neither Irene nor I had eaten since breakfast and it was now past eight o'clock, so I was glad when she offered to go and cut us all a plate of sandwiches. The offer of an additional five hundred pounds had obviously gone some way towards easing her irritability. A few moments later I joined her under the pretence of making the coffee, which gave us a few moments to decide that we should accept their offer. A delay of three weeks was neither here nor there, and five hundred pounds would almost buy a brand-new small car. Indeed our still near-new Landrover had only cost six hundred and fifty five pounds.

Gwen and Harold were over the moon when I said that subject to written confirmation we would accept their offer. It was quite dark when they finally left, and when I enquired if they had found somewhere satisfactory to stay they seemed surprised.

"Oh no! We aren't staying, We're going directly home to the farm. We hired a helper for one day, but we can't afford to pay for a second day. We'll be back in time for feeding, have no fear!"

We did however have fear, or at least we were uneasy. The Powells had seemed a certainty, and I had no doubt that we would hear from their solicitor.

And so we did, in the same post as a letter from Gwen neatly setting out all that we had agreed. I passed this correspondence on to our solicitor, asking him to consider the offer and saying that I would telephone later. When I did so, I found his advice indecisive, even vague. He was only returning our thoughts to us: that both offers seemed genuine. We finally decided to go along with Harold and Gwen, whose name we had now learned was Lees. I telephoned Mr Powell and gave him the news, which he accepted with no more concern than if I had been a newsagent apologising for the non-delivery of a newspaper. Perhaps after all Mr Powell had not been serious. The three weeks that followed were an eternity.

CHAPTER TWELVE

A Cause for Celebration

In the three weeks since we had set it going, the ancient planing machine had done Trojan work. Day after day Mick and I had fed the timber through the rollers, and day after day it had emerged from the cutters with a little more of the multiple moulding process complete. It was one of the most satisfactory jobs I have ever undertaken. On countless previous occasions I had machined timber into (just for example) skirting boards, architraves and picture frames, but this was quite different. Perhaps i was the sheer size of the timbers, or the novelty of making a moulded section so different from any before.

Whatever the reason, it was exciting work. Because the cutters in the machine are revolving, and therefore describing a circle, their actual shape is not exactly that of the finished moulding. The shape of the cutter is in fact a complex geometric exercise. Each cutter in these old machines has to be hand-made, a painstaking process of hand-grinding which, in the case of the very large cutters which were necessary for transforming our logs, had taken many hours. But now the reward of all our efforts lay before us. As we had started each operation, we had taken the timber from one stack and begun another so that every few days the great pile appeared in some other place in our yard, with yet another section of moulding complete.

Today we had reached a very significant stage of the work, for this would be the very last time the timbers passed under the rollers of the old machine and, instead of starting the now-familiar second pile, we were going to stack the finished logs in order of length. The day was hot (it was now early summer), and by mid-afternoon Mick and I were exhausted. We stopped, partly for a break and partly to admire our work: the profile of each log was so perfect, and the colour and grain of the wood so beautiful, that I could not help but stare at it.

Just as we were about to sit down amongst the timbers, Irene burst into the yard.

"Quick! quick!" she shouted. "There is a man on the phone and he has been robbed. I'm sure he needs help."

I quickly straightened up and made a dash to the 'phone. It seemed absurd to say "Hello" under such circumstances, and as soon as I had caught my breath, I think I said: "Are you still there?"

I imagined that I was talking to some poor unfortunate who had been battered by an opportunist assailant and who now, half-reeling from the blows, could remember only our number (but why our number?). I thought I recognised the voice as it shouted "Of course I'm here!", but it was yelling with such emotion that I could not actually pin it to anyone in particular.

"Try to be calm," I urged. I barely got the words out before the voice was yelling again.

"I've been robbed, robbed, daylight robbery! Thieves, nothing but crooks!" the voice wailed.

"Try and tell me your name, and where you are," I said.

"Dear god!" the voice shouted back. "Who in the world d'you think I am?"

I don't know whether I was surprised or plain shocked by the answer. It must have been shock, for I felt the skin of my face and forehead tightening and a feeling of light-headedness creep over me.

"For god's sake," the voice ranted on, "it's Harold! Pig troughs a shilling each, hurdles five bob a time! I just don't know what's to become of us!" he wailed, and then in a voice that sounded as if I might be to blame for all his woes, he said: "Can't buy your property now. That's definitely off."

I felt as if the blood-supply had been cut off from my head. It was not that the sale was off, although that was bad enough; it was that in my heart I had known that it was never on, but I had persuaded myself that it was. I walked slowly back to where Irene was waiting.

"Whatever has happened? You look terrible!"

I related the whole story. Apparently the Lees hadn't been able to bear to see their property sold in the manner they had themselves chosen, and so they had gone for a walk while the auctioneer had done his best. On their return, they were at

171

first pleased to see that even the farm scrap was being loaded onto a lorry. They thought that that meant that everything had been sold – as indeed it had. But the auctioneer in the absence of any reserve-prices had just let property, land and equipment go to the highest bidders. For a moment I felt sorry that such a thing could happen – if that is what really did happen.

I sat in a daze whilst Irene went to make that panacea, a pot of tea. She brought it down, together with a bottle of aspirins. She looked calm and quite unconcerned as she said:

"Take two of these, then I will tell you what we are going to do, or at least what *you* are going to do."

With a mind bereft of all rational thought I had not the faintest idea what to do. "What do I do?" I ventured to ask.

"Simple," was the reply. "You're going to ring Mr Powell."

I recall my reply with some shame. "No," I said. "I can't do that, after the way we turned down his very generous and correctly submitted offer. No, I couldn't possibly."

Irene's answers were always direct.

"Why?" was her uncompromising response, and before I could think why I was being dragged to my feet and all but marched to the phone. Irene looked for the number, dialled and passed me the handset. I might have just put it back down, but I heard Mr Powell's voice. I can recall starting rather awkwardly.

"I've a bit of bad news and perhaps a bit of good. We learned today that the people who had offered for the property do not have the money." I distinctly heard a very nasal 'umph'.

"So you're offering it to me now," said Mr Powell in his flat emotionless voice. Before I could reply, he went on: "My plans have changed. ... Hang on."

He obviously had not consulted anyone, indeed the 'hang on' was superfluous as he returned to the conversation immediately. I was absolutely amazed at what followed.

"If you would stay on until mid-October, we could put the solicitors on to the job in the morning. Is it a deal?"

"Yes," I said. "It's a deal."

Mr Powell just put the phone down, and I stood rooted in disbelief. We had not exchanged a single irrelevance.

"The property is sold," I said to Irene, as the blood finally began to flow back to my head.

"There now, that didn't hurt, did it?" she said. Irene was very strong on intuition, and I believe she had foreseen the course of events from the outset.

Strangely, the sale of our home suddenly meant very little to us. There was no doubt that the strange circumstances had something to do with our lack of feeling: losing the sale, and then abruptly regaining it. There was also the remoteness of the Powells. We had still learned absolutely nothing about the soon-to-be owners of this property that had brought us so much happiness over the years. We couldn't explain our feeling of finality; perhaps in the future, instead of being like other people, looking back with fondness to the place that had been our home, we would look back to find that it had been just a mirage.

Two days later, a note from our solicitor confirmed the sale. The indifference that had beset us came to an end, and this aspect of our adventure was now firmly under control. Perhaps a little celebration was in order: Irene had done well with her advertising spread, for the housing market had moved a little – but only a little, and our two prospects had been the only ones. Of course, selling the property was not the only thing for us to celebrate: it had just been a month since Mick and I had dug out the old planing machine from the store where it had lain for years. We had wondered whether it could be adapted to machine the logs, but we need wonder no more. The last log had just been placed on the last pile, and the hardest part of the work was done.

Yes, it was certainly worth celebrating. It had been little more than six months since the idea of moving to the Highlands had been born, and what had taken place in that comparatively short space of time undoubtedly constituted an adventure. We had sold our business and now had a purchaser for our home. We had acquired one of the most beautiful coastal sites in the north-west Highlands, and we had designed a Scandinavian-style dream house. Nothing could stand in the way of our building it, for we had also obtained our planning consent. Perhaps most exciting of all, at that very moment the most difficult of all our tasks lay before us completed.

So a celebration we had, although after working so hard for so many months we didn't feel like dressing up for a big occasion. We therefore did as many a countryman had done for ages past on the completion of some seasonal task: we went, as we were, to the Cider House. It was just a few miles away, and was a unique haven of good will and good cheer. No one knew when it had been established: it was simply very old.

It was no more than a cottage, hidden in a maze of Shropshire's most typical countryside. There was no car-park; the field gate was always open and you drove in – at your own risk. If it was wet, then it could be difficult. The doorway was low, so you ducked as you went in – and suddenly you were in another world, the world of the past. Farmers, labourers, saw-millers, the blacksmith and other country artisans were gathered there, some with wives and girlfriends, all with one thing in common – the celebration of another good day. The hay might be safely in, or the crops progressing amazingly well, or the animals in extreme good health. The laughter and the chatter were immediately infectious, and there was no need to ask what everyone was drinking: there was only cider, the most natural of all drinks. Cider of every variety was stored in the back room of the cottage – rough, medium, sweet, champagne cider, and many more, too numerous to mention. The landlady knew everyone and offered you your usual as soon as you entered the room.

There was just the one room at the Cider House, a room in which the household lived during opening hours as well as when the place was closed. It was cool in the summer and snug in winter, when a blazing fire greeted drinkers in from the cold, and there was always someone celebrating the results of working with nature's bounty.

Within sight stood the plantation where the trees had grown that were now the basis of our future home. A new moon was just visible; soon it would be a harvest moon. As we made our way home, tired and happy, we looked forward to the next phase. Tomorrow is another day.

Our next task was one that we had really looked forward to. It was fortunate that our parking area was a substantial area of tarmac, as the time had come to lay out the logs into the respective sections of the house. It took time to sort out the lengths most suitable for the varying sections of the structure, but gradually every wall, those of the exterior and those of the interior took shape. We could visualise walking through doorways, looking through windows. Irene imagined certain curtain materials against the wood, I imagined the copper-canopied fireplace in the gap in the logs where the stone chimney-breast would be built. We had before us a gigantic full-size plan upon which all the facets of the house could be seen.

I had not realized that there were others interested in this novel way of showing the elevations of a house. Mick nudged my arm as he whispered: "You got visitors."

Yes, indeed we had. Standing back from the entrance but still able to see part of our display, were Captain Whitmore and the Colonel. The Captain came forward as I opened the gates. Once he could see the whole of the timber they had supplied, he just stood stock-still a little way inside. He was obviously pleased with what he saw. A smile crept across his face, and it was some moments before he had finally said:

"This is all quite extraordinary. I had absolutely no idea that you had the facility for undertaking such work. The Colonel and I would be most interested to see your workshops, that is if it is convenient. What do you say, Colonel?"

The Colonel had so far not spoken a word, but now he apologised for his silence, and went on: "Yes, by all means – we must see how all this has been done. I have truly never seen anything quite like it before."

We chatted on for some time whilst I pointed out certain of the design-technicalities, particularly the means of controlling the differential shrinkage between the inner and outer surfaces of the timber. Gradually I managed our progress around the sections, until we were standing with our backs to the planing machine. It had been cleaned of all the dust and shavings and its appearance revealed nothing of the rôle it had played in producing what we were inspecting. I had waited for a suitable moment to confess:

"There were no workshops. The whole of the work was done with nothing more than the machine at our backs."

Both men smartly wheeled around and, if they had found the machined timber incredible, their look now was one of complete disbelief. The Colonel touched the machine as if to test that it was what he thought it was and muttered:

"It's a planing machine", and then doubtfully added: "I think."

"You're quite right," I said. "It is just a old planing machine, built in the days when planing large sections of timber was commonplace."

They seemed fascinated that such a relatively small machine should be capable of such work. I opened up the bed of the machine so that they could see the moulding cutters and to demonstrate just how the cutters had produced the profile of the log. The Captain was inspecting every minute detail of the workings with the utmost interest. Suddenly he straightened himself and rather surprised me with a request:

"This is all too interesting not to be seen by the men who were engaged in the varying aspects of producing the timber. What would you say to my letting them have time off just to have a quick look? Perhaps they could come down two at a time? I assure you they would be extremely interested to see their timber used for such a worthy cause. Makes a change from the usual fence-posts and packing cases, hey Colonel?"

"Quite so, splendid idea," replied the Colonel. "I'll see to it." Then turning to me: "That is, of course, if you are agreeable."

Certainly I was agreeable. In fact I had had it in mind to go up to the sawmill myself to see whether anyone would like to have a look. Mr Elcock's words on that first day ("And when did you last handle a fresh-sawn log?") may have been said in jest or simply as a warning, but they had rankled. It was arranged that the dozen or so mill-workers and foresters should come in pairs, the first couple arriving soon after lunch.

What followed was one of the most enjoyable days of the whole time it took to produce the log house. I had known from way back that Captain Wolryche-Whitmore had spent years publicising the rôle of forestry and country-sawmills, but to arrange for one's employees to see the uses to which their raw materials might be put was indeed innovative.

The first of the sawmillers arrived in the early afternoon and the others followed at regular intervals, with a military precision which I suspected was due to the Colonel. My suspicions were confirmed when, as the last pair left, they told me that they had a message from him. He was sorry that he had not managed to fit in the whole contingent. As I had had no real idea of how many to expect, I had been unaware that they hadn't all come – except that I *was* aware that Mr Elcock had not been among the number. This, as you may imagine, was something of a disappointment. However I did not like to enquire how many more were still to come, as I did not wish them to think I had had enough of them. But just as this final pair was leaving they suddenly remembered that they were to enquire if it would be all right if Mr Elcock came that evening, as he had been unable to get away during the afternoon. I naturally said yes.

At about seven, a car pulled up at the gate and there at last was the man who I had hoped would come. He had been brought along by a relative who was also interested in timber. Like most who had already viewed the unusual display of what the Colonel had called forestry woodwork, they said little as I ran them through the various procedures, including a look at the old planer and the moulding cutters.

"Well, I'm damned" was the first really positive comment to come from Mr Elcock. Then, looking me straight in the eye, he said: "You lost me five bob. I bet the sawyer five bob that you wouldn't do it. I just could not see how you could handle the fresh timber...."

"You got to admit the weight would take most people by surprise, and although we didn't tell you at the time, Douglas Fir is one of the most abrasive timbers in the forest. Plays the very devil with cutters. You must have been sharpening regular... And one more thing – them knots might look fancy, but they'll break some cutters as easy as look at em, and the shock of hitting big uns'll break them old flat belts."

Most of the later comment was addressed to his colleague, as he could tell from my nods that he was telling me things we had learned the hard way. But Mr Elcock had not finished.

"Now, what I'm going to tell you is the absolute truth," he said as he inclined his head in a way that suggested seriousness. "I said to the sawyer, 'He has no idea of what he's taken on. I bet you five bob that when he's found out a thing or two, he'll be back and wanting us to offer him something for what we supplied.' To be fair, the sawyer was on your side, but I said 'If the loads come back, he can't have but half their value. Even if they're resawed, there is bound to be a lot of waste.' Now I've told you, and you've proved me wrong. I'd like to shake your hand. You're a hero!"

The very next morning we started to take the sections apart, an easy job as only the tongues and grooves held them together. We started at the bottom of each section and as each log was removed it was given a letter and number: thus N1

indicated that it was the first log of the main north-facing wall, or S6 for the sixth log up from the bottom of the south wall, and so on. When all the logs had been similarly numbered and placed into a single stack we put a simple cover over it, just to protect the top. Right then, we had a cloud burst. There was no wind, and the rain came straight down in bucketsful, hitting the ground with such force that the spots were bouncing at least a foot high. It was the first rain for weeks and was desperately needed for the growing crops.

The dry weather had been perfect for us, as it had helped the timber slowly lose its surface-moisture and thus had made our load just that little bit easier each of the hundreds of times we had carried the logs backwards and forwards across the yard. We had carried the wood to the machine, from one pile to another and then to yet a further stack, as the operation was slowly completed. For a while, as we stood sheltering from the rain under the lean-to, we felt lost. For a month we had toiled in the warm sunshine, which was now totally obscured by leaden clouds. After a time they gave way to the familiar blue of recent weeks, and a sun which was hotter than ever. Soon everything was steaming, and we were assailed by that wonderful scent of parched earth that has just been blessed by summer rain.

The realization that a major phase of the work was now finished brought with it the further realization that the stack of logs could in fact be transported to the Highlands if we wished. This was yet another milestone along the road of the adventure.

Of course we were not ready to start the move. Our temporary accommodation was not available until October, and by sheer good fortune the Powells had made it a condition of their purchase that we remain in occupation of the

Bridgnorth house until the hand-over. We could have not asked for more it was a perfect arrangement.

But it was time to reassess our position. We still had three months in which to complete the rest of the log house. I intended prefabricating it in every possible detail because once we arrived on site at Creag nan Cudaigean there would be no luxury of electricity. There were no mains anywhere near, and although a generator was always a possibility they were expensive and needed specialized installation. No, I had decided that we would do all we could whilst we had the electricity on line, and then when we were without electricity in our new home we would manage quite well. Indeed Irene was looking forward to a degree of self-sufficiency: cooking on her new solid-fuel cooker was at the heart of her dream of living in such a remote spot.

The next objective was obviously the roof structure. This consisted of open rafters supported on great natural round-log ridge-poles. If the logs of the wall had been heavy, then these were almost impossible to move. We rolled them, slid them and levered them, until at last they reached the stage at which on site they would (we hoped) just slide into position. Another item was ready to go.

There was plenty of time still available, but we were always conscious that as the hours and days went by, time would speed up – like the last grains of sand in the egg-timer, disappearing at an ever-faster rate. Windows and door frames were made and joined the other materials that would eventually go north. We left nothing to chance. Nearly everything we needed we would take, for we had no idea of what would be available, despite having gone to considerable trouble to write to innumerable suppliers in the Highlands. We were told, for example, that only a plumber registered in the Highlands could obtain plumbers' materials, and furthermore that it was doubtful if they would agree to obtain goods unless they themselves were fitting them. I did not necessarily disagree with the practice, but I had heard tales of people waiting years for things to materialize. (These delays were a sort of tradition in the remoter parts, dating from the days when roads were too poor for normal transport. That great symbol of inter-island communication, the puffer – a small steam-driven cargo boat – would come in perhaps only once a year, sometimes just running up the handiest beach. Then it would wait until the tide had left it high and dry, allowing the crew to throw the goods down to the eagerly waiting recipients.)

By this point, we had either located a suitable supplier in the north with whom we would deal at the appropriate time, or we had obtained the items locally and added them to the ever-growing mountain of materials set aside for dispatch. The mountain included the log house (which was now a near-complete package, with the fully machined logs all neatly numbered, the pre-cut roof materials, and the stack of window- and door-frames), and Irene's much-prized solid-fuel cooker. I had not even begun to sort out my precious collection of ancient woodworking machines. It was clear that however we might load the array of goods, it would not take fewer than three average lorries.

Irene had many skills at her fingertips, but few would have guessed that she was conversant with road-haulage, particularly abnormal loads. In the months just prior to our getting married, Irene had worked as a freelance temp and had taken on some very diverse and challenging commissions. The most formidable was the temporary management of a haulage company specializing in the transportation of heavy plant and machinery. The owner-manager of the company had decided that in order to boost his business he would go on a grand tour, calling on potential plant-and-machinery customers up and down the country. He obviously saw his proposed adventure as something of a holiday: what would be wrong with working in a little golf if it helped to get to know a possible client?

He had worked out all the details except one. His assistant, to whom he had intended to entrust the running of the company for the period of his absence, had taken fright at the idea and promptly left. Not to bother, the adventurous businessman had said to himself, he would get a temp. Weren't the 'employment wanted' pages full of ads offering temporary solutions to every employment situation known to the business world? It might even be an opportunity to poach a permanent replacement for the assistant – as long as it was someone with experience. His search amongst the agents had been fruitless, but he was undeterred. Our intrepid businessman placed an advertisement in the local newspaper: 'Temporary manager required to take charge of small heavy-haulage company; male or female; must be experienced'.

Irene had seen the advertisement, thought it sounded exciting and presented herself at the office of the company. Unknown to her at the time was the fact that she was the only applicant. She had expected to be summarily dismissed on account of perhaps her youthful appearance and lack of experience. The man had received her courteously and listened intently as she related her qualifications and experience.

"But do you have any experience with vehicles?" he had coaxed.

Her reply, which she later admitted to have been somewhat brazen, had been: "What experience is wanted? Surely it's only a matter of lorries, loads, distances and quotations?"

The haulier was so staggered by Irene's reply that he offered her the job, subject only to a week's trial. At the end of the week, she was very excited.

"He's leaving me to it – going away on Monday afternoon! He'll keep in touch with me by phone of course, and try and let me know where he is so that I can contact him in an emergency."

Monday arrived, and by the afternoon I could think of nothing but Irene trying to run a haulage business single-handed and without any real experience. In my mind I saw a muddy wheel-rutted yard, with piles of bald and cut tyres, scrap axles and worn-out engines; there would be hefty mechanics in greasy overalls, to say nothing of disgruntled drivers and perhaps irate customers. 'Haulage is a tough business,' I kept saying to myself. 'How is she managing?'

My office was only a few miles away. By four thirty I could stand it no longer and drove off to find out for myself. I had not previously concerned myself with where Irene's new office was. All I knew was that it was off Market Street in a nearby town, so I was somewhat surprised to find that 'off Market Street' was a smart area next to the town library. I soon found the stylish sign declaring that I was at the address Irene had given me. There was no muddy yard, no lorries, no men; indeed the address was virtually in the centre of the town where there was hardly room to park cars, let alone lorries.

I entered the foyer where photographs of smartly painted low loaders lined the walls to illustrate the many and varied loads that the company had handled over the years. It was all very impressive. A discreet notice and arrow pointed up the carpeted stair to reception. Half way up I heard Irene's voice and on reaching the landing I could see her through a glazed door which proclaimed the company and its business in gold letters edged in black. The door was slightly ajar and I walked cautiously into the office.

Irene was seated in a large leather-covered executive chair behind an imposing desk. She was in deep conversation with someone at the other end of the telephone line, and she motioned to me to take a seat. I felt as though I was waiting to be interviewed for the vacant assistant's job – it was as though Irene was not even aware that I was there. I could only look and listen as she aggressively interrogated whoever was at the other end of the line.

"Now, look here. Shall we start again, with you being a little more precise with your requirements?" She raised her eyes to the heavens. "Right!" she snapped. "Let's see if I've got it. Two tar-boilers, each one seven and a half tons. Any tar in them? … About a ton. Then they are eight and a half tons each. Why didn't you say that in the first place? Give me the dimensions." She shook her head slowly. "Good. Now you say you're in Worcester. Where in Worcester? Ombersley!" she almost screamed at the enquirer (I'd assumed by now that it was an enquiry). She caught her breath and went on: "You expect me to give you a price from Worcester to Gloucester, when in fact you are nowhere near Worcester?"

I could just about hear the chap at the other end making excuses for misrepresenting the length of the journey in order to avoid paying for the real mileage. The person at the other end seemed to be a man, and now Irene was pacifying him. The fellow had, I thought, had enough.

"Okay, okay," she was saying in a sweeter voice. "Just tell me who's loading." She nearly shot out of her chair when she repeated in a voice of alarm: "With a *dragline*! Okay, okay, you'll take responsibility. And there's a loading gantry at the other end? ... Thanks for the enquiry. I will come back to you within the hour."

Before I had had time to enquire how she was getting on she was off again, this time talking to me.

"Do they think I was born yesterday? First they try to do you on the weight, then on the mileage. Pigs to load, tar-boilers!"

I thought 'Is this the Irene I once knew?' She looked puzzled as I reminded her of how she had dealt with her enquirer, I remember well her expression when she said:

"I said all that? Well, I don't want the job anyway. I'll lay it off."

By her second phone call she had found someone with an empty vehicle going down the next day. They gave her a very good rate to which she added a handsome profit, and the tar-boiler man accepted her quote without query.

"Irene," I said. "You're brilliant! Where and when did you learn this business?"

She looked up from writing something that had just come into her mind, and smiled. "Where?" she said, with a slight look of innocent surprise. "Oh, just sitting where you're sitting now. And when? Last week."

We laughed and celebrated Irene's first day as a transport manager by having high tea at Lyons and then going on to the opening-night revival of *White Horse Inn*.

Irene stayed with the haulage company only for the three weeks she had contracted to work. The owner offered her a permanent position, but she had had the excitement she always craved and moved on to yet another challenge.

As for the lorries at this company, there had been five, all beautifully polished Scamells. Their base was an immaculately concreted yard, but being long-distance hauliers, they were rarely there. The yard had a single bay workshop manned by a foreman-mechanic. He looked after the practical side of the operation. There were no piles of old tyres, no old axles or engines, only the orderly signs of a operation run by men whose last job may well have been to keep Lancasters flying on even longer missions than the present low-loader fleet.

CHAPTER THIRTEEN

Sorting out the Transport

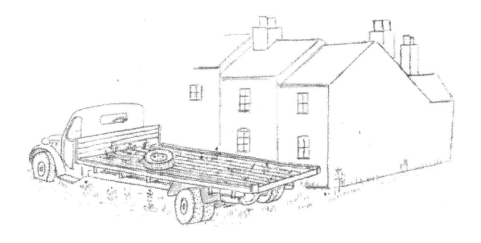

Although time remained on our side, I still had lots to do. There was for example my collection of old woodworking machines to drag out of the store and prepare for loading; and there were innumerable tools to box and perhaps just as many to discard. The latter task doesn't sound too difficult until one comes to decide: should I take the old forge or the scaffolding? would the costs of transport amount to more than the items were worth? did I in fact need them at all? ... And so it went on as each piece of equipment, lovingly cherished for years, fell prey to practical considerations.

Meanwhile, Irene began her search for a suitable haulage contractor to transport the log-house materials and our other effects to the Highlands. It was obvious, as my last chapter will have made clear, that Irene was the one to tackle this problem – for problem we had no doubt it was going to be. It would definitely require three loads, and we felt it would be more practicable to use a haulier local to us in Bridgnorth. We wanted to keep the work within the community, and this way we would also have a better chance of discussing possible problems and of overseeing the process: adequate packaging and security was essential. Furthermore, a local man almost always makes less clamour about getting things loaded and this would have many advantages, not least with everything having to travel so far and over roads as poor as those in the north.

Irene began her quest by simply telephoning all the companies within easy distance and then calling upon them in person. This was far easier than trying to explain everything over the phone. Each day she would return and disconsolately report her lack of success. Within the week she had seen everyone on her first list – which had covered a radius of something over ten miles from our home. These were the firms which she had regarded as truly local, but not one had even offered to consider the job. Most were sympathetic to Irene's enquiries, but the typical reaction was: "Where's Ullapool?" Mostly they had wall-maps, and it should have been easy enough to point out the location – but almost invariably the maps only showed the southern part of Scotland, even the most far-reaching only extending as far as Inverness. When maps were not available, they would ask if the actual distance was known. Of course Irene would say: "It's a one-thousand-and-fifty-mile round trip exactly."

Silence would reign whilst a transport manager would try to relate the journey to their usual daily runs to Manchester, Nottingham, Bristol or some other well-known destination. Then he would gasp out:

"God! That's more than a week's worth of runs to Preston!" – or wherever he was most familiar with. By now others would have joined in the discussion, usually with some story about how the firm they used to work for had practically lost a vehicle they had sent to Glencoe. "Of course," they would add, "that would be a lot further than this Ullapool you mentioned."

Irene would inform them that Glencoe was only *en route* to Ullapool, and then resign herself to their lack of commitment. The manager would begin to make his excuses. Sometimes it was that they did not have drivers to undertake such a journey: "It's hard to find men who'll stay away more than a couple of nights." Others had regular runs and, although they could always fit in other work, it would be difficult to have their vehicles away for what might be more than a week. Irene decided that the mirth that greeted her enquiry in the lesser companies was prompted by the unimaginability of their lorries even getting halfway without a breakdown.

So it was clear that the first round of enquiries had failed. It was time for a new initiative. Irene knew that there were more serious contractors out there somewhere, but it would be too time-consuming just to call and hope. A written enquiry would be more economical, and would surely find someone interested. Letters were sent, and gradually our enquiries were returned, with polite refusals to quote for the work. The usual reason was that it was beyond the normal field of their activity.

We were well into the second week when the very first and, as events would reveal the only, positive reply arrived. It was from a contractor some twenty miles distant. Irene had not written to him, but someone to whom she had written, and who had not replied to us, had passed it on to him. The note was simple: they were interested, but for such journey they thought it first necessary to agree a timetable. Excellent! Here at last was someone who knew what they were doing!

Irene set off in high spirits to meet the owner-manager. She came back less enthusiastically. I was puzzled, and immediately thought that she had found the lorries tied up with string or some equally off-putting situation; but no: it was something we had not even considered. Crestfallen, Irene explained that the company seemed sound; the only lorry in the yard was nearly new, the owner was very positive and had gone to a great deal of effort to draw up an itinerary for the journey.

"Well, is there a problem?" I'd said, somewhat impatient to hear whether we were going with them or not, and then suddenly realised that Irene might be just teasing me. So I smiled and said: "Go on! I'm all ears."

Irene began: "Drivers are the problem. They can't afford to have them away on Wednesdays and Thursdays, because on those days they have a regular contract that they could not ignore. But that isn't the obstacle. The owner was prepared to bring his spare lorry over on Thursdays for loading, and he appreciated that this might occupy most of the day. His two drivers would then be able to drive up to Ullapool on Friday and Saturday, returning Monday and Tuesday."

"Great!" I said enthusiastically. Irene still looked glum. A second thought suddenly came into my mind. "Cost several thousand pounds I suppose?"

Irene continued to look searchingly at me, but I didn't know what else to say.

"Don't you see? They want to unload on the Sunday!" She added, in case I needed more prodding: "The Sabbath!"

The implications struck me like a bombshell. I'm no Sabbatarian, but the act of even thinking about working on the Sabbath in Ullapool, never mind actually doing it, was beyond the pale. Irene smiled as she recalled the time Angie Allan had tried to sell newspapers on the Sabbath. The event had quickly reached the ears of the minister who, together with a posse of Kirk elders, had marched on the newsagent's shop to remind the wayward Angie of the wickedness of his doing. The minister declined to enter the shop but had harangued him from the street. Angie just stood silently in the entrance of the shop. When the minister had repeated himself several times and generally lost the thread of his sermon (as ministers frequently did when engulfed by emotion), he stopped, perhaps hopeful that his parishioner would repent. Angie is a big man and standing on the step of the shop, towering above his accusers, he seemed even bigger. "Well minister," he had begun. "You have been a good customer all these years. In fact, as I look around, you have all been good customers. Now, I hear what you say, and I hope that this is not going to mean that you will not be here for your Monday paper, as you have been for years."

The minister took this as Angie acknowledging the errors of a Sunday paper indiscretion and nodded, affirming that he would of course be taking the Monday edition as usual.

"Well minister," Angie continued, "I think you ought to know that the papers you so eagerly devour on Mondays are in fact printed on the Sabbath."

A goodly number of the community did not collect their Monday newspaper, but strangely Angie sold out as usual thanks to the many small boys who collected the papers for someone who couldn't manage to get in that day....

Irene telephoned the haulier, and explained that she'd waited to discuss the Sabbath situation with me, and that we had agreed that unfortunately we couldn't go ahead on that basis. He said he was sorry to lose the business, but understood the situation perfectly. He'd spent the war at Loch Ewe, only a few miles south of Ullapool. He had heard it was a beautiful place, but he'd never managed to get there.

The transport situation was getting worrying, although I had confidence that Irene would think of something. Her next step was to seek advice from the office she had managed on a temporary basis a few years back. Low-loaders, which was their stock-in-trade, were not an option for us, but the firm was very knowledgeable about the industry. She came back with what seemed the perfect solution.

"Don't know why I hadn't thought of it before! Why not the railway? We could have a closed wagon, safe, easy to load and probably competitively priced," she said.

"Umph!" I countered. "That's all very well, but the railway doesn't go to Ullapool." My mind was not able to come to grips with railways so suddenly after a couple of weeks of considering lorries daily, but when it did get into gear, I began to see the possibilities. 'It's an interesting idea, though. Loading and unloading might be a bit of a problem."

"Not at all," Irene assured me. "You can rent the wagons for a month if you wish. They just shunt them into a loading bay and you load and unload at your leisure."

I really began to warm to this novel solution. It was true that it had disadvantages: the Highland line ceased at Garve some thirty miles short of Ullapool. This could be an advantage in disguise, however. We would be able to take the load on from Garve in very small consignments, which we would have to have done in any case. There was no way at present that any vehicle could get down onto the Creag nan Cudaigean headland. We had always known that we would have to stockpile the loads in the village and take small consignments from there. I began to get really enthusiastic about the railway notion.

"It's a great idea," I said to Irene. "Where do we go from here?"

Irene was on top of the world again and fielded the question with nonchalance. "Oh I'll just go up to the station and discuss it with the goods manager. In fact I might as well go now."

Mick and I got on with extricating the last of my machines. We cleaned several years' grime and dust away, and greased the bright parts. Well, perhaps they were not very bright, but going as we were into a sea-air environment the grease would provide a little added protection. After about an hour, Irene returned from the station with the news that everything was in hand. A quotation and conditions would be in the next morning's post. It was as if a mist had suddenly lifted.

The summer was turning and we had entered the balmy days. Fruit was on the orchard-trees, the garden vegetables were in their prime, the grain crops were stooked in the fields and swallows skimmed the river, gorging themselves on an endless supply of insects, building up reserves of energy to sustain the long migration south. The cuckoo had already left. Its supply of hairy caterpillars had become scarce, and its crop was so full of hair that it had done no more than croak farewell. These soft days, and the sense of having done almost all our preparatory work, put us in a holiday mood. The pressure to organise every last detail had eased, and we were now just coasting along, taking care of the last few items.

Out in the yard, amongst the neat piles of our stuff, a few very long logs protruded from the tarpaulin cover. They were at just the right height for a seat, with a shorter length making a perfect back-rest. We sat there in the early morning sun, mugs of coffee in hand: just sitting around, a new-found pleasure. On top of everything, Irene produced a large box of chocolate-digestive biscuits: what luxury! Life was indeed pleasant. The gate clicked, as the postman entered the yard.

Irene pounced on an envelope which was obviously from the railway, and opened it. She read it and then danced around, waving it in the air in triumph.

"Problem solved!" she sang, as she passed the documents to me.

I read through carefully, then went back and reread. Irene was deeply engrossed in something else as I tried to come to terms with the specification of the railway wagons, and in particular the bit that said: "Closed top and sides, side loading, 16' 0" long x 6' 6" wide." I gazed at the details for what seemed several minutes and then slowly read it out.

It was Mick who confirmed my worst fears when he casually asked: "If the doors are in the middle, how will we be able to load the lengths?"

"Indeed – how are we going to get eighteen-foot lengths into a sixteen-foot wagon at all?" I said.

Irene couldn't think what all the fuss was about. "They'll surely have other wagons! Go and ring them yourself. You can explain better than I can."

I did ring. No: they were sorry, but that was it. There *were* special wagons, but they were few and far between; there *were* open wagons, but they were not recommended for our type of goods.

As I came from the phone with the devastating news, Irene thrust another letter into my hand. It was from the supplier of our roof-tiles. The quotation was just as I expected. Irene then showed me the back of the accompanying letter. I began to read the relevant words. "These particular tiles, which are the only ones suitable for your application ... are not available in Scotland ..., we are not able to arrange delivery ..., we will give every assistance to load your vehicle at our Cheshire works."

I slumped down heavily beside Mike just as Irene reappeared with a large bottle of aspirins and a grin from ear to ear.

"Come on, Mick!" she said. "You're the only one who hasn't had a go at this problem yet. What would you do?"

Mick looked incredulously first at me, then back to Irene.

"Me do?" he gasped, as if we were asking the impossible. "Me do?" he repeated. "Why I'd buy my own lorry."

It was our turn to look blank. I suddenly suspected that Mick had been quietly thinking over our problem for some time. He was a quiet lad and kept his thoughts to himself, although if asked for his opinion he could always give one. We were nevertheless stunned by his simple answer. In fact for a moment I could not say anything. I had given up jumping to conclusions. Thinking that we may not have appreciated what he had said, Mick said again:

"I'd buy my own lorry, use it, then sell it. At least I'd get my money back."

He'd already answered part of the question I was about to ask. I only just managed to say: "Well, wouldn't it be a big outlay all the same?", when Mick announced that he knew where a suitable lorry might be for sale.

At that moment I knew for certain that all the time that Irene had been wrestling with our haulage problems Mick had been secretly pursuing an alternative strategy. But for Irene's desperate appeal to him, his plan would have remained undisclosed: we had not consulted him. And it was a plan, not just an idea. We sat captivated whilst Mick revealed its practical foundation.

Apparently a lorry had been parked in the yard of a local pub called the Malt Shovel for more than a year. The landlord wanted it moved, and he'd had words with the owner to the effect that if it was not moved it would be sold. To the landlord's amazement, the owner had said: "Well sell it then, and give me twenty-five quid out the proceeds."

"When was this?" I wanted to know.

"Months ago," was Mick's flippant reply.

I was getting more and more interested as each moment passed. "Then it's still there, and unsold?"

"Yep. No one wants it. It's a petrol-engine model. We could easily go and see it if you have the time."

We certainly had time. We piled into the Landrover and in no more than a few minutes were at the pub looking at the object of our sudden and now all-absorbing interest. We did not get out of the car, but just viewed the truck from a distance. Although I had always had a passing interest in commercial vehicles, I could not really claim to know much about any particular make except one, the long wheel base Bedford seven and a half tonner. Memories of an earlier period of my life suddenly flooded into my mind.

My first practical experience of the building trade had come shortly after I had qualified as a surveyor. All those years of study had not been wasted, but I had soon realized that the professional office was not for me. I craved the opportunity of practical creation – I wanted to manage the restoration of great houses, to enter green-field sites and raise landmark buildings – in short, I wanted to build. So I had then secured a position as assistant contract-manager with a substantial and long-established building company. Being only the assistant it was my job to be in the office before seven and to provide answers to any problems arising, whilst the contract-manager partook of a leisurely breakfast at home and arrived an hour or so later. On my first morning I had stood in the yard-office, just observing. I could only marvel at the efficiency with which the operation ran. The yard-manager marshalled lorries, vans and men; he was seeing to it that each foreman with his squad and supplies got away to their respective contracts in one or other of the open lorries. For fifteen minutes, it was a hive of activity. More than two hundred men climbed into the backs of lorries. Storemen passed up parcels of all manner of small sundries, and took note of the daily needs of one or other site. One by one the vehicles departed, until only one was left. The men who should by now have departed on it stood around expectantly. The foreman talked urgently with the yard-manager, who after pointing in my direction came hurrying over. It was my cue to go out and meet him.

"Problem?" I enquired.

"Yes, driver's not turned in, and there is no spare. What about you taking the lorry down to Worcester?"

I was to get to like the yard-man, as he was called. He was the vital link between administration and practicality, with a very engaging manner. He could usually be relied upon to persuade the men to do whatever was asked of them.

"I've never driven a lorry!" I protested.

"Come on," he coaxed. "It's our newest vehicle. Be quite an experience for you, and give you the opportunity of seeing the Worcester site."

I was slowly being ushered towards the now open door of the still shiny new vehicle. The yard-man bent near to me and, at the last moment, whispered: "Feather in yer cap for initiative lad. I'll see the gaffer gets to hear of how you volunteered."

I suppose it was that which made my mind up. I started the engine and made gingerly towards the entrance gates. They offered little view of oncoming traffic, and I had to stamp on the brakes as a car appeared out of nowhere. That was my first experience of the power of servo brakes: the lorry stopped instantly, the contract-foreman and I nearly went through the windscreen, and there were cries of anguish from under the green canvas tilt behind us. That was my first lesson: lorries are designed to react as though fully loaded, and so they must be treated with respect when travelling light.

Like any new vehicle, the Bedford (for a Bedford it was) was a joy to drive. I soon got the hang of things and we had no more mishaps.

"Well, what do you think?" Mick was asking.

"Think? I think it's worth a closer look. Do you know the owner?"

"Yes. It's old farmer Davis."

I had heard the name, but couldn't place the farm.

"Don't do anything now," Mick urged. "Just drive slowly by and then drive off."

"There's a good crop of grass growing out of the wooden platform," Irene noted as we passed alongside.

"Spect its last load was hay," Mick riposted.

"Well, where do we go from here, Mick?"

I need not have asked. I had no doubt now that his plan of action had been under consideration just as long as we had been pursuing the question. Mick knew Ron, who was the new foreman at Corkindale's (which as you will recall was the new name of my former business). Ron was a regular at the

Shovel (as the Malt Shovel was affectionately known locally) and he would ask the landlord if he could look the Bedford over just to see what it might be worth for scrap. Mick raised his hand as I was just about to remonstrate on the question of scrap.

"Hear me out," he said. "If it all looks sound and the engine will turn, Ron will um and ah for a bit, then offer just the level twenty-five pounds.

"When are we supposed to put the plan into action?" I asked. The bridge-clock had just struck twelve forty-five.

"He'll go now for the price of a pint of best. I could just catch him."

I gave Mick a pound.

When he returned smiling after lunch I guessed there was news, and there was.

"Did he go?"

"Yep."

"Well?"

Mick was determined to keep us in suspense.

"Well?" I prompted for the second time.

"Well you now own a lorry and we are to go up at half past five to collect it. We'll tow it with the Landrover, and Ron can steer the lorry, but we will have to go very slow. The engine's free but wouldn't start and without it there are practically no brakes. You'll need twenty-five pounds."

CHAPTER FORTEEN

Countdown

The sight of the lorry standing in the yard on the following morning was something of a shock – not that I hadn't expected it to be there: I'd thought of little else during most of the night. It was just such a long vehicle, or at least it seemed so to me, or maybe it was that it dwarfed our Landrover. It had certainly all been a bit of a bolt from the blue. Less than twenty-four hours before we had not had the slightest idea that we would ever be the owners of such a vehicle. And now we indisputably were.

We had not had the least difficulty coming down from the Malt Shovel. Ron had handed over the twenty-five pounds in exchange for a receipt and a promise that the registration documents would be found in due course. Meanwhile, Mick had attached the tow-rope. Before the bridge-clock had struck six we had brought our prize home.

First glance had revealed no deficiencies and I hoped that it would take little effort to get the lorry operational. However, this sudden turn of events had solved one problem only to activate another: the timetable. We knew that in six weeks' time we would have tenure of Corry Point, a beautiful wooden bungalow on the shore of Loch Broom and about a mile from our own land. This would be our base over the winter whilst our log house was being built. As far as the let was concerned, it did not really matter when we took occupation, but it did matter that in six weeks' time the Powells (who had now contracted to purchase our present property with vacant possession) would be here with all their furniture and expect to find us gone. This became the defining date, which was precisely six weeks and one day away. The haulage firm that had wanted to unload on the Sabbath had proposed a six-day schedule: a day to load, a day to unload and four days' driving with two experienced drivers. For my part, I could not see why I could not drive north in two days, and returning empty should be easy. So, my simple calculation was that I could do the three journeys that our load needed in three weeks. That left exactly three weeks and one day to restore the Bedford to working order, plus the various formalities of moving house. I wrote out my draft timetable on a piece of scrap plywood, and gave it to Irene to enter into the diary in which we were charting events.

Irene looked incredulously at what I had written and in no uncertain terms announced: "Daftness."

She went on: "Are you seriously proposing to spend three weeks loading, unloading and driving?"

"Yes," I said, somewhat deflated.

"Madness," came her quick reply. "We had better be on the way with the first load not later than one week from today. Come on: I'll start weeding the grass from the lorry platform and you can get on with whatever you had in mind."

What I had had in mind was giving the lorry a good service. I had reckoned on a couple of days doing all the usual things that one does to ensure that the controls work and in particular that the electrics are in order. The nights were already drawing in, and some travelling would of necessity be during the hours of darkness. What I was most concerned about was the fact that Ron had said the brakes were binding (although he had hardly had to use them during our journey from the Malt Shovel).

Irene had only been pulling the grass from between the boarded joints for a few minutes before she straightened up and declared the work a waste of time.

"You'd better come and have a look at this. I've put my foot through the boards. They're rotten."

I'd feared that they might be and had there not been so much muck and grass I might have been able to confirm my suspicions earlier. Mick got up beside Irene and together they soon had the débris cleared, revealing the extent of the problem. The deck would have to be renewed. The job is no more bother than re-laying a boarded floor in a house, but preparing it, obtaining the material and fixing it would require maybe three days. With two days for servicing the lorry and two days for the brakes Irene's timetable was already in peril. But her approach was without doubt more sensible than mine.

We had to act quickly. We left Mick with instructions to remove the rotten deckboards and to clean as much of the chassis as he could. Irene and I drove off to Shrewsbury towing a borrowed trailer on which we intended to bring back a supply of hefty tongue-and-grooved boards and a few other things that had become necessary for our new enterprise.

We left the trailer at the timber merchant's with an order for the boards whilst we went in search of tarpaulins and ropes. On the north-west side of the town, just beyond the Welsh bridge, in buildings two centuries old, there was a great black-and-white painted sign high up on a gable: "POTTERS: fine-quality tarpaulins, ropes and twines of all descriptions." If I had to make a list of merchants whose wares give me the most sensual pleasure, then Potters would be near the top. Here is a shop and warehouse that probably has not changed since it was first established. From the moment you enter, the senses are assailed with the evocative smells of a bygone age: Stockholm tar for dressing ropes, linseed oil, tallow, proprietary liquid proofing, new canvas and the more delicate scent of natural fibre ropes – coil after coil, from the size of your little finger to great hawsers as thick as your arm: manila, hemp, sisal and white Egyptian cotton; rack upon rack of large balls of binder twine, tarred yarn for seizing, brown string for hefty parcels and fine bleached string for the shopkeeper, reels of thread for the saddler and shoemaker. It is a sort of greengrocer of the hardware trade, for practically everything in stock has been *grown*. It is one of the few merchants where you hope that no one will come too quickly to attend to your needs: there are so many interesting things to look at – rolls and rolls of leather belts, some not much more than an inch broad, some several inches wide, brown and glistening in expectation of conveying power to the revolving shafts of countless mechanisms; reels of small round belts for sewing machines – and here's a more modern type of belt: layered canvas bonded with the very exotic-sounding gutta-percha.

We went through to the warehouse to see the tarpaulins. There were shelves mounded with rolls of many shades of canvas. The most conspicuously attractive were the colourful stripes intended for deck chairs. We headed for a pile of green covers and selected two that we judged would not only cover our large load but provide sufficient slack to wrap around the ends and give total protection for the load. I was completely taken aback by the weight of our purchase.

The warehouseman laughed as I struggled: "Put him down a bit and have a try at one of these."

He led us through into yet another workshop where piles of reddish-brown covers littered the floor. So thick was the material that it would not fold, but just bent. To me they were quite immovable, and I did not need to be told that they were railway-wagon covers, in for refurbishment. I felt better about our tarpaulins. With a little help we put them in the back of the Landrover, together with a large coil of soft pliable rope.

There is nothing quite so satisfying as to be loaded up with tarpaulins, ropes, picks, shovel and buckets. They are the staples of pioneers. We had had a busy afternoon and, although we had done nothing ourselves directly with the lorry, we were happy and felt that somehow the adventure was under way.

Whatever work we had done was more than equalled by what Mick had accomplished in our absence. The rotten deck had gone, and the oak crossbearers were clean and ready for the replacement deckboards. Not only that, but the lorry-chassis, extending naked behind the cab, had been scrubbed, and looked to be in a remarkably good state.

One day gone.

In the event, it took only a day to deal with the servicing.

Two days gone.

Getting the wheels off and freeing the brakes began at six in the morning, and was finished in the dusk of that autumn evening.

Three days gone.

The weather had been remarkable, with day after day of perfect conditions. Sometimes there had been showers during the day, but they had been short-lived, and the hot sun that followed the rain had quickly steamed the damp away. Once there had been a cloudburst, accompanied by thunder and lightning, but even this had taken no more than an hour from its ominous start to its abrupt end – as sudden as a tap being turned off.

Whilst Mick and I toiled with the rehabilitation of the vehicle, Irene had been no less busy trying to tie up the formalities. For one thing, we needed to sort out the insurance and the road-licence. I had realized that purchasing a vehicle without the registration documents was a risky business, but I hadn't for one moment doubted that farmer Davis had the papers. The problem of course was whether he knew where they were. The simple answer was that he knew they were *somewhere*, but that as he had now, at last, sold the vehicle it didn't seem too important to him to find them. Because it was vital to us, and because it would take too long to get a copy, the only thing for it was for Irene to go and sit on the farmer's doorstep, as it were. Finally her persistence paid off and she came home in triumph, waving the elusive document.

Somehow or other we had found time to repaint the dark-brown cab in a much more attractive beige. What with that and its new platform, the lorry really did look workmanlike.

On the evening of the sixth day, with a new battery installed in the lorry, I turned the key. The engine went silently round for a few revolutions and then, with a cough and a splutter, burst into life. After a few moments it settled down to a steady tick-over worthy of a new vehicle. Proudly, Irene affixed the tax disc; but in the darkening evening I opted to await the morning before taking it out for a trial-run.

The morning came. At the beginning, in organising all that went into preparing our move, we had used critical-path analysis, which the fashionable business-consultants of the day guaranteed would take you from A to B by the shortest route. Perhaps better management, or management regardless of cost, would have kept us more closely to the path, but whatever the reason, our wall-chart looked like the first draft of Birmingham's Spaghetti Junction, at that time regarded as the ultimate in British road-engineering. In short, critical-path analysis was not a great success, and we had been using it less and less. My firm belief was, and remains, that one does better making lists, crossing the items off as they are accomplished. We had made one such list for the lorry, and now only three items remained: check tyre pressures; fill tank; and test-drive. In the next hour or so, I would be able to score off each item as done. All that was left, on the log-house list, was the floorboards.

The narrow Oregon-pine floorboards that I was having specially machined were the only items on our list of materials for the log house that had not yet come to hand. These could probably have been produced in Inverness, but I was leaving nothing to chance and had placed my order with a reputable firm in a town not too distant from Bridgnorth. I assumed, not unreasonably, that it was dealing with my boards, but I was beginning to be a little worried. I'd ring the supplier: maybe they were on their way at that very moment, and that would be the final item scored off.

The mill foreman, whom I'd known for a number of years, answered and no sooner had I mentioned my name than he announced the boards were ready, adding: "You're going to be pleased with um. Tham out of clear an betta straight up from Bristol, special, but we can't deliver just yet. Ain't got a worthwhile load your way for the moment."

'Clear and better' was the highest grade of timber: not a knot in sight and close-grained as straight as a die.

"I'll fetch them," I said in a rash moment, looking out of the window at our new toy.

"Just as you like mate, any time. We close at five."

"Come on, Mick, we're going for a test drive."

The engine started at touch of the button and sounded very reassuring as I gingerly reversed into the lane. Just a touch of the brake pedal brought an instant response, and once more I relived that morning when for the very first time I had driven such a vehicle. However one thing was quite different: it was taking all my strength to turn the steering wheel. I knew there was nothing mechanically wrong and so I was puzzled, or, rather, worried.

"The tyres need a bit more pressure," Mick assured me and I agreed.

We crept towards the petrol-station a quarter of a mile away. First, we filled the tank. Mick had calculated that I would need one hundred and four gallons for the round-trip to the Highlands, which was a bit of a shock. However it was still substantially cheaper than putting the job out to contract and, what was more, we were going to operate to our own timetable, a timetable that would leave us in control. Then we looked at the tyres. As Mick had suggested they were quite down and we put that right. I started to manoeuvre the lorry off the forecourt.

But despite the correct pressure I noticed little difference with the steering.

"There must be something wrong. I'm going back to the petrol-station."

I knew they did a bit of local haulage work with a similar lorry. I wrenched my way back onto the forecourt and went in search of the owner. After a cursory look under the vehicle and a ritual shake of the wheels, he shouted for a lad to bring a trolley-jack. This easily lifted the wheels off the ground. There was another inspection underneath and yet more shaking of the wheels, and finally a check for play in the steering. There followed even more head-shaking and then the pronouncement that nothing was wrong.

"You wouldn't think that if you were trying to drive it," I said, trying to justify my misgivings.

"Soon give it a run down the road, if you think that will help."

I said "Yes", and quickly got into the passenger seat.

A mere touch of the button and the engine was purring. The mechanic pursed his lips as he nodded approval of the engine-note. He slipped it into gear and away we went. The muscles of the mechanic's bare arms bulged as we rounded the first island with the greatest of ease. Now, as we took a steep right-hander, I watched the driver closely. Yet more muscles were brought into play and the unladen vehicle literally bounded up the hill, round another traffic island and back onto the garage forecourt. I waited for the verdict uneasily.

"It's in good nick. Nothing wrong at all!"

"Well, it's not the first Bedford I've driven and I'm certain that the one I drove was much easier on the wheel."

"Maybe the one you drove had newish tyres. That always makes em feel easier."

"It was a new vehicle!" I volunteered with pride.

"Oh well, that's it then! Stands to reason – anything new is usually better. Take it from me – this lorry is in fine shape. What about trying a bit of spinach?"

I was not particularly amused.

CHAPTER FIFTEEN

The Great Trek North, Again and Again

The weather had changed; the seasons were progressing. Although it was fine and dry, it was now cooler than of late. When I got up this morning, somewhat later than usual, there was a slight foreboding in the air. I was decidedly stiff from the exertions of the previous day, and I thought what a blessing it was that Irene had had the good sense to suggest a later start. I had slept soundly, lulled perhaps by the fact that for the first time in months I did not have to rush out and start any one of a hundred jobs.   At the same time, this unaccustomed lack of urgency quite unnerved me. Was I dreaming still, or had I just forgotten where I had got to in the program of things? There was only one way to find out: go and have a look.

The first thing I noticed was that although it was a grey morning the cloud was high. That was a good sign, and I began to feel better. Round the corner was the Bedford, just as we had left it: neat and loaded. Considering it had been nearly dark when the last of the ropes were tightened, it looked a pretty professional job. I walked around the lorry. Its load struck me as being rather high in relation to its width, but no more so than on many other similar vehicles I'd seen in the past. Maybe at this eleventh hour I was looking for excuses – but if I was, I didn't find any. I tried the engine, and it started instantly. The lorry was ready to go, and so was I.

I wandered back to the house and reported to Irene that everything was ready for the start. We could have started there and then. It was still only eight o'clock. But Irene was adamant.

"If we start now, you will be driving all hours. We'll start at one and you can drive for a hundred miles. That will take us to Preston."

I nodded acceptance of what we had already agreed, but felt at a bit of a loose end. The aimless feeling did not last long, however: I came to earth with a bump when Irene passed me the checklist I had written just before we had gone to bed the previous night. It was mainly about dealing with the odd bit of correspondence, a stray account.... So in the event, the morning passed by all too quickly, attending to the kind of thing I was used to getting out of the way before we went on holiday. To some extent of course it did feel like going on holiday. However when this holiday finished we would not return home to the familiarity of Shropshire but would wake up one morning to find we had really and truly transplanted ourselves into the Scottish Highlands.

And then it was time to go. We made a last-minute check to see that we had everything, which wasn't much: the grip with a few overnight items and Irene's trusty picnic-hamper. That hamper could be guaranteed to feed us for days if need be.

Mick and Joe Corkindale had come down to see us off. It was just after one o'clock when, for what was only the second time in my life, I edged our lorry gently astern into our lane. The first time I had executed this manoeuvre I had been able to look out of the rear window of the cab, but now my view was blocked by the load. It was time to start learning those most essential skills of the HGV driver: the use of the mirrors and the exercise of patience. I had been told to take my time when reversing a heavily laden vehicle, and so I did. At last we really were ready to go.

The lorry was certainly overloaded, but I felt less anxious than perhaps I should have done because the Bedford that I had briefly driven all those years ago had regularly carried consignments of timber in excess of nine tons – not far off the weight I had on board now. All the same, it felt like being in charge of an elephant as I took my time along the unmade lane. I could see myself riding comfortably, my feet tucked neatly behind the great flapping ears, whilst somewhere behind a great lumbering body gently swayed from side to side. Nor was this all my imagination: the cab was relatively stable, but behind us, as the vehicle repeatedly adjusted itself to the innumerable pot-holes along the lane, the load was indeed rolling from side to side as the long chassis flexed. It was Irene's first experience of the lorry and she was sitting very quietly. I could tell that she was nervous, and this encouraged me to put on a show of confidence. Deep down I was probably even more worried than she was.

At last the lane reached the main road. Mick had been walking behind us, just in case – although I don't suppose any of us knew what he could have done had we run into trouble with the load. I had been moving so cautiously that Mick had almost kept up with us. At the junction, I paused before we turned north. Irene waved, Mick waved, and the journey had begun.

This was my first experience of driving quite such a load. The first surprise was how quiet the Bedford had become under the influence of its cargo. There was none of the rattling and banging of the empty unit of yesterday, when it had skipped and jumped at every undulation. The words of Harry, the driver who had brought the timber down from the sawmill, suddenly came to me.

"She'll be all right when she feels the load."

And she was. I felt greatly reassured.

For the first mile after the junction, the road skirts the Severn. As the river gently meanders between the willow-lined embankments, and watering places where the cattle come down to drink, you pass deep dark pools interspersed with faster, rippling water traversing the frequent shallows. The scene is particularly dramatic above the town bridge. Here there is almost a wooded grotto, formed by the near-vertical sandstone face of High Rock. As we drove by, shafts of miraculous dappled sunlight streamed through the branches of the trees that clung to the rock and arched above us.

The level road came all too suddenly to an end, and we began the long climb out of the valley. The river was soon lost to sight as the road bore us smoothly away and steepened. The lorry immediately lost momentum, and I was quite perturbed at the thought that I might run out of gears. I had quickly dropped to third, and then to second. It settled at that, and I let it have its head.

Slowly we made the ascent. In the steepest section of the hill, the road bent away to the right and, from seemingly nowhere, a car came zipping past, diving almost under our radiator. I glanced in the mirror and was horrified to see a tailback of at least a dozen cars. I felt terribly embarrassed that I should be the cause of such a hold-up, even though I knew there was no help for it. I sat back in my seat and tried to relax; but I couldn't. At last the road began to level out as the top of the hill came in sight: up into third and then back into top gear. At the first long straight stretch, the tail-back cars began to pass one by one. I kept glancing in the mirrors to catch the faces of the drivers as they came alongside, and was relieved to see none showed any resentment at the enforced delay. I told myself that I had been held up under similar circumstances on hundreds of occasions, and that it was all part of the experience of driving on busy roads. I asked myself why I was worrying, and said to myself, again and again, that the Bedford was only a medium-sized lorry, and that there were thousands on the roads twice as large and perhaps even slower. This self-administered pep talk did little however to allay my misgivings. Indeed I never got over the mortification of causing long streams of traffic to trail behind my truck.

We were bowling along quite steadily when it suddenly occurred to me that we had had no lunch. The mental and physical exertion had made me hungry. Irene obviously had the same feeling as she was already reaching for the trusty hamper. An hour had gone already, and a signpost pointing back towards our starting point showed that we had covered only twenty miles. It wasn't far, but soon we would be on the flatter roads of Cheshire. With every bend and incline, my confidence was growing. As the afternoon progressed, Irene also seemed more relaxed. We had negotiated the busy centre of Warrington when I noticed that Irene was absorbed in the road atlas, and was scrutinizing every signpost as it came into view.

Guessing rather regretfully that she was already looking for a place for the night I ventured to say: "I thought we might make somewhere around Preston for the night."

I was relieved to discover that my assumption was wrong, but before I had a chance to inquire further, the reason of her interest in the local geography came into view.

"There it is!" she cried, and in case I was in any doubt cried again: "There! There! Look!"

I had no doubt what I was looking at. I was just as excited as Irene at the sight of the enormous signboard. 'DIVERSION M6 NORTH'.

"You knew all along", I chided Irene.

"Yes, but I wanted it to be a surprise. I heard it on the radio just this morning."

I peeled off to the right, and in a few miles we were on an enormous stretch of brand new highway. It was not the first motorway, because the M1 had been opened three years earlier. In fact it was not even the first *northern* motorway, because the Lancaster by-pass had just stolen that distinction. However this new section did have one claim to fame: it was the location of the first M6 service-station, at Charnock Richard. Irene told me that the American-style restaurant had received great publicity, being hailed by food writers as the way ahead and a model for future fast-food outlets. We had no idea what to expect, but we soon found out.

At this time, the only access to the new road was the route we had just taken. In consequence, and with such a wide carriageway, the traffic seemed very light. What a pleasure it was to glance in the mirrors and, for perhaps the first time since we'd started, to find we were not being tailed! Nor were we disappointed with our first view of Charnock Richard. There were vast and near-empty car- and lorry-parks, and veritable forests of fuel pumps. We had never seen so many before, and it seemed amazing that anyone should imagine that there might be sufficient traffic to warrant such extravagance. We were astonished again when we walked into the restaurant. No roadside café had ever looked like this before. The main window of the area looked out over the motorway and one could sit leisurely at conventional tables watching the traffic zoom by.

But the real novelty was to be found by those who took advantage of the fast-food facility. We sat around long double-sided food-bars which extended into the main body of the café like so many fingers. It seemed such an easy and obvious arrangement. Each bar had a circulation space down the centre which allowed a waitress ready access to everyone seated around the counter top. Below the counter the there was every conceivable item of cutlery, crockery and glassware that might be required. The food itself was all typically American: Aunt Mary's apple pie with a mountain of cream, enormous jam doughnuts, waffles, hamburgers and lots more, all with as much coffee as you could drink. Roadside heaven!

We stayed rather longer than we had intended, dazzled by the novelty of the experience. Already the long afternoon was becoming evening and the light was fading. We agreed that the time had come to take the very first possible turning in order to find somewhere comfortable for the night. It was disconcerting to find that there were no turnings-off. Under a darkening sky we were obliged to trundle on towards Preston. The lorry's headlights were completely ineffective in the descending gloom. It wasn't that they didn't work; it was that the vast scale of the road provided nothing for the meagre beams to focus on. One could only stay between the lines and hope that somewhere up ahead lights would provide direction. The traffic was still very light, but occasionally a car passed us and we would gratefully watch its lights until they were no more than pinpoints in the distance. Eventually the lights of Preston loomed in the distance and then at last, and thankfully, we were under the street-lamps of a conventional road.

I drove slowly on into the town and out again. We were actually heading back in the direction whence we had come. There was a surprising lack of suitable accommodation: when we did see something that looked suitable it would turn out that there was nowhere to park. At last, about a mile out of town and down a side-street, we saw a small illuminated B&B sign. It turned out to be a comfortable little pub, but like the other places we'd seen, it had no parking. The landlord however assured me that somewhere over to the right they were knocking houses down and that I could park there– "But watch out for the open cellars!"

The headlights which had proved almost useless on the vast open space of the motorway were little better in the pitch dark of this side-street, but eventually we found the demolition site. I drove cautiously onto the rough ground until it was comparatively level. When I had turned the lights off I realized that we had forgotten to bring a torch, so we were extra-mindful of the cellars as we gingerly stepped down from the cab. It was only then that we discovered that the door-locks did not lock, so we took what we could along to the pub with us. We consoled ourselves with the thought that if there were anyone foolish enough to try to investigate our vehicle they would probably end up in the cellars.

We had no idea how true this was until the next morning. After a hearty Lancashire breakfast, we wandered down the street to find the Bedford perched between two gaping holes, and half a dozen workmen gazing incredulously at it. In the pitch darkness we had parked within inches of disaster. Irene stood in the road as one by one and sometimes in chorus the workmen guided my return to safety of the street's tarmac.

The morning was surprisingly pleasant after the ominous and premature darkness of the previous evening.

Irene joked: "Baptism by fire, and we are still here. Now everything's going to be just fine."

We went back to the motorway for its last few miles, and then suddenly we were into the confines of the old road for a few miles – and then, much to our delight, onto the new Lancaster by-pass. We were really doing fine, and the whole day was ahead of us. We were about a mile from the end of the by-pass when there was a loud bang, and the lorry lurched to the right.

"Damn! We've got a burst."

I steered gradually onto the hard shoulder, and slowly we came to a standstill. The burst tyre was really no great problem; luckily it was an outside one. It was just inconvenient when we were getting along so well. I soon had the jack under the axle and was glad that I had had the wheels off before: it was thus an easy exercise to remove the offending wheel.

"We'll be off in five minutes."

Famous last words, as they say. However I struggled, I simply could not lift the spare wheel onto the studs. I brought the axle down so that I only had to lift the wheel a whisker, but still I could not get it in position. A police-car slowed as it passed down the opposite carriageway, then sped off in a burst of acceleration.

"Just like the police – never available when you want help," I muttered.

We heard the siren before we saw the police-car. It was now racing down our side of the motorway towards us, with no apparent chance of its stopping to help at that speed. Then, when it was almost upon us, the wailing siren stopped and the car screeched to a halt in front of the lorry; simultaneously the doors were thrown open, and two officers leapt out. One made straight for the cab and the other came aggressively up to where Irene and I were standing, beside the punctured wheel.

"What's this then?"

"We've got a puncture."

"Don't be funny. What's in the load?"

"Timber," I replied in all innocence.

"Where've you come from?"

"Preston."

He was a mean-faced man of slim athletic build, the sort that never smiles, the sort of chap with whom you would not readily pick a quarrel. He was looking at the number plate.

"Where before Preston?"

"Shropshire."

And so it went on. He completely ignored my requests for an explanation. In the corner of my eye I just caught the other officer descending from the Bedford's cab. His hat had fallen off, and I could see that he had close-cropped ginger hair. His plump oval face looked amiable enough, and as his feet touched the ground, I saw his head give an almost imperceptible little sideways shake. Obviously he had been searching. His aggressive colleague picked up the signal and immediately softened his attitude.

"I'll have to see under the cover. We'll start at the back."

Ginger had already started.

"Just timber," he reported.

Irene stood quietly by, a look of frustration on her face. "I don't know what they think we've done."

"We're the first people to have dared to stop on a motorway," I joked.

Our aggressor returned from inspecting the small section of the load Ginger had uncovered. His features seemed to have softened.

"By, there better be some good explanation."

I gave them the gist of our story and remarkably they listened as if they were really interested.

"Now, let's get this straight. You bought some trees and turned them into a house that you want to build in the Scottish Highlands, but you couldn't find a haulage-contractor to do the transport, so you bought this lorry. Right?"

"Yes," I replied.

"You can of course prove this, shall I say, fairytale?"

"Yes, it's a fairytale," Irene chipped in. "And it is true. Just a minute and I'll prove it to you."

She fetched a slim raffia shopping bag from the cab. In it were a couple of magazines, the maps, yesterday's newspaper and an envelope file. She thrust the file into the officer's hands.

"Just take a glance through a bit of our correspondence. It all relates to what we are doing here. Then see whether you think what we've told you is the truth."

Irene stood defiantly at the policeman's side as he took in snippets of our story from the various letters. After a short while he handed them back.

"I'm sorry. I can't say more than that, except that we seriously suspected that you were connected with the Great Train Robbery."

He tried to smile, but Irene's eyes said only one thing: 'you stupid man'. The look was so effective that the officer was immediately on the defensive.

"Now see here! We have a job to do, and we have been on Red Alert since the weekend. Escaping by driving in a heavy goods vehicle would be novel. You don't even look like lorry-drivers. In fact, you stick out like sore thumbs."

A faint smile flickered across all our faces at this point, but for Irene it was relief rather than mirth. The whole mood changed. We learned that Ginger's name was Doug.

"Get the sheet tied down again for them, Doug, and get it tight. I'll give 'em a hand with the wheel."

The serious one was Allan. He was trying hard to make amends and joked: "If you're going to try another escape for goodness' sake get your lorry-driving act sorted out, particularly changing wheels. I'll give you this, you've got the wheel in position, but obviously you can't lift it. So here's how it's done. Pass me the jack-handle, please, and the wheel-brace. Just slip them under the bottom of the tyre, and lever upwards. Easy when you know how."

The wheel just slipped on. Allan proceeded to fit and tighten the nuts; he removed the jack as I watched.

"There! Ready to roll. I should get the pressure checked though. There's a garage as you come off the motorway."

They got in their car. Allan leaned out of the window. "Sorry again. Only doing our job. Have a good journey! Cheerio! See you again maybe."

"I hope not," Irene mumbled.

I did as Alan had suggested and checked the tyre. It was time to fill up with petrol anyway. At last we were ready to go again. We had lost about an hour, but it was still only mid-morning and the sun was shining.

"Let's go!" I turned the key, and the engine sprang into life. Just as I was about to engage the gears, whoosh, there was another police-car across our bows.

"Oh no! I can't stand this," Irene groaned in desperation.

We sat waiting. There was only the driver and he slowly eased himself out of the car, straightening his hat and uniform as he did so. He sauntered over in a rather arrogant manner, and with chin held high and in a rather stagey voice addressed us.

"You're trailing a loose rope. It's an offence to have an insecure load. Get it done up before you go onto the road."

He returned to his car and drove off. We sat bemused for some moments and then burst out laughing.

"What did I say about not wanting to see that pair again?" said Irene. "If I ever do, I'll kill that Doug."

Being stopped on suspicion of being train robbers is a rather serious business. We might have been at risk of any sort of treatment, not to mention the implications of the flat tyre that we had failed to deal with. Perhaps, in retrospect, the search of the cab and the inspection of the load had been only cursory. At the time, it had seemed tedious, not to say overbearing, but now, as we sped on our way, we began to see the funny side. In fact it was many miles before we talked of anything else.

Once we had cleared the congested main thoroughfare of Carlisle, the incident was set aside. Our thoughts turned to the implications of the delay. The plan had been to have cleared Glasgow at least before stopping for the night. In fact I had our usual stop at Crianlarich in mind, but this now seemed over-optimistic. On and on, the miles slipped slowly but relentlessly by. Our lorry had little chance of ever overtaking anything, so we just settled down to our place in an endless procession of vehicles. They came from all parts of the country, mostly conveying export goods to the Glasgow docks. From time to time Irene raided the trusty picnic-hamper. Her prepared sandwiches and the two large flasks we had had replenished back in Preston kept us going for the rest of the day.

We arrived at the southern outskirts of Glasgow in the evening rush-hour. Every other vehicle seemed to be a loaded lorry, or one of those wretched trams that would peel off left or right without the least warning. As usual, they stopped and started, loading and unloading their multitudes of passengers in a way which was doubtless normal for Glaswegians, but which was a nightmare to an apprentice lorry-driver like me. To add to my misery, a fine rain began to fall from the ever-darkening sky and, if that were not enough, we discovered that the rubber in the windscreen-wiper had perished: it failed to remove any water.

The northern suburbs of Glasgow went on for miles. I was creased with back-pain brought on by my unaccustomed wrestling with the Bedford's heavy steering and, not a little, by the fruitless attempts I had made to change the punctured wheel earlier in the day. I was tired. Eventually we cleared Dumbarton and left all vestiges of street-illumination behind. The road ahead became pitch black, and the rain was now a deluge. For some reason, however, it was not as bad as it sounds. The headlights, which on the motorway's vastness had found nothing to focus upon, now glinted reassuringly on the rain-sodden embankments and rock-faces of the tortuous and narrow road that skirts the shore of Loch Lomond. Such is the nature of this continually winding road, hemmed in as it is by woodland and rock, that any lamp capable of shining twenty feet will always have something in its beam. Moreover, this was not our first experience of Lomondside in such conditions.

At eight thirty, we reached the head of the loch. We were still short of my objective, but an illuminated car-park and a welcoming hotel-sign beckoned, and we gave way to good sense.

By the morning, the overnight rain had given way to bright sunshine, but there was a decided nip in the crystal-clear air, and the bracken on the mountainside had begun to turn gold. Autumn had come to the Highlands. We had entered a land remote from yesterday's troubles, and by evening we would be in Ullapool.

We were in high spirits as we drove on: mile after mile of mountains, moorland and loch. Our first sight of the sea was as we dropped down through Glencoe to the familiar shores of Loch Leven and Loch Linnhe. At Fort William we ate our lunch sitting at the very edge of the water. Curlews called in the distance, and overhead wheeled black-headed gulls, already in their winter plumage. They dived at every crumb we discarded. Mac and Jenny had again asked us to stay with them when we arrived at Ullapool – the typical Highland invitation which says 'We'll expect you when we see you'. This was just as well, for we could not resist walking around Fort William, just to savour the joy of being in the Highlands again, and on such a gorgeous day. The sun was now gloriously warm, and the waters of the loch so calm that they reflected the outline of the surrounding mountains.

At a great height, up in the mountains, a golden eagle soared effortlessly on the rising currents of warm air. We had no need to remind ourselves that this was what had drawn us to the Highlands. Time loses its meaning in so perfect a world. These mountains have stood since before human life evolved, and by the side of that fact another minute, hour or day has no significance. Yesterday's schedules, timetables and average speeds were totally unimportant.

The road up through the Great Glen was almost devoid of traffic. At one moment we were at the water's edge, and the next we were passing through dense pine forests. From our high driving position in the Bedford we amused ourselves with imagining that we were in an old four-litre Bentley, on a grand touring holiday. The engine at least had some of the car's characteristics, and the exhaust note was very reminiscent. In the ecstasy of the drive, I had almost forgotten my back-pain. It is no wonder to me that there is never any shortage of long-distance lorry drivers: I wouldn't deny that a driver's life is full of hardship and untold hours of work, but the bonus is that their cab is their dream-world, and the open road represents freedom from the outside world. So at least it was with us on that glorious autumn afternoon.

At Inverness we had a brief stop for supplies. Then we headed north-west as we had done so many times before – but never, until now, in a lorry. We recalled the fears of all the haulage companies with whom Irene had tried, and failed, to arrange our removal. Every transport manager had argued that to send their vehicles so far north and into such remote areas was a gamble they simply could not take. Our last sixty-five miles were nevertheless uneventful – except for one small incident, at what appears to be an insignificant hill at the Falls of Rogie. This was the one and only occasion in over five hundred miles that I had to slip the lorry into the lowest gear. I was mightily thankful when we just crawled over the summit. Soon it was virtually all downhill. In the gathering twilight we ran easily down the Broom valley. Ahead, on its promontory, we saw the village and, far out to sea beyond the Summer Isles and beyond the horizon, the familiar afterglow of the sun.

We had telephoned Mac from Inverness, and he had anticipated our arrival to a nicety. He was standing there at the open gate ready to greet us. As they say in the Highlands: 'What a night that was!' Well, what a night that was, indeed. We had made the journey despite the set-backs. In expectation of our success we had purchased a bottle of MacAllan's in Inverness: twelve-year-old single-malt whisky. We make no excuse for having nearly drunk it, together with our hosts, to celebrate our achievement.

CHAPTER SIXTEEN

Bonfire Night

Good fortune smiled upon us following our triumphant drive. Mac had been trying to organize somewhere for us to store our load, as it was impossible for us to get onto our own land for that purpose: there was no road down there and there would not be one for some time. He'd decided that it would be best to stack the material in their garden, and to that end he had cleared a substantial patch for us between the trees and laid down a number of heavy battens to keep everything clear of the ground. The best of our good fortune was that their lads Sandy and Donald were home from university. With their help the whole load was safely stacked and covered by coffee-time the following morning. Jenny begged us to stay on at least until lunch, but we had a long way to go, and with such a time-advantage the bit was between our teeth.

We had, for example, taken an incredible risk by not doing anything about that burst tyre (which was now our useless spare), and we had no intention of continuing to tempt fate on the return-journey. I went, not for the first time, to Mackay's Garage in the village. Mackay's was a thriving haulage-contractor and also dealt with most of the local motor repairs; it was an Aladdin's cave of spare parts for seemingly every make of car, almost regardless of age. I've never forgotten arriving once in Ullapool towing a caravan with a collapsed axle-bearing. I'd had the same problem before, and so I knew the bearing to be the same as the back-axle unit of an obsolete Wolseley car. I had little hope of finding a spare in Ullapool, but no sooner had I ventured my request than old Mr Mackay was off into the cave, returning moments later smiling.

"There! Thought I had one. How will ten shillings suit you? Probably cost us five when we took it into stock before the war."

A bargain: I had paid three pounds for the previous one.

Nothing was too much trouble at Mackay's, father, son or any of the employees, and I had no doubt that this time they would again be able to help. Indeed they had many tyres in stock – but unbelievably not one to fit our wheel. Mr Mackay looked serious.

"Well, you cannot start without a spare. Only one thing for it – we will have to take a tyre off one of our vehicles. We can easily replace it tomorrow with one from Inverness. That would not be quick enough for you, but it is no problem for us."

Not only did we thus get the tyre, but they would take no payment.

"The tyre's part worn, and we could not make a charge for that." Mr Mackay's eyes twinkled with satisfaction as he bade us a successful journey. We filled up with fuel and were on our way once more.

Now relieved of its load the Bedford jigged and jumped like an eager filly waiting to be given her head. It was reassuring to have unfettered power available, but the driving was less pleasant. We frequently hit potholes and, without the load to dampen the action, the platform bounced up and down and every single component of the vehicle shook and rattled. I could think of nothing but to get back to Shropshire as quick as possible.

Irene for her part was busy working out what the journey had cost us in petrol. It can be rather startling to compare the figures with a car's until one considers that the lorry could carry a busload of passengers. Indeed Bedford buses, which were basically the same vehicle as the lorry, were a common sight at the time all over the country.

"There," said Irene. "Got it at last: five hundred and twenty-four miles, average speed twenty-seven miles per hour, and we used forty-six gallons of petrol. That can't be right! That's only eleven and a half miles per gallon!"

"Yes, it *is* right," I assured her. "And that's pretty good!"

"You've been unusually quiet," she said.

"I'm thinking," I smiled. Irene looked apprehensive. "I was wondering if we could make it back in one run."

Irene might also have been wondering how quickly we might get back. "Well … if you think you are up to it. There's no point in driving yourself to the point of exhaustion."

"We can always pull over if it gets too much," I replied with what I hoped was reassurance.

We passed through Inverness and out onto the A9. It was just after 5pm. We generally avoided this most tortuous of trunk-roads. On the map it looked pretty straightforward, over a hundred and fifty miles of road connecting Edinburgh to Inverness. It zigzagged a bit but gave no clue to what was in store for the unsuspecting driver. Perhaps it was the long journey with no notable objectives that made it seem endless. True, there was Perth, but the road quickly passed through an uninspiring part of the city and you hardly noticed when you left the city behind. Earlier on, Dunkeld and Pitlochry had been equally without interest to the passing motorist. To enjoy any one of these locations one would have to stop and explore, and we had no time for that. But the greatest drawback to the old A9 was the virtual impossibility of safe overtaking. For the most part the road twisted and turned, ducked and dived throughout its entire length.

However we chose the route now for the very reason that there would be other traffic, even through the night. With our poor headlights we hoped to be able to follow someone with better lights than us. There turned out to be less traffic than we had expected, but we need not have worried. Unlike the previous evenings, the sky was clear and beautifully starlit, and the moon was about half full. It took something over five hours to reach Perth, where we were greatly enlivened by the sight of a fish-and-chip shop still open. A fish-and-chip supper never tasted so good. We left the A9 after Perth and headed south-west through a sleeping Stirling. On and on south we went, until too tired to drive any further, we drew into a secluded village car-park at Abington. We had rejoined the main Glasgow route we had passed along only two days earlier.

We tried hard to get a little sleep, but the cold and lack of heat in the cab made it impossible. We drank the last of our coffee and after an hour reluctantly set off again. The moon had gone by now, but the night remained bright and in no time we settled in amongst the other night-drivers. They were taking goods south from docks and factories. At Carlisle there was a diversion south that took the traffic clear of the town. I noticed too late that the other vehicles were ignoring the turn, presumably because in the early morning the main run was just as quick. My inattention did not seem to matter: our road past the town was completely deserted. Near the end, when we had just passed another diversion notice ('South – 1 Mile), the engine suddenly spluttered and stopped. I did my best to see if there was any obvious cause but without a lamp it was an almost impossible task. As we had plenty of fuel, I tried the starter: the engine burst into life and we were off again – but only for about half a mile. We sat forlornly in the dark wondering what to do, looking at the lights of the main-road traffic up ahead. I remembered that there was a garage just south of Carlisle, but not whether it would be north or south of where we would be joining the road, nor whether it would be an all-night establishment, nor – and most importantly – whether the engine would start again.

Well, it did, again. And again, and again. After each run on the starter it would splutter into life and we would move on a little. I wondered how long the battery would hold out under this treatment. At the junction we chose to turn south, luckily. The starter was struggling as we limped onto the garage forecourt. It was in pitch darkness. Five o'clock on a cold morning and I was more tired than I had ever been in my life.

I came to with a banging in my right ear and completely disoriented. There was a face at the window mouthing something. I wound the window down.

"Sorry to disturb you. Could you back up a bit so that we can open up?"

Hazily the circumstances of our being there came to me.

"Er… sorry! The engine has given up."

I turned the key to demonstrate. The engine spluttered and stopped.

"It's petrol, starved by the sound of things." Our early-morning caller lifted the bonnet. "Try that."

It ran, but only for a moment.

"You've got fuel in I hope?" he called as he dived under the chassis.

"Yes, of course."

"Here it is!" he shouted. "Fuel pipe loose at the tank!"

He took a tiny wrench out of his overall pocket nipped the pipe-union tight.

"Try that."

It started first time.

"OK," said the man. "Can I open up now? Would you like a cup of tea?"

Would we just.

Our saviour turned out to be the garage-owner. Like old Mr Mackay he would take no payment, so I topped the tank up with ten gallons. After a very welcome freshen up in the new cloakroom facilities, we were on our way once more.

The bridge clock struck four-thirty as we alighted stiffly from the cab, our red rimmed eyes almost unable to face the bright afternoon sunlight. We had been on the road twenty-six hours.

The day after our return we had a surprise telephone call from the Major, who had heard from Mr Mackay at the garage that we had delivered the first load. Everyone was a little concerned as to whether we had returned safely. I assured the Major that we had and thanked him for his concern, but spared him the details. I said that we hoped to return in a few days with more of our belongings.

"Yes, so I heard," he said. "That's actually the second reason for my call. Corry Point bungalow will be vacant a week earlier than expected, and you would be welcome to use it ahead of your lease. Don't hesitate to use the garage as a store, if that would help."

Yes, it would all help. Indeed just at that moment it provided a much needed incentive to do the second trip. It went without a hitch.

Back again at Bridgnorth we had little time to spare, for now we had to vacate our home earlier than we'd planned. As we had no new home to furnish yet, most of our belongings had to go into store. What we needed for everyday use got packed under the tarpaulin of the last load, in amongst my collection of woodworking machinery, a concrete-mixer, a dumper and the load of roof tiles (which had been stacked on edge in every available deck-space). We probably had more weight aboard than in that first mammoth load.

It is difficult to hold a leaving party in a virtually empty house. By the time we finished packing, there was nothing left save a minimum of camping gear. We solved the problem by bringing forward our Bonfire Night barbecue.

We had had a barbecue every November for a number of years past, but how it all began is hard to say. It had just grown. We had a very convenient patch of land adjacent to our property, ample room for car-parking and a good safe area for the fire. We never advertised the event, but I think Mick used to put the word around: a few days before the fifth, a great variety of burnable material would start to accumulate. Often cars with trailers would sidle up to the site, arrange their combustible offering, nod to us if we were about and then shout "See you on the fifth!" Numbers of them we only got to know by virtue of their regular annual attendance. Our friends all came as a matter of course. They used to congratulate me on the effort I had made in arranging such a fire, whereas in truth I had done nothing.

Actually, that was not entirely true – Mick and I used to build the barbecue, which I suspect that had something to do with the attraction. We used to start by building a rectangular base with concrete blocks, twenty feet long, two feet wide and two blocks high. We topped this with a heavy steel mesh obtained from a nearby sand-quarry (now too badly worn, it had been used as sand screens), and then we raised the height of the structure with another course of block. Thus we created a waist-high barbecue pit. Into this, over the mesh, we placed a layer of kindling, topped with two hundredweight of blacksmith's breeze (i.e. fine washed coke). We would light this enormous forge-like unit at three o'clock in the afternoon. Whilst the fire was getting going, we would erect a scaffold over the whole affair and roof it with corrugated iron sheets, just in case of rain. A few Tilley lamps were strung under the structure and we were ready to go.

By darkness, the bonfire would be well alight, and the coals of our barbecue would be glowing over its length and breadth. Next we would fix a fine screen at a suitable height above the hot embers, for the food. We always had plenty of food for our friends and any number of visitors, but others would surreptitiously add more and more, until there were cooks stationed all around the cooking area. Amongst our guests were many of the children who when we had been machining the logs had enjoyed the nightly burning of the shavings. People added to the mountain of the fireworks (possibly providing the greater share), handing them dutifully to those I had put in charge of the pyrotechnics.

This year, our last at Bridgnorth, was a fine evening and we had a big gathering of old friends. A few of our usual helpers came to ensure that the occasion would be memorable. And it was.

At last it was time to say goodbye to the place we had loved for so many years. Yes, there were twinges of doubt as we gathered up our last few personal possessions. As usual Mick was there, just in case we needed any last-minute help. He had already volunteered to dismantle the barbecue and clear up after the bonfire. He was undoubtedly one of the most loyal friends that I have ever had the pleasure of knowing. We would miss him.

I gave Mick the keys to hand to the Powells, who were expected to arrive later in the day. We shook hands and Irene gave him a big hug. It was really a sad business, and all more so in that Irene and I were travelling in separate vehicles. I was driving the lorry and Irene the Landrover.

Driving in convoy is never satisfactory, so Irene went on ahead and the lorry just took its own time. We met up at prearranged meeting points through the journey, Irene always having drunk at least two coffees and read one more newspapers or magazine while she waited for me. It was not until the second day of our journey that it sank in that we were not coming back: we were in fact now going home, even if in practice we had yet to build it.

I can still remember the exact time and place where I was hijacked by this feeling that I had crossed my Rubicon. We had stopped there many times previously: by the side of Loch Linnhe at the entrance to Fort William. I had no special liking for it, but it is interesting that Fort William is known as the gateway to the Highlands, although if travelling north one will already have been in the Highland for many miles. Are there ley-lines somewhere deep below the highway, or some other force that urges travellers to stop here? Later that evening, toasting our success and comfortably ensconced by a roaring log-fire at Corry Point, I mentioned the possibility of ley-lines to Irene and asked if she had felt anything similar. Was there any point in the journey when she had felt that she had *arrived?*

"Yes – the moment I came through the door, and smelt the old familiar pine-board scent!"

We did not rise at our usual early hour, for even I with my restless need to get on with the work had, for the moment, done enough. Together we had achieved what many who visit the Highlands only dream of doing. It still felt a bit like a dream to us, to tell the truth, as we sat in the window of Corry Point and gazed out over the Loch towards the inland mountains. They had their first white caps of winter snow: it was settling early. We had worked incessantly during the last year; when we weren't actually engaged in manual toil we were planning or organizing some aspect of our project. And there had been all the travelling: it is easy to underestimate this aspect of uprooting oneself as we had. Irene used to complain in good humour that she felt like the Flying Dutchman, doomed to travel the Great North Route for the rest of her life.

But by mid-morning we felt lost in our new-found freedom and craved for something to do.

"I know what we must do – go down and let Mac and Jenny know we have arrived!"

We found them sunning themselves on the bench beside where the French windows should have been. We joined them and knew that we had indeed come to the place of our dreams. Mac seemed subdued, almost brooding, and he left Jenny to fill us in with the news of their builder.

Her attitude towards him seemed to have somersaulted since we'd last seen them, not that that is an unusual thing to happen. A builder may not have come up to expectations; words may have been said; and he probably couldn't get away from the job quickly enough – but there will still be, there always are, outstanding perhaps essential matters to be dealt with, and in areas where builders are few and far between, one very often has to change one's tune.

"What's the good of falling out with your builder? OK, we haven't got a proper staircase and what we have is in the wrong place. OK."

The builder had apparently smoothed over that small deficiency by telling them that because they only had a loft-ladder the council would not rate them on the two attic bedrooms.

"We'll see," Mac suddenly interjected with an air of fatalism.

"As for the French window," Jenny was saying, "I can see now that it would have been totally impracticable. You should see the way the wind drives the rain when there's a storm! We would have been flooded every time it rained."

Mac looked up and raised his hand towards an old fisheries protection ship that had just steamed in. "I shouldn't think their wheelhouse door floods the ship every time it rains."

Jenny stared at him. His point was either lost or she was lost for words (but that was unlikely).

Mac went on: "What about the underfloor heating in the bathroom, or should I say the underfloor heating under the bath?"

"Mac, you're just splitting hairs! The builder says that the heat will travel across the floor to where we stand, especially if we leave it on all the day."

"Oh well, I suppose he would know. It's probably not the first time they've made such a blunder."

Jenny ignored the comment and turned her attention to Irene. "The builder's men are really very nice. I've persuaded them to come and do all sorts of little jobs for me. In fact I have them coming tomorrow to put up more shelves."

Mac had had enough and caught me by the arm.

"Come and see what you think of this!"

We marched off through the birch trees until we came to the furthermost boundary fence.

"What do you think of that?" Fences in the Highlands serve basically one purpose, to keep the marauding sheep out and, if they are high enough, deer as well.

"It's a good stout fence," I ventured.

"I know that!" Mac replied grumpily. "Come on up by the house."

I followed, somewhat puzzled. When we reached the house he turned and looked back, this time down the line of posts and mesh. The fence followed a meandering watercourse which continually changed direction. Viewed from where we were standing it did go back and forth a bit, but that's the nature of fencing over such ground. Mac didn't wait for my comment but just turned on me in a way that I thought rather aggressive and very uncharacteristic.

"Don't suppose you were ever on convoy duty?"

"Only exercises," I answered, although I could not see the point.

"Then you'll know what I mean by zigzagging."

"Yes, dodging about to avoid submarines."

"Quite so," Mac continued. "I spent weeks, months, no ruddy years at it, decoding signals, giving orders – "Port eight miles, starboard fifteen," "Port twenty" – and always at random headings so as to confuse the enemy. And still our ships went down, sometimes just abeam and often with someone aboard that you knew."

There was a long pause in which I dare not speak in case I should say the wrong thing. Clearly Mac was getting agitated, and this was a side of him that was unknown to me. At last he spoke again.

"What do you think comes into my mind every time I look down the course of that fence?"

I could only imagine. I tried hard to think of what might be done. "What about having the fence taken down and re-erected on a straight line? What does it matter if you lose a few yards? You've got acres!"

"Take it down!" he shouted. "I can't take it down! It's not mine! It's the damned Major's!"

I felt cornered by a problem I did not fully understand, and I was glad when Irene appeared to tell me that we had to go and shop before they closed for lunch.

"Jenny's quite worried about Mac. He's involved himself in some feud with the Major, something about a fence," Irene said.

"Yes, I know."

Irene was as anxious to start the new house as I was. I had been thinking of having a few days off, but by the time we had spent the afternoon exploring our estate we had caught the bug and vowed to start on the following day. For one thing, we had little idea yet of how to read the local weather-signs and for all we knew winter might start in earnest any day soon. Our plan was that each day I would have an early breakfast and then walk to the site, whilst Irene would deal with the household jobs and drive down later with elevenses and a picnic lunch. It was a routine that was to work well. We vowed that tomorrow we would start.

CHAPTER SEVENTEEN

Hogmanay

We must have looked a silly pair as we made our way to the site on that very first morning: I was sitting on our tiny dumper and Irene was driving the Landrover, towing the dumper with a sagging over-long rope. What did it matter? It was only a mile of very quiet road. We went gently round the first bend with the long rope clipping the offside verge – and there, by a hundred-to-one chance, was the road-repair squad, busily clearing the side-ditches of the verge. They looked in amazement as we passed, doffing their caps in all seriousness, and equally seriously we exchanged greetings. Then the sag in the towline was suddenly taken up and I was catapulted on at great speed. We passed two more locals walking into the village and yet another walking out. All this along a mile of road that rarely sees a soul from one week's end to the next. Within the hour every detail of our comic progress (no doubt much exaggerated) would have been broadcast around the village and out-lying areas. Any hope that we might have had of being regarded as normal would now be out the window.

Ah well. We arrived at the edge of our estate. We realized that whilst it had been difficult enough unloading the half-ton dumper from the lorry, what we were now proposing was downright dangerous. There was absolutely no vehicular access from the narrow single-track road down to the level platform of land where we intended building the log house. The embankment dropped away at far too steep angle. Nothing could ever drive over that bank without ending up in the sea – yet this was precisely what we were intending to do.

Irene precariously balanced the parked Landrover on the narrow verge whilst I prepared to drive the dumper over the edge. This might have seemed potentially suicidal, but I had no foolhardy intention of risking death. I had a cunning plan. The tow-rope would now be attached to the rear of the dumper and Irene would give the rope a couple of turns round the Landrover's bumper. This would enable her to ease me over the edge and down the precipitous slope a bit at a time. The first yard was nearly a disaster: as the rope took the strain the dumper jerked forward uncontrollably. The sudden snatch dragged the Landrover to a point where it almost teetered on the edge and threatened to follow me down. Irene gasped in horror.

The very moment of my plunge coincided with the road-squad returning to the village. Their lorry nearly joined us as the driver's disbelief caused him to lose control. The lorry veered from one side of the road to the other before it finally went into the ditch over the way from us. The men standing in the open back fell all over the place, and more than one unfamiliar Gaelic word was uttered. But the lorry did not stop. Perhaps the Gaelic utterances had been prayers; if so they had been answered. The vehicle simply drove out of the ditch as neatly as it had driven in. It was now clearly a matter of urgency that they be the first to relay this latest incident to the village. These newcomers were indeed mad.

Irene had had the foresight to hang onto the rope and now, aided by judicious use of the dumper's powerful brakes and by the grip of heavily cleated tyres, she eased me down the slope, inch by inch.

Our priority was to build a road down to the site. The 'main' road was too narrow for a conventional tipping lorry to discharge filling material over the embankment. Even if it had been possible to do this, it would have taken hundreds of tons of material to start a ledge from which in time a road might be constructed. Our solution was to build a drystone retaining wall parallel to the road, and then fill between it and the verge. There was a great deal of loose stone on the land and the dumper would bring it up to the new wall. It would be a big undertaking. For a start, the retaining wall would need to be sixty feet long and eight feet high at its tallest, and at least three feet thick.

We began at the point that would eventually be our entrance. It was the hardest section but, this portion of the wall once built and filled to road-level, we would at least have a decent parking-bay for the Landrover. As we were now obviously objects of local interest whose daily progress must be reported, we expected even worse distractions than the road-workers had provided. It was three weeks before Irene gingerly drove our precious car off the road and we feared no more for its safety. After another three weeks, a further milestone was reached: at last we were able to drive the Landrover down to the lower levels of the site, almost to the point where the log house was to be sited.

The first week of December arrived, cold and clear. Although we had had a few damp days I had lost no time on site – except of course I did not openly work on the Sabbath. On days when the weather was inclement Irene would stay back at Corry Point and get on with her baking. At one stage she made sloe gin, for we had been blessed with a fine crop of these tangy, damson-like fruits. In the chilly, bright conditions the loch would become mirror-calm in the late afternoon. The seabirds were like so many boating enthusiasts out for a leisurely paddle. Flotillas of eider-ducks would pass by, cooing 'ah-oo, ah-oo,' as if passing the time of day, and then at what seemed an unheard signal they would one by one disappear below the surface. We would wait expectantly as their reappearance grew overdue, then – plop, plop, and they would buoyantly bob back to the surface, calling again 'ah-oo, ah-oo,' nodding the time of day and then giving a repeat performance.

At a greater distance from the shore, the evocative, eerie wail of the great northern diver, that most handsome of the diving birds, would come floating across the still waters. Often these beautiful creatures would be so close to our shore that we could see every detail of their magnificent plumage: jet black head and a neck scored with a collar of thin vertical white stripes. However it is their upper body which gives them their greatest distinction –the formal white spotting covers their entire back and flanks like raindrops. This is why in some parts they are always referred to as 'the rain goose'. We never tired of hearing their calls.

As the afternoons wore on, all our usual bird friends would move in amongst the scrub for a last forage before selecting a roosting spot for the night. The secretive little goldcrest, a wren, blue tits together with their relatives the great and coal tits, a family of long-tails, would all flit noisily through the birch twigs then vanish. Out of the corner of our eye we might catch sight of the tree-creeper as it moved mouselike up the trunk of an oak. Agitated robins would call out to intruders daring to enter their territory. A gang of chaffinches rarely left our sides in the hope that we might take a break and drop a few crumbs. As the light began to fade and the winter evening closed in, the blackbirds would have one last session of noisy calling and then settle down for the long hours of darkness.

Often the last sounds of life were our own as we in turn scurried around gathering up tools before total darkness rendered the task impossible. Even then we were often reluctant to go. There was a magic in the air at such times. A stillness crept over everything as the last vestige of light in the west caught the snow-covered peaks of the high mountains, momentarily glistening a brilliant white against the ever-darkening sky.

A week into the last month of the year and the days became cooler, although never freezing. With cold air rolling down the mountain winter had begun to take a grip. We began going back to the cottage for our midday break, usually hot soup and perhaps a ham roll. On one of these occasions we slipped down to the village for supplies, and then headed back past the site for lunch. On such a bright crisp morning, one could see the head of the loch from just beyond our new entrance. As always during such spells of weather, the surface of the sea was like a mill pond.

"Look!" I half-shouted. "There's two dinghies out sailing."

"Where?" Irene questioned in disbelief.

"There!" I shouted as I caught sight of them again.

"Where this time?" Irene impatiently countered.

"I promise you I saw two dinghies near the head of the loch."

I was now so certain that I pulled into a passing place so that I might scan the water more carefully. There was an old school at the water's edge on the far side of the loch and the oblique angle of its white-painted gable could easily be mistaken for a sail close inshore. I now began to wonder whether what I had seen was the gable: for it was most unlikely that any one would be sailing at this time of the year.

Irene, still doubtful of my observations and with hint of sarcasm, questioned me: "You saw two images? Double vision." She looked me straight in the eye. "You've been shovelling too hard, barely drawing breath all morning. Here, let me drive. You're resting up this afternoon."

I was just about to do as bid when my apparition momentarily reappeared, disappeared, and in a second, there it was again. Or rather, there they were, for there were indeed two. Irene saw them at last, and her jaw dropped as she tried to comprehend the inexplicable sighting. Whatever it was, it was still at least two miles distant but each time it became visible it seemed nearer.

"They're whales," I shouted with excitement. "And they are heading our way!"

No question as to who was driving as I raced off towards Corry Point where we could get down to the edge of the sea. We dumped the vehicle at the house and raced down to the foreshore. They were killer-whales. We could see their huge swordlike dorsal fins and the white flanks as they surfaced with greater frequency. Suddenly there was a swirl of water at our feet and we had to flee up the beach.

Irene yelled: "My god! They're beaching themselves!"

We stopped some yards up the shingle our hearts pounding. The whales had in fact moved out from the shore but were still surfacing frequently. Occasionally they would lie on the surface just long enough for us to see every detail of their extraordinary fins. We crept back to the water's edge, and saw in the gin-clear water the cause of the earlier commotion.

"Young ones," Irene whispered. "Two."

"No, they're porpoises I think," I gasped in wonder.

They lay not a yard in front of us with their blow holes just at the surface of the water, gasping from time to time like hunted creatures that have gone to cover. The whales had for the moment vanished, but we continued to keep watch. When last we saw them they were heading out to sea. Irene wanted me to push the porpoises out into deeper water but, as the tide was coming in and there was little danger of them stranding, I thought it better to let them take their time. After lunch we again went down to the water's edge, and the porpoises had gone. It was too late by then to go back to the site, so we took the saw from the woodshed and had an afternoon cutting up driftwood at the shore.

With the site now accessible, I had begun the task of cutting a level platform for the loghouse into the sloping ground. It obviously had to be large enough to accommodate the building and our vehicles – both to park and, most importantly, to turn around. It is only when sees such an area marked out on steeply sloping ground that the full magnitude of the task becomes apparent. The method of excavating such sites is usually known as cut-and-fill. You cut into the embankment and deposit the excavated material on the lower level: this is the fill. The excavated area (where the 'cut' had been made) was where the house was to be built – where the virgin ground remained solid. Unfortunately, and perhaps unsurprisingly, there were no suitable excavating machines in north-west Scotland. Indeed JCBs and similar machines were still a novelty in the Highlands. There was nothing else for it: I would have to dig it by hand.

The first cut I made into the embankment was like starting a drift mine in the side of a hill. The top soil was minimal, no more than nine inches deep, and the ground below it was a hard moraine composed of clay and gravel, a glacial residue from the Ice Age. Every shovelful had to be loosened with a pickaxe. To add to the labour, the 'cut' soil all had to be wheeled away to wherever the fill was needed. I made the first cut six feet wide simply to give myself room to dig and load the barrow. As soon as I had created enough circulation-space, I intended to use the dumper. However, not only did I have to make space for the dumper to manœuvre, but there was a small ravine between where it now stood and the site of the excavation. My initial 'fill' task was therefore to level this gully.

The hard clay and gravel might have been difficult to extract, but it was excellent fill. At the end of that first week I was able to drive the dumper down the remaining stretch of road, over where the ravine had been. We were ready to start the second cut.

Irene stayed away from the site during that week of back-breaking toil and I was pleased that she had other things to do, things which she regarded as just as important. Christmas was only three weeks away, and she was not going to forgo the seasonal festivities: she was going to give a party. Corry Point Bungalow was the ideal place for one: it was spacious and its beautifully mellowed pine-lining gave it a character made for Christmas. During the week Irene discreetly mentioned the party to a number of the locals we had come to know over years and whom we regarded as our friends. For me, the thought of a week's baking conjured up rewards equal to my labour of digging, but we knew full well that they were likely to say 'Ach! We don't bother with Christmas. It's too much coming so close on the Hogmanay!'

Irene had nevertheless worked hard at her Christmas preparations despite the late start, but when I arrived home on the Friday afternoon I was disturbed to find her upset and tearful.

"No one's coming to the party! They can't abide Christmas!"

"Wait till they hear about your Christmas decorations!"

Irene let out a wail: "We didn't bring them! They are still in store."

I suddenly had an idea. "What about if we go south for the holiday and stay with your parents?"

"Yes, I'd like that."

When Irene told the very same friends of our intention to go south they were horrified lest we would not be back in time for *their* festivities. It would take time before we understood the full significance of the New Year to the Scots.

A little over two weeks before we went south a change in the weather brought summer-like conditions. Day after day I picked and shovelled, whilst Irene drove the dumper. If I did not shovel fast enough, she would jump down and help. It was a pleasure to be out in the open air, with the smell of the earth and the tang of the sea and the unreality of summer in the middle of winter. With such glorious conditions we returned to our midday onsite picnics again. It was undoubtedly one of the most productive periods so far, and certainly one of the most satisfying. In three weeks from the day I had started with the wheelbarrow we had, incredibly, excavated nearly two hundred tons of material.

We returned to the village on the thirtieth to find the north-west covered in a thin layer of snow. It was hard not to say that it looked like Christmas but, now that we had to learn to look forward rather to the New Year, Christmas might never be the same again. The dry powdery snow stayed put, and the next evening we walked into the village under a clear starry sky.

Of several invitations from friends who wished us to let the New Year in with them, we had chosen Dinah and George Lawson's. We thought it was appropriate that we should be with our longest-standing friends, and Dinah, the warden of the Youth Hostel, was possibly the very first person that we had met in the area. Moreover, her house was one of the special meeting places in the village – nothing to do with the house, and all to do with the personalities of the occupants. Dinah had been born and raised in that most Highland of all places, Achiltibuie, a straggling collection of crofts and cottages looking out over the strand to the Summer Isles a mile offshore, the whole area steeped in the magic of the west coast. What better to spend an evening such as this than with people who are part of that magic.

Quite a few friends were already gathered and more were arriving as the all-important time drew near. Five minutes to twelve and an anxious look amongst the gathering to make absolutely sure that everyone had a whisky or at least something in a glass. George was in the kitchen tuning the wireless and a silence fell upon the assembly. The BBC announcer spoke the last few words of the old year, and everyone waited expectantly. Then the chimes of Big Ben would ring out, followed closely by a Gaelic chorus of 'Bliadhna math ur, Slainth ma vore' – 'A good new year and great health'.

The warmth and sincerity of hand-shaking and hugging has to be experienced. There is no other way to convey the depth of emotion at this special moment of the year. The nearest would be to say that it is like welcoming a close friend home from an extended voyage at sea. Everyone is so anxious that the year that has just arrived will be the best ever. After a while, when everyone is satisfied that they have conveyed a personal new year's greeting to every individual present, it's time for the feast.

This is never a set meal but a running buffet that is replenished throughout the night. There will be many comings and goings as guests leave to visit other friends, and those who have been elsewhere arrive with their salutations. Sooner or later someone will produce a fiddle or an accordion, and the songs will begin: Calin Marunsa, The Waters of Kylesku and perhaps The Dark Island. That last usually brings a tear to the eye of older members of the gathering, for Hogmanay is not only a time to look ahead but also to remember the way it was long ago. It's almost always a signal for someone to tell a story. Callum calls across the room.

"Mind the time, George, when Sandy put the clock back?"

"Ach, that I do, but tell it again if you've a mind."

Calum is sitting next to Irene and as he is pretty certain Irene has not heard the tale before he addresses it to her as much as to the others – who know it off by heart anyway.

"Well now, Irene, it was like this on a Saturday night some years ago at Achiltibuie, when the Ross's kept the Summer Isles Hotel. There was a good gathering in the bar and the whisky was slipping down a fair treat. The songs and stories were coming one after another. I never enjoyed myself so much ever." Callum laughs as he recalls the merrymaking, then turns serious as he looks again to Irene.

"Now there was a problem in all of this, for it was a Saturday night and things would have to stop sharp at eleven o'clock. The morrow was the Sabbath, and it would not be fitting to be out on such a jaunt on the Lord's day."

The assembly looks grave as the story-teller gets into his stride. Those who know the tale or who may have been there on that memorable night, it's important that they relive the part to the full: it encourages the story-teller to add even more emphasis to his words and maybe a few new embellishments.

"Now I sees young Sandy behind the bar getting fidgety and wondering how he's going to call time with such uproarious goings on. And then I see, through the corner of my eye, Sandy taking a quick look round. Then in a flash I see him slip the hand of the bar-clock back ten minutes. I thought I saw him do it again, but I was not sure, and maybe the clock had been fast in the first place. The stories, songs and the drinking went on with everyone quite oblivious to time, but I had my eye on the clock and it was coming up eleven. All of a sudden a powerful voice boomed.

" 'Stop, stop, stop'. 'Stop this nonsense at once'.

"The loud voice was unmistakably that of big Huw. He stood there, a giant in a rough tweed suit. A formidable man now, holding his pocket-watch at arm's-length and glowering at Sandy.

" 'Man, your clock is wrong!' he bawled. 'It's already the Sabbath.'

"Red-faced, Huw turned to run for the door. Sandy shouted after him in the drawl of a Highland preacher.

" 'No use running. The Lord has already seen you.'

"Huw turned and, with a fierce expression in his eyes, and his voice shaking with emotion, he called out:

" 'Sandy, it's not the Lord that afears me. It's my sister Minor. She'll kill me!'"

Everyone claps. Well perhaps not everyone – the ending may have been a bit insensitive for one or two.

And so the festivities went on. Something after one o'clock we were persuaded to join a small party bent on visiting as many of the other meeting houses as could be managed. People whom we had never met before greeted us at these places with such enthusiasm that we might have been relatives or at least lifelong friends. We would stay a while to hear another song and more reminiscing about the old days as if they had gone forever. For Irene and me this seemed like the old days still, for we had never previously encountered such a community bond. People spoke passionately about acquaintances fifty or more miles away as if they were next-door neighbours, and would then add proudly that they were fifth cousins. We'd have yet another sandwich or a slice of black bun. 'Better take a wee bite,' a hostess would whisper, and add with a hint of disapproval of those who had ignored her counsel: '…or the drink might get to you.'

On we would go again, losing one set of revellers and joining another. At least half the villagers seemed to be trooping in and out of one or other of the houses as in a boisterous dance in which partners continually change. It must have been well past four in the morning when we decided that we simply could not go much further. At a moment when the street seemed empty of people we set out on the thin crunchy snow to walk the two miles home to Corry Point, under an even brighter, starrier sky than we had started out under.

Highlanders are not the only ones to have longstanding traditions. My father used to say: 'Start the year as you mean to go on', and that meant getting up early on the first morning It was also a tradition in our household that you had a good breakfast on New Year's Day. Somehow, despite the long night, we were up after a couple of hours and, in honour of our own traditions, had bacon, sausage, eggs, tomato and mushrooms for breakfast. We had nearly finished our first meal of the year when a knock at the front door startled us.

"Who on earth could that be?"

I got up and went to investigate. A young man of perhaps twenty or so stood out in the snow clutching a near empty bottle of whisky. I opened the door and as he stepped in he greeted me with 'A happy new year!' He greeted Irene similarly.

"You'll take a wee dram with me?"

Irene guided him to the fire which was just beginning to blaze. He had no top-coat on despite the cold outside, and we presumed he had been out or at least in and out of houses throughout the night. A wee dram did not seem quite appropriate with our bacon and eggs, so we persuaded our guest to have some breakfast and a cup of coffee. We learned that he was Jimmy Burns and his father was a gamekeeper on the other side of the village. Jimmy was our first new-year visitor and we were delighted to see him. After taking the merest sensation of whisky to seal the occasion he went on his way. No doubt far into the year he kept going until his bottle was empty.

The New Year is usually a week's holiday, but the greetings go on for ages after the event. Indeed I've been so greeted as late as March.

CHAPTER EIGHTEEN

Gelignite and Sun-Dogs

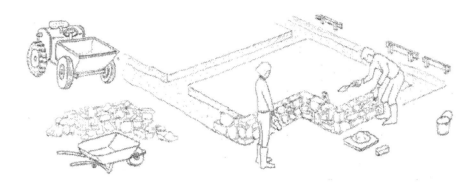

The thin powdery snow had almost gone when we resumed working at the site. It had soon been sent packing by just a little warmth from the wintry New Year sunshine. We had not quite finished the excavating, but enough soil and stone had been cleared to start working on the house-foundations.

Before we could do that, however, we had one last problem to sort out. In the final section of the road we had built there were two formidable outcrops of jagged rock. The dumper had just managed to clamber over these obstacles, but the lorries which would be delivering the sand and gravel would have no chance. There was also another large rock, the size of a dining table, standing in the way of an extension I wanted to make to a small tool-shed that I had put up soon after we had arrived. One way and another, I knew that there was nothing for it but to find someone with blasting experience and access to gelignite, but we urgently needed advice. Surely someone on the road-squad would know somebody who could come to our aid? We passed their little depôt whenever we went to the village, and as we did so late one afternoon, we noticed that the usually locked door was still open.

"Not much sign of life," Irene observed. "I'll go and have a look. Maybe there's someone."

There was. Eddie Fields was mending a puncture in his bicycle-wheel. Eddie was not a local – in fact he was from Reading, which was where he had met Sheila, a very pretty Ullapool girl. They had married and returned to the Highlands a couple of years before. I had first met Eddie within a few hours of his arrival in Ullapool. I don't think I have ever been so impressed in any young man's initiative as I was that day. I well remember working in the cramped engine-room of a our small fishing craft, *Rosebud,* beached in the mouth of the Ullapool river, about a mile's walk out of the village. I heard a call and looking up through the hatch I saw a slim young man, perhaps in his early twenties. I remember particularly that he was wearing drainpipe trousers and a bootlace tie. He introduced himself as Eddie; he said that he had just arrived on the bus and that the driver (whom he thought was named Kenny) had told him of me, and had thought I might have a job going.

I asked him where he lived and was astonished when he said that he was not sure. He explained that he had only just arrived in the town with his new wife. She had gone up to see her mother but he, having heard that jobs were hard to come by, had given priority to seeking me out. I was very sorry to have to disappoint him: I was only on holiday at the time and indeed was returning to Shropshire a couple of days later.

So we knew Eddie, and here he was in the Council depôt.

"I need a bit of advice, Eddie," I said.

"'Then you've come to the right place," he said, always sure of himself. "What can I do for you?"

I explained about the rocks and the need for blasting.

"Know just the chap! Davie. Any chance of a bit of part time, I'm available Saturdays."

What could I say but — "Come on up this Saturday, if you're free."

The following Saturday, as soon as it was light, Eddie was there. He eyed up the rock which was barring my shed extension.

"That'll be no problem," I said. "We can deal with it at the same time as the other rocks."

"No!" said Eddie. "I can do better than that. I've seen Davie and he can come and have a look late Monday afternoon. We finish at four, and I'll come myself then. Now if I bore a hole down through that rock today, and Davie brings a stick of gelly on Monday, you'll see how he performs."

"That's great," I said, cautiously. "But how are you going to bore a hole down through the rock?"

"With a hammer and chisel. How else?"

Eddie and the Council Depôt were a great resource.

On the Monday afternoon we heard the Council-truck stop at the top of the drive and when I walked up, there was Eddie and a rather underfed, thin-faced chap with dark curly hair and a bit of a stoop Eddie introduced him.

"This is Davie and he's got the goods."

I hoped that 'the goods' were not the dynamite, as Davie had a continual cascade of glowing ash falling from a cigarette in the corner of his mouth; but they were.

Said Davie: "Eddie said there's a shed so we borrowed this just in case."

He was referring to a great wire blast-net that they were dragging down the drive. At last they heaved the unwieldy net over the boulder and pegged it down. Eddie pointed out to

Davie the hole that it had taken him the whole of Saturday to bore.

"Ach, yer needn't have bothered," said Davie as a slick of hot ash fell from his cigarette onto the stick of gelignite in his hand. "We'll just stick this here on the side of the boulder and slice it off. Won't touch the shed, and if the rock shatters it'll all come this way."

Davie blew on his cigarette and casually placed the glowing ember on the end of the fuse.

"Come on – time to get out!"

Eddie grabbed me by the arm and we dashed for cover. Davie sauntered behind us, and only just made it to the shelter of an embankment before there was an almighty bang. Smoke was everywhere, and in the gathering dusk it was difficult to see what had happened. We waited a moment longer and then walked down. We stood in silent disbelief. The shed had completely vanished and the boulder remained.

"Thought to myself at the time the whole stick was too much. Half a stick would have been plenty. Ah well, you live and learn."

Davie's talk was pure bravado: the poor chap was shaking like a leaf. We bundled him into the Landrover and took off to the Caledonian Hotel where the solace of three large whiskies helped to ease our various states of mind.

At this time Davie was between jobs and, despite everything, I took him on. He had a purposeful way of going about things, and I quite liked him. He rarely spoke and was, I suppose, a loner. His work gave him little or no opportunity for conversation – he had to work alone, with the clatter of his rock-drill, and when he stopped to charge the drillings with explosives it was hardly a situation that encouraged companions. In the evening he usually sat solitary in the bar with his whisky and the inevitable cigarettes, escaping from the day's incessant noise and dust.

We hired a compressor and rock-drills and, as Davie had a blasting licence, we were able to obtain a supply of gelignite. In less than two weeks he had drilled more than one hundred holes in the bedrock that lay in the path of the road to the house site. Some were only inches deep, others feet deep. As each hole reached the required depth he would blow the dust out with the airline and then stuff moss into the top of the drilling to keep the dirt out. The rock, with so many little tufts of regularly spaced greenery, was an unusual sight. Charging the holes is a matter (I hesitate to call it a science) of hoping that you know exactly how much gelignite will be required. At each hole Davie would check his depth and then, as if it were candy, break off a suitable piece of explosive. Carefully he would insert the tiny copper-clad detonator into the soft explosive and then, taking care not to lose the end of the wire, he would lower it into the drilled hole and hold it in place with a small piece of clay.

At last the great day came to set off the charge. He was using delayed fuses so that the explosion would move progressively across the face of the rock, creating a giant shockwave designed to remove only as much material as would facilitate the new road-level.

When I was certain when exactly Davie intended to set off the charge I went down to the village to seek Sergeant Grant's advice.

"Three o'clock? That's fine. I'll stop the traffic at the village side, and you do likewise on the Inverness side."

At three we were all in position. Davie had trailed his wires up to near where the Sergeant stood. I could see them from my position about a quarter of a mile east and, at a prearranged shrill of a whistle, Davie pushed the plunger. We saw the first rocks begin to rise, and then the sound-equivalent of World War Three engulfed our ears. Salvo after salvo; the rock shot into the loch, sending up great plumes of water. The noise reverberated around the mountain for what seemed an age and rumbled on like distant thunder. I could not believe that our little road had been the source of such a symphony.

When Davie was quite satisfied that it was at last safe, we crept back to examine the works. Nothing could have been more satisfactory. What was left of the rock lay neatly piled along the line of the track. It was a masterpiece of skill and experience. Even the Sergeant was impressed, and we celebrated the event in the way one does in the Highlands.

The next day being a Saturday, Eddie came down to the site in the morning to help clear the rubble. By the end of that afternoon Irene was able to drive the Landrover right up to where our front door would soon be situated. It was another milestone, for with this access secure, we could actually start building.

We had been very lucky with the weather: it had been so mild that every day now we expected to be overtaken by winter storms. Even the old respected weather-prophets were at a loss to say why the winter had been so open. Some thought that the early snow over the tops had had a settling effect, but the other sages said that they had seen the mild weather coming in the sun-dogs. Unfortunately, as they had each seen something different it was rather difficult to be confident about their method, but the sundogs themselves are an interesting phenomenon. A sun-dog is created by a patch of ice-crystals in the upper atmosphere and looks like a tiny portion of a rainbow – a selection of the spectrum. It is not uncommon, but it generally goes unnoticed. However, once you have seen one you tend to be on the look-out for them, and they become easier to find.

As for the principles on which the old weather-prophets based their forecasts, they were not very logical, but on the other hand these observations have been going on for centuries and more often than not, in my experience, they prove correct. Interpretation is mainly a matter of the position of the dog in relation to his master the sun. If the dog is to the lower left, it is said to be obediently trailing its master; if to the lower right, then it is leading its master: these sightings are favourable. A dog above the sun is apparently not so good a portent. Sometimes the dog is so wayward that it is not anywhere near its master – it might even be in the opposite realms of the heavens – in which case, watch out! Additionally, and unfortunately for the lay-forecaster, the colour of the dog and the time of the year also have to be taken into consideration.

On holiday years earlier, I had observed one autumn evening a sun-dog of a deep and sickening green hue in the eastern sky. I could not wait to seek out Murdocan Macleod, one of the last great exponents of the art; I described what I had seen, and exactly when and where. "O man, o man," he moaned, shaking his head slowly from side to side. "Snow! Just into the new year, and plenty of it, deep, real deep." It started to snow in the first week of the following year and went on until a depth of fifteen feet was recorded in some parts of the Highlands.

This year, no such prediction was around, but everyone expected the mild spell to break. Our work was going smoothly: with three months gone, we had reached the halfway stage exactly to plan. The remaining task was of course building the house itself, and that was far more sensitive to the weather than the jobs so far had been. Bad weather before we got the roof on would be a real nuisance, but getting that done in time seemed a forlorn hope when we hadn't even started construction yet. As I lay awake during the early hours, everything seemed doubly urgent. It all went round and round in my head. I listened to the wind, trying to detect a change in its direction, but the steady blow remained from the south-east.

I was up before dawn. Today was a significant point in the project. Today we would cut the first sod, as it were. If we had been on a greenfield site we might have had a little ceremony but, as we had already spent three months building the road and excavating the site, the novelty of digging holes was wearing a bit thin. Nevertheless, as soon as there was a flicker of light in the sky, I started digging the foundation trenches. I told myself as I toiled that this was the last of the digging – well, that's if I didn't count the drainage-works, and I told myself that as they weren't yet in the plan, they didn't count.

At lunch-time I heard a lorry coming gingerly down our new road. I had ordered sand, gravel and cement in good time, and here came the gravel. Ian Ross had a small fleet of tipper lorries just the right size for awkward places like ours, and he treated the job as no more difficult than a delivery straight off a proper road onto a tarmac drive. In the space of ten minutes we had five tons of gravel, our very first building materials.

Ian did not hang about. "I'll try to get your load of sand here before dark," he said.

The days were now perceptibly beginning to lengthen and I was taking full advantage of the extra daylight, working on until dusk, but all the same the nearest sand quarries were some forty miles away. There was no sign of Ian, and I had almost given up and was already putting the tools away, when I heard the now-familiar sound of the tipper picking its way down from the road.

"Said I'd make it! Get your cement tomorrow."

In the gathering dusk he and I examined my day's progress.

"Hardly ready yet. Sure you want the cement tomorrow?"

"Yes!" I said confidently.

"Oh well," he said, as if in agreement. "Best get it in before the snow comes!"

During the hard work of the day, I had hardly given the weather a thought, but now it once more began to crowd my mind.

The cement duly arrived as promised. We had two more fine-weather days, days of frantic activity, which saw our concrete foundations laid. It was yet another milestone and one which we should have paused to celebrate, but so paranoid had I become about the weather that in the last glimmer of the fading light I dug two drainage ditches from the foundations out over the bank in front of our embryo building.

'There,' I said to myself. 'Rain, snow, whatever; at least the foundations will not get flooded!'

It was dark as I made my way wearily on foot up the steep incline. Irene used to come down to the site on most days, but as the afternoons had become colder she had retreated to the bungalow. This meant that by the time I arrived home there was a blazing log-fire and, on the table, a traditional Highland refreshment in my favourite tumbler. How I looked forward to that moment after a hard day's toil! Some days Irene would leave the Landrover so that I might drive back, at other times I would walk. On this particular evening I was walking.

The last section of our road was particularly steep, so when I reached the main road I stopped for a while, primarily to catch my breath. I was also however trying to get my bearings, as I had never experienced a night so dark. Despite the fact that this road bore the grand name A835, it was no more than a single-track lane with two strips of tarmac for wheels to run on and grass everywhere else. Tufts of grass grew in the centre of the roadway, and the verges were high. It looked more like a railway than one of the county's main highways. An occasional iron-post topped with a white diamond marked passing places. The odd formation of the road was a blessing that evening. I just walked on the tarmac and if my boots touched grass I simply altered course accordingly.

After a few hundred yards I reached the high ground. From here I could look back to the sparkling lights of the village. Although they provided no illumination to help me on my way they at least seemed friendly and I felt less alone. I lingered there for a while. The air was unusually warm, and there was only the faintest breeze from the south-west. South-west! The wind had veered after being in the south-east for weeks. By the time the lights of home had come into view the breeze had strengthened and the temperature had noticeably dropped. A few spots of wintry rain whipped by in the wind. The weather had changed at last.

It was a wild night. Gale-force winds and rain battered the window-panes, and the fire smoked. I could not help but worry that we were going to face an enforced delay. I had no useful indoor work to occupy such time. The countless sketches of future projects I was given to making would do little to assist on the practical front. By morning the gale had eased, but the wintry rain continued to fall. We could hear the roar in the nearby burn as the water fought with the boulders that impeded its raging progress from the rain-soaked mountains and moorlands towards the sea. All around us, the bare twigs of the birch-trees dripped, dripped, dripped. Wherever the level of the ground changed, small rivulets made miniature waterfalls. At least it was not snowing.

I have always been told (if I have not always believed) that everything happens for the best. I had a sudden inspiration. There was *one* thing I could do, despite the rain. We were determined to use as much natural material as possible in the new house, and to this end I had decided to build the foundation-walls in local stone. Now that the concrete foundations were complete, the next job (weather permitting) was constructing those walls to the damp-course level, and then, in the fullness of time, the logs would be laid on top of them. But before I could build the walls, I needed the stone. All the good stone on the site had already been used to build the huge retaining wall at the road entrance. But the road-verges north and south of the village were littered with masses of just the stone I sought. Why not put our lately redundant lorry to use, and go out in this wretched weather and collect a load or two?

This sudden brainwave not only gave a much-desired continuity to my labours; it actually saved me a great deal of time. The stone I discovered on this expedition was far superior to any still unpicked from our own land. At the time I hardly enjoyed being thoroughly soaked, frozen and covered in mud, but at the end of the day I had several tons of perfect building stones stacked on the platform of the old Bedford, and made my way the few miles back towards Ullapool. Somehow, I had managed to steer this same vehicle, loaded to the gunwales, over three thousand miles, back and forth from Bridgnorth. Surely I hadn't gone soft after four months of muscular work in the Highlands? I was baffled by how hard I found the short trip.

"It's nature's way of telling you to slow down," Irene explained in her usual logical way.

Her advice to rest was enforced at least for a time, as the next day was the Sabbath. However, I was so pleased with my stint as a stone-gatherer that I could hardly wait to start building. Moreover, the rain had stopped and the sun had reappeared through gaps in the cumulo-nimbus cloud drifting in from beyond the Outer Hebrides.

As if to reinforce the message that things always happen for the best, the sun was still shining on the Monday, and everywhere began to dry up after the storm. By the time Irene came down to the site with the coffee it was like spring. The setting-out lines were already strung from the corner-profiles, mortar was on the mortar-boards and a sample corner had been built to damp-proof height for Irene's approval, something she quickly gave.

"It's beautiful!" she enthused.

She was so taken with this first visible sight of the house that she stayed on as my labourer. The stone was unbelievably easy to build with, unlike that on our site which was an agglomeration of totally irregular shapes, each one of which would have required trimming before it could be laid. The stone I had brought in from north of the village was a sedimentary slate that had broken up at a lower level maybe millennia ago, and had since lain unprotected from the weather. Much of it was a dark grey, almost like black house-bricks, with edges beautifully rounded, worn smooth by countless centuries of exposure to the elements. Irene soon got the hang of this building in random courses, and began to anticipate my requirements. What I had dreaded might take weeks took only five days. Maybe things are always for the best.

We had not seen Mac or Jenny for perhaps three weeks. In fact we had been staying clear of them in the hope that the fence-dispute between Mac and the Major might be resolved in the meantime. We passed Altt-a-Choire daily, and every day we would see the fence which so upset Mac, and every day we hoped to see Willie the fencer re-erecting the posts and mesh along a more acceptable line. But it was not to be. The Major, a man with a strong belief in getting on with the job oneself, was genuinely interested in our progress, and we saw him regularly. I never mentioned the question of Mac and Jenny's fence and was taken aback when on one of his visits he suddenly came out with:

"Just had words with that damn fellow at Altt-a-Choire, moaning about a fence which he claims is in the wrong place or something. Told him in no uncertain terms, boundary was set out by a chartered land surveyor, its position is correctly on the estate land and there it stays. There's a principle at stake – can't have the likes of that sort of chap throwing his weight about, what, what?"

I could see the Major was as affected by the incident as Mac himself, and I was relieved when the Major said he had an idea.

"Can't go on like this. I put an idea to him. Told him you're a surveyor and that if he asked your opinion you'd soon put him right."

"What did he say to that?" I enquired with considerable misgiving.

"Just walked away and left me standing there."

This was serious. Just how serious, we were soon to find out. We saw Jenny picking her way down our steep drive, now rutted by the lorry and the wet weather over the last weekend. All she said was:

"Mac was wondering when you intended to move those logs. He wants to work on that part of the garden now, that's all. Perhaps you'd call in some time and let him know what your plans are?"

"No point in putting it off," Irene said.

Somewhat apprehensively we popped in our way home that day. Mac almost pounced upon me as we entered the little porch which led to the kitchen and which, thanks to their thoughtless builder, was now their main entrance.

"Saw your friend the Major this morning," he began, none too promisingly to my ears. "One of these days I'm going to have to pull rank on that fellow. Do you know what the cheeky beggar suggested? Suggested that if I put this fence business to you, you would soon tell me that he was right and that I was wrong!"

My mind went blank. I could not think of anything sufficiently diplomatic to be worth saying, but I was saved when the door burst open and in came their son, home from University for the week end.

"How's the house going?" he cheerily demanded of me.

"Oh fine," I said, my mind still on his father's fencing problems.

"Just let me know when you want the logs brought round," he said impervious to my preoccupation. "Ready anytime you are!"

"What about tomorrow?" I ventured.

"Yes, fine! My brother will be home later on this evening, and he can help me."

"What time shall I bring the lorry down?" I enquired.

He thought for a moment. "Better not make it before ten o'clock. There's a few lads I want to see in the village a bit later on, if you understand my position."

I said that yes, of course I understood, and was grateful for his help; but I was not sure whether his evening out was to escape from the fence problems.

CHAPTER NINETEEN

How to Make Your Own Log House, Part Two

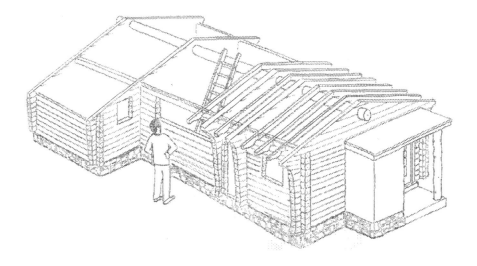

Each stage of the work had produced its own excitement, week by week. There had been the day when we had gingerly lowered the dumper over the edge of the road; there had been the laying of the first stones of our great retaining wall, and the first time that Irene had driven down our driveway. Later, after the blasting, there was the time when we had first been able to drive right to the very spot where one day we would step into our new home. And then there had been Irene's joy on the day she saw the first corner of stonework rising from the ground, after we had laboured so long to produce the level standing for the building.

Now progress was measured day by day. What words could describe how we felt about this daily materialization of what had once existed only in our dreams? At ten-thirty on Saturday morning I edged the lorry down Mac's drive. True to their promise, there were the two rather bleary-eyed boys and our great pile of logs. Joinery, rafters and joists had migrated from their winter resting-place, ready now to be transported to our site. There, over the next few days, they were assembled into a house the like of which may never have been seen in the Highlands before.

All those days back in Shropshire when we had worried about the trees being felled when in fact I had not even placed the order! The days on which Mick and I had struggled with the machining, and the hours Irene had put into trying to arrange transport! All were now only memories, and like all memories they had mellowed with age. The pain and distress ease, and successes are magnified into triumphs: or so it was that morning, as we began to erect the logs.

It took the rest of that day to get the first timbers level and square on the damp-proof course, but our patience all those months earlier, when we had crafted each log for its final position, had its reward when we began the actual assembly. We were both staggered by the speed with which each component just slotted in. There was, obviously, a predetermined order in which everything had to be fitted together. When the components had been loaded on the lorry at Bridgnorth we had taken great care to place every item in an exact sequence in order to ensure that we did not have any problems retrieving them precisely as needed. Alas! the off-loading at Altt-a-Choire, the reloading back to our lorry that Saturday and then the final off-loading at the site had conspired to produce a degree of disorder. I spent my time building the structure, whilst Irene went searching for the next and all-too-often wayward timber. But these were the only delays we had at this stage.

Previously of course we had only seen the log walls and partitions laid out on the ground, but now they were rising vertically. What was particularly pleasing was to see the interlocking corners taking shape, and creating a structure which was as strong as a fortress. Incredibly we reached the window-cill level on only the day after we had brought the logs in.

Working with the logs was such a pleasure. Although they were now considerably drier than they had been at the sawmill, the weight of a single length still buckled your knees. It was nevertheless addictive work, building a sort of domino tower – except that no way would this tower ever be knocked down. Much as we would like to have worked into the now lighter evenings, tiredness and backache would get the better of us, and so we would make our way back to Corry Point happily forecasting where we would get to on the morrow. Usually we did get there.

I will never forget the moment when we dropped in the windows with their glass already fixed. There is no moment like it in building your own house – that first window of the new home framing the scene that will be yours for as long as you live in that place. And what a view we had! On that still, bright afternoon somewhere between winter and spring, the loch was mirror-calm, as it so often was in the latter part of the day. Far out on the Otter Bank, a favourite fishing mark, a local fisherman was hand-lining for haddock; beyond, on the opposite shore and up the dark hillside to the mountain tops, the setting sun had turned the pure white snow to pink icing sugar. I tried hard not to think of the days to come when we would be out there fishing. It was a beautiful thought, but it would have to remain a thought for the time being, as we had more important things to attend to for now.

By lunchtime the following day we reached the eaves, and before the evening closed upon us the whole log structure was complete, including the great ridge-poles which when they were freshly cut Mick and I together had not been able to lift. We had now slid them into the building; with the aid of pulley-blocks and a derrick pole they were the last members to be put in place before starting on the roof.

'Please!' I kept saying to myself, 'just two more fine days and you can send whatever weather you have a mind to send.'

By the Friday the clear sky had given way to dark clouds. The previously calm surface of the loch was ruffled by a fitful breeze that every now and then produced cats'-paws amongst the wavelets. But despite its ominous appearance the day produced no more than a few isolated spots of rain. With everything pre-cut it was as usual not difficult to get all the rafters and the eaves-detailing in place. That was as far as I could get without Eddie's help. Tomorrow he would be here.

Under the Scottish Building Act, roofs have to be watertight independently of whatever is intended as the final roof-covering, be it slate, tiles or whatever. To achieve this doubly protective state, boarding is laid over the rafters and a stout waterproof felt-covering is fixed in a manner quite as good as if the felt were the final watertight barrier. To make sure the felt stays in place a network of battens and tile-laths is fixed in preparation for the final finishing material. It was normal to use ordinary timber boarding for this first covering, but I had decided on something different. STRAMIT was a very ingenious roof-boarding material composed entirely of compressed and bonded straw, two inches thick and covered on both sides in a stout shower-proofed paper. The sheets were large and heavy, but had the great advantage of being easy to fix and thus allowing large areas to be covered in a short time. This was just as well, for as Eddie and I worked, yesterday's isolated spots of rain became more frequent. We fought with the felt as we unrolled short sections in a rising wind that at times threatened to pitch us off the roof. Hurriedly we nailed the battens down as the spots of rain became ever more frequent and heavier. Quickly we gauged the tile-laths into their allotted positions as Irene brought up fresh supplies.

"Come on, Eddie!" I urged. "We have got to get it finished before the rain gets worse." I heard myself repeating the weather-lore that goes: "Long foretold, long last. Short notice, soon passed."

It was raining steadily as we finally hammered the last of the roof-nails home and climbed back down the ladder. It was only mid-afternoon but already half-dark under the lowering skies. The mountains above the far shore had vanished in the mist, and small waves on the loch had breaking white tops. The mournful cries of the sea-birds, disturbed by the growing storm, were now almost drowned out by the rain battering on our new roof. What a week, what anxieties, what satisfaction!

Day after day the rain fell, but what did it matter? Occasionally the mist would clear from the hills and it would seem that an end to the wet period was in sight, then the mist would re-gather and down would come the rain again. Mostly the rain was light, sometimes no more than a wet mist which on first contact seemed nothing to worry about until five minutes later you noticed that you were soaked. What did it matter? The rain only added to our satisfaction: we worked away in comfort, snug inside, completing our home. It is all too commonplace to detail here; suffice it to say that whatever the trade, we took it in our stride, as the wind blew outside and the rain streamed down the window panes.

It was not all hard work and no play. The new year saw the beginning of the social season. There were many private supper-parties, but the real highlights of the winter season were the fortnightly dinner-dances arranged by the various village organizations. Some of these organizations were active only now, vying with each other to provide the most splendid gathering, and there was always great anticipation to see which group had drawn which date. The principal members of each organization were responsible for the draw, which was done in an apparently open and above-board manner, although I always suspected a little horse-trading – somehow either the Sailing Club or the Badminton Club always opened the season.

One facet of these functions was open to very significant enterprise on the part of the sponsoring organization: the choice of band. Without question it had to be a top-class Highland dance band, but the organizations had to compete to engage a suitable group, not only with each other within Ullapool, but also with other organizations across the Counties. Woe betide the dilatory society! And the expense was considerable. The nearest band was nearly fifty miles distant and many others had to come more than a hundred miles, and what with travelling expenses and overnight accommodation, it all added up. The village favourite was undoubtedly the Strathpeffer Dance Band. They were excellent musicians with every traditional Scottish tune at their fingertips, and in Eck Wilson they had a brilliant compère guaranteed to make any night a wonderful occasion. Almost as popular was the Wick Band or, as they liked to be known, the Wick Broadcasting Band. They were also brilliant musicians, but maybe they were a little too formal.

The two bigger hotels took turns to stage the events. This was not only so that the business might be equally divided; as these occasions usually involved not fewer than one hundred and fifty guests, and as in the off-season neither hotel had sufficient staff to cope, the sensible custom of the respective managers had always been to pool their resources (including the staff). Hugh Grant at the Caledonian and Brian Maglennon at the Royal Hotel were the very best of friends, and both organized these events with great flair. However, there was a considerable professional rivalry between them, to the definite advantage of those attending.

It was a delight to find that the highest standards of etiquette were always maintained, and the admission-tickets were printed on large gilt-edged cards in the manner of an invitation to attend. They were good enough to display proudly on one's mantelpiece. Dress was always formal: most of the men wore full Highland evening-wear and their ladies long tartan skirts and fine lace blouses. Irene would go similarly attired, donning a 'permissible' tartan (having no clan attachment). Her favourite was Black Watch. The few men (including myself) who were in a similar position wore normal evening dress.

This particular year, our first living in the area, the honour of starting the season had fallen to the Sailing Club. They had secured the ever- popular Strathpeffer Band, and the venue was the Caledonian Hotel. This was our first Highland ball, an event to rival a Royal Gala performance, and an occasion that we would never forget, but it was also typical.

Most of the village lived within easy walking distance and on a fine winter evening the streets would be thronged with couples in full Highland dress. The hotel, whichever it was, would be decorated with whatever flowers could be got from Inverness at a reasonable price, made up with a little local foliage and trimmings; there would be a little more lighting than usual. On these nights, the cocktail lounge would overflow into other parts of the hotel, and everyone would take a few drinks before dinner. When dinner was over the Master of Ceremonies would call:

"Take your partners for the eightsome reel!"

This was not perhaps the best dance to engage in following a big meal, but it was nevertheless calculated to get everyone on the dance-floor at the start of the evening. While the band quietly played the tune in the background, the stewards would rush around making sure, firstly, that every one was on the floor; secondly, that we were actually grouped in eights; and, finally, that the eights were spaced well apart. It can be an energetic dance. That done, the stewards would scurry to their partners. A moment's pause. Someone nods ready. The band strikes a long chord, the music begins and you're off.

It was a wondrous sight to behold, perhaps best seen from a balcony where you could look down on the dance-steps neatly executed in a whirl of tartan and fine lace. However, observing thus from the outside is one thing. Being in the middle of it for the first time is something else. I had never danced an eightsome reel before, in fact I had hardly ever danced anything other than a quickstep and an old-fashioned waltz. I was at a definite disadvantage, a fact underlined by the roomful of experts around me. That I acquitted myself without undue disgrace was all down to my partner, Mrs Smith, who patiently nursed me through the intricate steps and to whom I will always be grateful.

The excitement of the eightsome is such that no sooner is it over than you are ready to try your hand (or should it be your feet?) at some other dance. Irene, who had a natural dance rhythm, was also getting hooked, but we could not dance with each other as neither of us knew any of the steps. Next was a Highland Schottische, a kind of polka. Then came the Gay Gordons. The name was well-known to us, but the steps were another matter.

At last there is an old-time waltz, and Irene and I can dance together. As we slowly walk back to our seats, the master of ceremonies rises:

"Ladies' choice! Strip the Willow!"

Before I know it, I'm whisked away by Eddie's pretty wife Sheila. It's a vigorous dance with two lines of partners who step their way through a complicated pattern of set moves. By now, and with the aid of a few whiskies, I feel I can dance any dance that's called. I'm amazed when it's the last waltz. Irene and I smooched around the floor with the rest of the assembly, tired, happy, and never more sure that the Highlands was a great place to live and play.

The rain continued day after day, rarely more than a drizzle and more often just a wet mist. A certain amount of outside work could be undertaken but it was limited to jobs where being soaked through with water streaming down your face was no hindrance. We chiefly stayed indoors, and worked on what now had all the signs of a comfortable home. The raised hearth had been completed, made of slate with a herringbone fire-brick back. The chimney of the tall copper smoke-canopy was ready to receive the smoke (or would be once conditions allowed me onto the roof to complete the chimney top – and for that matter to fix the roof tiles). I had laid the beautiful Oregon-pine floors, and we were more than pleased at how its golden coppery sheen brought warmth to the rooms. Now the plumbing was complete: water- and drainage-pipes dived under the bathroom floor and emerged neatly into an outside trench – but as yet they had nowhere to go.

The final destination of the system was clear: Eddie (who now came every Saturday) had been dealing, amongst other things, with the drainage-trenches and the excavation for the septic tank. As I looked out through the misty rain I could see water running down our slopes into these trenches. The whirlpool which had arisen here was an exciting if unwanted feature, but it only temporarily checked the flow.

This was all very entertaining for an onlooker. What concerned me most here however was not the trench-bound river nor even the whirlpool, but the mud from the waterfall. The waterfall overflowed and cascaded down to the shore, where at slack tide a large area was becoming stained with mud. This mud came from somewhere, and my fertile mind had no difficulty in envisaging that our modest excavations for the trenches had become cavernous. Until the rains ceased, there was no way of knowing if I was right, and no amount of speculation would help. I consoled myself with the thought that it was only a matter of time: the drains would be dealt with in due course.

The situation I faced over the water-supply was rather different. A special feature of Creag nan Cudaigean was the lack of a reliable supply of fresh water. Obviously, from the very beginning, this lack had never been far from my mind. Right now what I had was, in the words of the Ancient Mariner: 'Water, water everywhere, but not a drop to drink,' but I knew full well that within a month or two the land would in all probability be dry, the burns reduced to a trickle. The first anglers arriving to fish the rivers would bemoan the fact that there was no water and pray for rain. The problem, which is not peculiar to the Highlands, is that what top-soil there is is so thinly spread over the rock that it offers little or no storage capacity; water collects only where the rock forms natural basins and lochs are formed. Unfortunately we had no nearby loch or suitable burn.

What we needed was a spring. Despite the concern that Mr. Stewart at Dingwall had expressed about the reliability of the marked issue, I had been encouraged to think that a good source must exist nearby, because we were not the first settlers to have thought Creag nan Cudaigean a good place to live. On our initial, fleeting visits to the site it had been so overgrown with scrub and bracken that searching for water had been impossible, and since we had cleared the site, there had been water everywhere. I needed really dry conditions to show up the tell-tale damp patch. If looking for a needle in a haystack is difficult, then I can tell you that trying to locate a tiny spring in a seven-acre site drenched from weeks of rain is impossible. I gave up for the time being. Somewhere, however, I knew that there must be a cool hollow, lush with green moss which, once cleared, would reveal a steady trickle of pure, clear water.

Irene meanwhile had turned her attention to the log-house ceiling – or, more correctly, to the roof-space. The massive ridge-poles and the rafter system are all exposed to view, and are an attractive feature of this kind of building. The beautiful Douglas fir of the rafters had been left in its natural state with only a thin coat of varnish to protect its surface. Between these rafters the smooth underside of the STRAMIT roof-boarding formed ceiling-panels and it was these that Irene was decorating in her favourite colour, a pale Wedgwood blue. The effect of the timber against the blue was stunning. With the rain still pouring down outside, I was adding a touch of this blue to the recess where the Rayburn now stood in the kitchen. Irene came in to see how I was getting on.

"Oh, I can't wait to get a fire going in the cooker and feel the warmth!"

"And have a kettle at the boil all day," I added in a voice that trailed away as the last syllable came out. I realized none of this was possible without water.

CHAPTER TWENTY

A Kettle on the Hob

April arrived, and with it the spring and its soft warm
sunshine. The rains ceased, and gradually the water in the
burns fell to a gentle trickle and the drainage ditches began to
dry out. Skies were blue and for the first time in weeks the
inland peaks were visible, still glistening white with the remains
of the winter's snow. Suddenly it was another world, and if
our progress had faltered during the long period of enforced
indoor activity, now we found new enthusiasm and the energy
to get on and get finished. We were not actually behind with

our program, but circumstances had forced us into an illogical sequence of work.

There was no doubt at all as to where we should channel our efforts on this first day of a belated spring. The interior of the house was almost complete: I had got as far as fixing up the curtain-rails so that Irene could begin work on that part of the project which was exclusively hers. It was only when we saw the curtains being measured that the full extent of the Alice-through-the-Looking-Glass quality of the house dawned upon us: a beautiful copper-canopied fireplace just waiting to have a fire on its hearth, but, beyond the roof level, no chimney; a Rayburn cooker just waiting to be lit and feel the gentle warbling of a boiling kettle upon its hot plate, but no chimney and (I recoiled to think) no water.

The chimneys were my priority. Outdoor work began once more with the last of the stone I had gathered on that very wet day north of the village. The stonework above the roof-level provided just the right aesthetic touch. What a pleasure to be out in spring-weather! And what a difference a couple of days made to the general appearance of the house!

Traditionally a topping-out ceremony is in order at this stage of the work, and so Irene and I sat up on the roof drinking our morning coffee. The warm sunshine was bliss. We looked out over the shimmering waters of the loch to the harbour where the village was going about its normal morning's activities. But there was no time to remain idle for long. The great pile of tiles lying alongside the house had to be brought up onto the roof and fixed in place. It was hard work but easy by comparison with many of the other tasks we had undertaken. Indeed, with the tile-laths already fixed, it was only a matter of placing the tiles in position and clipping them down with a single nail. The ridge tiles were cemented into position atop the roof, and the verges were pointed.

The house was complete.

It was one of the most satisfying moments of the whole process. Suddenly the house looked finished and unaccountably larger as the overhanging eaves and verges emphasized its outline. This effect was especially evident looking down on the property, the view from which it would most often be seen, nestling amongst the trees at the loch-side.

Back to the outstanding problems. You'll remember that water had been cascading down the drainage-trenches towards the whirlpool where the septic tank would eventually be: that torrent had subsided, and finally dried up. Having seen the great clouds of mud staining the sea at each low water, I fully expected to find our trenches ten feet deep and the tank-hole bottomless. I was greatly relieved to find the worst of these fears unfounded. The water had had little effect on the *depth* of the trenches. However, the *sides* had been so undercut that, for example, in the septic-tank excavation, which was more than six feet deep, you could actually take shelter under the overhanging turf. No other constructor of drainage works ever had so much elbow-room, and I took full advantage of the novel situation.

Two weeks into the glorious April spring the end of the project was in sight. Our timetable had been driven by the fact that we had to vacate the Corry Point bungalow (which had been our home for the winter) at the end of April so that the Estate could begin letting it for the summer season. At each excursion between Corry Point and the new log house, we would pack the Landrover with yet a few more of our possessions. We began to see our new home extending its invitation to us to take up residence, but we knew that it is wise, if at all possible, to avoid moving into a property that is still under construction. At the same time we knew that there are of course always things to do even when properties are on the face of things finished.

Irene's precious Rayburn stood in the beautiful kitchen, still unused. The moment when we would light it was almost a daily topic. We sat out in the sun, its rays noticeably increasing their intensity as the weeks passed. But Irene's dreams at times like these were not *always* for the day that the kettle would first sing on the cooker-hob. She had quietly nursed another dream: a large kitchen-garden where at any time of the year there would be an abundant supply of fresh vegetables. It was during one of those lazy sun-drenched lunch-time breaks that Irene began a line of questioning that seemed to be leading up to something although I couldn't think what.

"If the water question was settled, we could move in, couldn't we?"

"Yes…"

"How long would it take to run the water from wherever we eventually decide is the best option?"

"Half an hour, initially. I would only dam up one or other outfall and wedge the pipe into the pool. If it doesn't hold out we can try elsewhere. It's as simple as that. What *will* take time will be the filling of the four-hundred-gallon storage tank. May take a day." I thought that was a fair assessment of the water-problem and Irene seemed satisfied.

"We won't have to watch it filling, will we?"

"No, of course not." The question seemed superfluous.

There was a pause in her questioning, then: "Could you postpone dealing with the retaining wall at the back of the house?"

"Well, yes, of course, if there is something more urgent." Now I knew something was afoot.

"What about if we start the veg garden? We are still in time. They plant late up here. I saw a man in the village yesterday planting potatoes and putting seaweed in the drills and Kenny's hardware has new seeds in stock. Please can we, just a small garden?"

Who could resist such enthusiasm? But I did not give in immediately. That would have been an anti-climax after all Irene's pleading. Secretly I had nursed the same powerful desire to plant some seeds now that the time was right – something to do with past generations of my family having been farmers. Perhaps it is in the genes.

So we eventually agreed that the retaining wall could wait. A new enthusiasm engulfed us as we walked up to an area we had long ago earmarked as the possible site for a garden. All our land had an ideal southern orientation, but it was so undulating and timber-strewn that we had had little choice – especially given that there was no question of cutting down any trees. So we had nominated the only regular, clear piece of land: a section about forty feet square which was level across the site but sloping towards the sea at an angle of about one in four. This steepness had the advantage of achieving naturally what the great Victorian gardeners had sought to do artificially and at great expense: namely to increase the angle of the crops to the sun and thus promote early growth. The slope was also well drained.

There was no visible sign of this plot ever having been cultivated, although as we had noted on our very first visit to the land, there were marks of past workings in small pockets elsewhere. I needed to see what depth of top soil existed in our would-be garden, and so I went down to the newly built tool-shed. (It was newly built because, as you may recall, Eddie's friend Davie had blown up the previous shed when he failed to dynamite that boulder earlier in the year.) The only spade to survive the blast was an incongruously lightweight affair, but it would have to do.

The ground I was testing had previously supported only bracken. A solid mat of roots had accumulated over the decades, or centuries. Irene was in her element, raking clear small patches where I might make trials. To a gardener, the smell of the earth in the afternoon sun was like champagne. I rammed the spade down at the exposed surface of the ground. The flimsy tool shuddered, and left a faint mark. I set the spade squarely at the point where I wished to make a start, took a deep breath and jumped once more on the erring implement. This second effort produced hardly more of an impression than before. Bracken's root-system lies near the surface and is difficult to break up by hand. The problem was not new to me, but this was by far the most difficult I had ever encountered. Irene had by now fetched the sharpest of our pickaxes.

"Have a try with that."

I soon learned that it was no good burying the tool to any depth, as it was impossible to lever it out. The only workable technique was to tackle a few strands at a time. It would take weeks to clear the whole patch in this way. I worked at maybe half-a-dozen tiny patches: at most there was a scant nine inches of unusually dry, sandy topsoil. This was not in the least promising, but it was what we were stuck with. Like all good British workpeople faced with such a challenge, it was time for a cup of tea and a think.

We needed a plan and, as we got as much fun out of making plans as executing them, we did not begrudge the rather extended break.

"What about a day off tomorrow?" I said.

Irene looked incredulous. "Now, look here! It's the first time for ages that I have had an idea, and all you want to do is to run off!"

"Hang on! Hear me out! We need a bit of specialized equipment if we are going to tackle this job. A heavily forged spade for a start, and a mattock."

Irene looked vague.

"You know, one of those pickaxe like tools that have flattened ends. If you can get a start at the bottom of the land it's no problem to pickaxe your way up. We'll need fencing as well, and netting and posts. We can get them from Rose's sawmill at Contin. When we're in Inverness you might like to call in at the nursery: there might be things you can think of. After all, you're in charge of planting. I'm only the garden labourer."

"What a good idea!" Irene was mollified. "We'll start early."

We had no trouble in rounding up all these supplies. On the following day we set to with the same eagerness with which we had begun the work first on our road, and then the log house.

By now Irene was cleaning out the Corry Point house in preparation for our imminent transfer to our new home. I decided that there was no point in the old Bedford remaining any longer at Corry, and so I drove it down to the 'site' (as we still called it). The poor old lorry – the vital link between our former Shropshire home and our new abode – had been good to us. It was now something of an intrusion amongst the wildflowers and delicate green foliage at Creag nan Cudaigean, but its future would have to wait. It certainly owed us nothing: the total expenditure on it – the original cost of the vehicle, tax, insurance and fuel, plus the new platform – was still less than the lowest quotation we'd had from the reluctant hauliers. It wasn't that they had been quoting high because they did not want the work; Irene knew what was fair and what was not from her brief employment in the business.

The mattock proved the perfect tool for breaking up the tangle of bracken root in the new vegetable patch – that and a drain-drag. The drain-drag was an implement quite new to me: it was like a very thick walking stick with four strong metal fingers set at right angles at its end. Working up the slope was easiest as there was less need to bend. I would break up about a square yard, and then hook the drain-drag into the mat and pull. Every yard produced at least a barrow full of debris; it also reduced the depth of the top soil.

Every so often I would pause. I had never felt so at peace with myself. Surely there could be no more beautiful place to be making a garden. It was so quiet. Small birds flitted amongst the surrounding trees and shrubs as they went noiselessly about their nesting duties. Occasionally a robin would drop down at my feet and explore the newly turned earth. As the sun climbed higher and warmer, patches of short grass nibbled by the roe deer and rabbits would slowly turn from a pale fresh green to the most delicate blue, as the speedwell's tiny flower created a magic carpet that would disappear as quickly as it had appeared when the sun went down.

I was just getting well into yet another patch of roots when I heard a softly spoken voice from somewhere behind me.

"Looks like a lot of hard work!"

I turned, startled. A short stocky man stood smiling up at me where I was perched on the slope. I knew the man by sight but had never spoken to him: he was from Achiltibuie and brought the post in daily from that remote area. I simply could not think what he might want to see me about. I climbed down and we shook hands and said the usual things one says when such a surprise meeting takes place. He turned towards where the lorry was just visible amongst the trees.

"Old Bedford's been good to you," he began. "Three loads I heard tell as how you brought up from the south, and now you'll be finished with her I shouldn't wonder?"

I managed a nod but no more before he went on.

"Had my eye on her since you came. Reckon you're wanting rid of her now, so I've come to make you an offer."

He walked over to where the lorry stood, and started a cursory examination with the tyres.

"Not much life left in them."

I felt almost annoyed at this stranger suddenly turning up and telling me things about my vehicle that I already knew, but I mellowed somewhat as he ran his hand over the deck – the deck that Mick and I had hurriedly built when Irene had found the original to have gone rotten.

"Must have cost something to have that done."

I was warming to what I recognized as the subtleties of Highland bargaining, but the comment about cost seemed a bit lax.

"Of course," he went on, "you will have got it back many times over with all the miles you've run up. Does it start ?"

"Yes. The key's in."

Any moment now I would be offered a ridiculous sum, and I was not even sure I wanted to sell. The engine started and ran perfectly. Five minutes later I began to think that my visitor had come just for the pleasure of sitting in the cab and imagining he was out on the open road. It was clear that that was what he was imagining. But I suddenly also sensed that he really did want to buy.

I decided to sell and started mentally preparing myself for the fray. The engine stopped and my would-be purchaser opened up the business with a pile of notes in his hand.

"There! Count it."

"Just tell me what it is," I said as calmly as I could. The sum proved to be greater than I would have asked.

"Take it or leave it," he said. "I'm not haggling."

"Well," I muttered, "I suppose it would save me the trouble of advertising."

"No one will come out here to see an old lorry anyway. So you'll take it then?"

"Yes," I said, with what I hoped was a little reluctance in my voice. "You've a good vehicle there."

"Oh yes, I know. And if you don't mind I'll be on my way. Get the registration book next time I pass. Seems to be enough petrol to get me to the village."

He turned the lorry and tackled the steep drive with more expertise than I had ever acquired.

I don't doubt he was delighted, and beyond doubt so was I. As the lorry moved out towards the village, Irene arrived from the opposite direction with yet another load of our personal bits and pieces. In complete bewilderment she jumped out of the Landrover.

"I've just seen our lorry driving off to the village!" As if I might not know.

"Yes. It's sold."

"Sold?! How much?"

"More than the total outlay of our entire move."

"I can't believe it!"

"It's true, and what's more, he's got a bargain."

I could see that Irene was pleased, for we didn't need the lorry. When the time came for us to think what to do about an income I would not have suggested road-haulage.

Occupying our new home was now the thought uppermost in Irene's mind. Only our overnight things remained at Corry Point. Tomorrow night would be our last there. Over at our new house, surface water still poured down the many ditches that criss-crossed the land but, despite a daily round of all the likely spots, no spring was to be seen.

On this day, Irene climbed up the steep bank above the house to where the profusion of catkins was now at its best, amongst the thickets of sallow. Within moments she came racing back, almost losing her footing as she scrambled down the steep bank.

"The water off the roadside ditch has stopped running!" she gasped.

"Yes, things are drying up nicely."

"No – you don't understand!" she cried in frustrated excitement. "The water at the top by the road has stopped, but it's still running down here!"

The significance of Irene's observation suddenly struck me. There must be a spring somewhere in between. I dropped the mattock, and we climbed as quickly as we could back up to the ditch. There it was! – a bubble of water welling up right in the middle of channel where, until only hours before, its presence had been obscured by the surface-water from the higher ground flowing down and under the road.

Weeks earlier, I had promised Irene that it would only take half an hour to connect a supply to the tank. In fact it took less. We dammed the ditch with turfs just below the spring (which was, luckily, well above the level of our storage-tank), and pushed a pipe through the dam. As the pool filled, muddy water soon began to exit the pipe. Within a few minutes it was running clear, and I was able to make the final connection into the tank.

Everything was happening so quickly: no sooner were we at the tank-side than the inlet began to pour out crystal-clear water. First it just made a pool in one corner; then, spreading out over the bottom of the big tank, it began to rise. The progress was almost imperceptible but we were mesmerized, unable to take our eyes off this simple matter of water filling a tank. How long we watched I'm not sure, but it was soon clear that, as I had forecast, it would take some time to reach a level that would overflow into the service-pipe which ran to the house. It was amazing how the water-supply had, for the moment, taken over our lives to the exclusion of all other things. The wait was going to be some hours, yet we could not settle to other tasks. Every ten minutes or so we would have to go to have another look lest the flow should have stopped.

But it did not stop. The spring was going to bring the lifeblood into our home. It did this at exactly five forty five that evening, when the open tap at the kitchen sink began to run. It gurgled, stopped for a moment whilst air cleared from the line, and then ran steadily. If there is such a thing as a twosome reel then Irene and I danced it; or perhaps it was a jig? Whatever it was we danced it in sheer joy: the last obstacle to our occupation of the house was removed.

I dashed around looking for possible leaks but there were none. As the water rose through the pipework, we heard it trickling into the header-tank in the compartment above the Rayburn. There was a distinct bubbling as the boiler finally filled. Then the ball-valves closed off the pipes, and said 'Enough', and the incoming water finally fell silent.

Irene was hopping about with excitement and a box of matches. When I was at last quite certain that we had no boiler-leaks, I gave the go-ahead.

"OK, you can light up!"

For Irene this was the culmination of the dream that had begun a year ago at Olympia, where she had seen this particular cooker on show. The oven had been ready to light for weeks, and at last Irene could put a match to the kindling. In moments the flames were roaring up the chimney. We could already smell the heat which is the great attraction of such cookers. Next to the cooker there was a pile of wooden blocks from the hoard that we had been accumulating from almost the day we had started work on the site. Irene took from this to add fuel to the thriving fire.

It was amazing just how quickly the hot plate was ready for use. There is somehow a visual entertainment in such appliances, and we continued watching the kettle until it boiled.

"Have we moved in?" Irene said in an emotional whisper.

It was not just a question but a plea, just in case I might have pressed to spend the last night of our let at Corry Point.

"Yes, we've moved in," I conceded. "I'll go and get the last bags from the bungalow and lock up there. Have we got something for supper here? Anything will do," I added carelessly.

Anything would *not* do for Irene. She had been planning this meal for weeks.

There was something nostalgic about those last moments at Corry Point as I tuned the key in the lock for the last time. It had been our home not only throughout the past winter, but also on the many previous occasions we had spent our autumn holidays there. With our new house only a mile away, it was unlikely that we would ever stay there again. I drove slowly away from the old house. A chapter of our lives had come to an end, and a new one was about to begin.

The early spring evening was cool and I arrived home with the fading light. As I opened the door I was greeted by a gorgeous smell of cooking food and an unfamiliar but friendly hiss. Irene had lit the Tilley lamps, whose soft light added to the cosy feeling of well-being and comfort. When I lit the great sitting-room fire and its flames flickered in the lamplight, our satisfaction was complete.

Irene and I were home. A dream lived and fulfilled. Tomorrow would be time enough to think of the future. But where on earth would I take Irene for holidays now?

The End